VISUAL BASIC .NET FOR BEGINNERS: A STEP-BY-STEP GUIDE TO LEARNING VB.NET

Anshuman Mishra

Published by Anshuman Mishra, 2025.

ABOUT THE BOOK:

VISUAL BASIC .NET FOR BEGINNERS: A STEP-BY-STEP GUIDE TO LEARNING VB.NET IS AN EASY-TO-FOLLOW, COMPREHENSIVE GUIDE DESIGNED SPECIFICALLY FOR THOSE WHO ARE NEW TO PROGRAMMING OR ARE TRANSITIONING TO VB.NET. WHETHER YOU HAVE LITTLE OR NO PROGRAMMING EXPERIENCE, THIS BOOK WILL TAKE YOU THROUGH THE BASICS OF VB.NET AND GUIDE YOU TOWARD MASTERING ESSENTIAL PROGRAMMING CONCEPTS. STARTING FROM THE VERY FOUNDATION OF VB.NET, THE BOOK GRADUALLY BUILDS UP TO MORE ADVANCED TOPICS, OFFERING PRACTICAL EXAMPLES, TIPS, AND EXERCISES ALONG THE WAY.

THE BOOK COVERS ALL KEY ASPECTS OF VB.NET, FROM UNDERSTANDING THE BASIC CONCEPTS OF EVENT-DRIVEN PROGRAMMING TO ADVANCED FEATURES LIKE OBJECT-ORIENTED PROGRAMMING AND DATABASE CONNECTIVITY. EACH CHAPTER IS CRAFTED WITH CLARITY AND SIMPLICITY IN MIND, ENSURING THAT EVEN THE MOST COMPLEX CONCEPTS ARE EASY TO GRASP. BY THE END OF THIS BOOK, YOU'LL BE EQUIPPED WITH THE SKILLS NEEDED TO DEVELOP FUNCTIONAL APPLICATIONS USING VB.NET AND UNDERSTAND ITS ROLE IN THE BROADER .NET FRAMEWORK.

BENEFITS OF STUDYING THIS BOOK:

1. **BEGINNER-FRIENDLY APPROACH:** THIS BOOK IS SPECIFICALLY WRITTEN FOR BEGINNERS, ENSURING THAT EVEN THOSE WITH NO PRIOR PROGRAMMING KNOWLEDGE CAN FOLLOW ALONG. EACH CONCEPT IS EXPLAINED STEP-BY-STEP, WITH PLENTY OF EXAMPLES TO HELP REINFORCE LEARNING.
2. **COMPREHENSIVE COVERAGE:** YOU'LL LEARN EVERYTHING YOU NEED TO KNOW TO GET STARTED WITH VB.NET, INCLUDING CREATING USER INTERFACES, WRITING EFFICIENT CODE, WORKING WITH DATABASES, AND UNDERSTANDING OBJECT-ORIENTED PROGRAMMING PRINCIPLES.
3. **HANDS-ON LEARNING:** THE BOOK INCLUDES PRACTICAL EXAMPLES AND EXERCISES THAT ALLOW YOU TO PRACTICE WHAT YOU'VE LEARNED. THIS HANDS-ON APPROACH HELPS SOLIDIFY CONCEPTS AND BUILDS CONFIDENCE IN CODING.

4. **Real-World Application:** Through examples and practical projects, you'll gain the ability to write real-world applications, making your skills immediately applicable in the workplace or personal projects.
5. **Clear Structure:** The book is organized into clear chapters, with each chapter building on the previous one. You'll be able to develop your knowledge in a logical, structured way.
6. **Error Handling and Troubleshooting:** Learn how to debug and handle errors effectively, which is an essential skill for any developer.

ABOUT THE AUTHOR

ANSHUMAN MISHRA, AN ACCOMPLISHED ACADEMIC AND EDUCATOR, HAS OVER 18 YEARS OF TEACHING EXPERIENCE AS AN ASSISTANT PROFESSOR IN COMPUTER SCIENCE. HE HOLDS AN M.TECH IN COMPUTER SCIENCE FROM THE PRESTIGIOUS BIRLA INSTITUTE OF TECHNOLOGY, MESRA. CURRENTLY SERVING AT DORANDA COLLEGE, RANCHI, HE SPECIALIZES IN PROGRAMMING LANGUAGES, SOFTWARE DEVELOPMENT, AND COMPUTER SKILLS, INSPIRING COUNTLESS STUDENTS WITH HIS PROFOUND KNOWLEDGE AND PRACTICAL INSIGHTS.

ANSHUMAN IS A PASSIONATE WRITER WITH EXPERTISE IN CREATING EDUCATIONAL RESOURCES FOR STUDENTS AND PROFESSIONALS. HIS BOOKS COVER TOPICS LIKE JAVA PROGRAMMING, SQL, OPERATING SYSTEMS, AND COMPETITIVE PROGRAMMING, REFLECTING HIS DEDICATION TO MAKING COMPLEX SUBJECTS ACCESSIBLE AND ENGAGING.

BEYOND ACADEMICS, ANSHUMAN IS A MOTIVATIONAL THINKER, A LOVER OF MYSTERIES, AND A STORYTELLER AT HEART. HE HAS AUTHORED WORKS RANGING FROM SELF-MOTIVATION GUIDES TO CHILDREN'S STORIES AND BOOKS DELVING INTO THE RICH HISTORY AND CULTURE OF JHARKHAND. HIS ABILITY TO WEAVE KNOWLEDGE WITH INSPIRATION MAKES HIS BOOKS A TREASURE FOR READERS OF ALL AGES.

"Programs must be written for people to read, and only incidentally for machines to execute."
— Harold Abelson & Gerald Jay Sussman, *Structure and Interpretation of Computer Programs*

Copyright Page

Title: ***VISUAL BASIC .NET FOR BEGINNERS: A STEP-BY-STEP GUIDE TO LEARNING VB.NET*** IS

Author: Anshuman Kumar Mishra

This book is published for educational purposes and is intended to serve as a comprehensive guide for MCA and BCA students, educators, and aspiring programmers. The author has made every effort to ensure accuracy, but neither the author nor the publisher assumes responsibility for errors, omissions, or any consequences arising from the application of information in this book.

BOOK TITLE: VISUAL BASIC .NET FOR BEGINNERS: A STEP-BY-STEP GUIDE TO LEARNING VB.NET

TABLE OF CONTENTS

HOW TO STUDY THIS BOOK:

1. **FOLLOW THE CHAPTERS IN ORDER:** SINCE THE BOOK IS STRUCTURED IN A PROGRESSIVE MANNER, IT'S IMPORTANT TO STUDY EACH CHAPTER IN ORDER. START WITH THE BASICS AND GRADUALLY WORK YOUR WAY THROUGH MORE ADVANCED TOPICS.
2. **PRACTICE REGULARLY:** PROGRAMMING IS A SKILL BEST LEARNED BY DOING. AFTER READING THROUGH EACH SECTION, TAKE THE TIME TO CODE THE EXAMPLES PROVIDED. MODIFY THEM, EXPERIMENT, AND TRY CREATING YOUR OWN SMALL PROGRAMS TO REINFORCE YOUR UNDERSTANDING.
3. **WORK ON EXERCISES:** AT THE END OF EACH CHAPTER, YOU'LL FIND EXERCISES DESIGNED TO CHALLENGE YOUR UNDERSTANDING AND TEST YOUR KNOWLEDGE. THESE EXERCISES WILL HELP YOU APPLY THE CONCEPTS IN REAL SCENARIOS.
4. **SEEK ADDITIONAL RESOURCES:** IF YOU ENCOUNTER A DIFFICULT CONCEPT OR NEED FURTHER CLARIFICATION, DON'T HESITATE TO CONSULT ADDITIONAL RESOURCES SUCH AS ONLINE TUTORIALS, FORUMS, OR OTHER PROGRAMMING BOOKS. SOMETIMES, A DIFFERENT PERSPECTIVE CAN HELP CLARIFY CHALLENGING TOPICS.
5. **USE A PROJECT-BASED APPROACH:** ONCE YOU'VE COVERED THE BASICS, START BUILDING SMALL PROJECTS USING THE KNOWLEDGE YOU'VE GAINED. BUILDING YOUR OWN APPLICATIONS WILL GIVE YOU PRACTICAL EXPERIENCE AND KEEP YOU MOTIVATED.
6. **REVIEW AND REINFORCE:** PROGRAMMING CONCEPTS CAN SOMETIMES TAKE TIME TO SINK IN. DON'T HESITATE TO REVISIT PREVIOUS CHAPTERS, ESPECIALLY IF YOU FIND CERTAIN CONCEPTS TRICKY. REPETITION AND PRACTICE ARE KEY TO MASTERING PROGRAMMING.

CHAPTER 1: INTRODUCTION TO VISUAL BASIC .NET

1.1 What is Visual Basic .NET?

Visual Basic .NET (VB.NET) is a modern, object-oriented programming language developed by Microsoft as part of the .NET framework. It is the next evolution of the classic Visual Basic (VB) programming language, which has been around since the early 1990s. VB.NET was first released in 2002 as a major upgrade to Visual Basic 6. It was designed to modernize the language, incorporate advanced programming concepts, and take full advantage of the powerful .NET framework, which provides a robust platform for building a wide range of applications.

Key Features of VB.NET

1. **Object-Oriented Programming (OOP):** VB.NET is an object-oriented language, meaning it is built around the concept of "objects" (collections of data and related functions). This allows developers to structure their code in a modular and reusable way, making it easier to manage and maintain large applications. VB.NET supports core OOP principles such as inheritance, polymorphism, encapsulation, and abstraction.
2. **Simplicity and Readability:** One of the key design goals of VB.NET is to make it easier for developers to learn and use. The syntax is straightforward, with a clear and human-readable structure. This makes VB.NET an ideal choice for beginners, as the language closely resembles natural English in its command structure. For example:

```
Dim x As Integer = 5
If x > 0 Then
    Console.WriteLine("Positive number")
End If
```

3. **Modern Programming Features:** Unlike older versions of Visual Basic, VB.NET supports modern programming features, such as:
   - **Automatic memory management** (via garbage collection).
   - **Structured error handling** (using Try...Catch blocks).
   - **Type safety** to prevent type mismatch errors.
   - **Multithreading** and asynchronous programming support.
   - **Access to powerful libraries** within the .NET framework.
4. **Versatility for Different Application Types:** VB.NET is a versatile language that can be used to create various types of applications, ranging from:
   - **Desktop applications:** Using Windows Forms or WPF (Windows Presentation Foundation) to create graphical user interfaces (GUIs) for PC software.
   - **Web applications:** Using ASP.NET, which is part of the .NET framework, to build dynamic, data-driven web applications.
   - **Mobile applications:** Through Xamarin (a cross-platform mobile app framework) or UWP (Universal Windows Platform), VB.NET can be used to develop mobile apps for Android, iOS, and Windows.
   - **Cloud and enterprise-level applications:** VB.NET can also be used for large-scale, cloud-based applications, thanks to its integration with Azure and other cloud services.

5. **Integration with the .NET Framework:** VB.NET runs on the **.NET platform**, which is a powerful and flexible software development platform developed by Microsoft. The .NET platform includes:
   - The **Common Language Runtime (CLR):** The runtime environment that executes .NET applications, providing services such as memory management, garbage collection, and exception handling.
   - The **.NET Framework Class Library (FCL):** A comprehensive set of reusable libraries and APIs for handling tasks such as data access, file I/O, networking, security, and more. The FCL is a key reason why VB.NET is so productive—developers don't have to reinvent the wheel to perform common tasks.

   Because of this integration, VB.NET can leverage all the benefits of the .NET framework, including cross-language interoperability (i.e., being able to call code written in other .NET languages like C# or F#) and strong security features.

6. **Cross-Platform Capabilities:** While VB.NET is traditionally known for building Windows-based applications, recent developments in the .NET ecosystem (such as .NET Core) have made it possible to run VB.NET applications on different operating systems, including macOS and Linux. This makes VB.NET a viable option for cross-platform development as well.
7. **Backwards Compatibility and Easy Transition from Classic VB:** VB.NET was specifically designed to be a better and more powerful language while remaining familiar to developers coming from the classic Visual Basic. For those who have experience with VB6 (the predecessor of VB.NET), transitioning to VB.NET is relatively easy because VB.NET retains the event-driven model that made classic VB so popular, but it also introduces modern programming paradigms such as OOP and structured error handling.

Why Use VB.NET?

1. **Ease of Learning:** VB.NET is known for its simplicity and readability, which makes it ideal for beginners. Developers don't have to struggle with complicated syntax or obscure rules. It's easy to pick up, and its intuitive design allows new programmers to quickly start creating useful applications.
2. **Wide Range of Application Types:** Because VB.NET is part of the .NET framework, it can be used to create desktop applications, web applications, mobile apps, and even cloud-based enterprise solutions. This versatility makes VB.NET a powerful tool for a wide range of programming tasks.
3. **High Productivity:** The .NET platform provides a wealth of libraries and tools that simplify development. VB.NET developers can make use of these pre-built features to quickly assemble applications without having to code every single component from scratch.
4. **Strong Developer Support and Resources:** Since VB.NET is widely used, there is an abundance of resources available for learning and troubleshooting. Microsoft provides comprehensive documentation, and there are many community-driven websites, forums, and tutorials where developers can seek help and advice. Visual Studio, the official IDE

for .NET development, provides excellent support for VB.NET with features like IntelliSense (code suggestions), debugging tools, and project templates.

5. **Integration with Microsoft Technologies:** For developers working in Microsoft environments, VB.NET is a natural choice because it integrates well with other Microsoft technologies. It works seamlessly with Microsoft SQL Server for database applications, and it can be used to create applications that interact with Microsoft Office products, Windows Services, and Azure cloud services.

Example: A Simple VB.NET Program

Here's a basic VB.NET program that demonstrates the simplicity and ease of the language:

```
Module Program
    Sub Main()
        Console.WriteLine("Hello, World!")   ' Output a message to the console
        Dim name As String
        Console.Write("Enter your name: ")    ' Prompt the user for input
        name = Console.ReadLine()            ' Read user input
        Console.WriteLine("Hello, " & name & "!")   ' Greet the user by name
    End Sub
End Module
```

In this example, the program:

- Outputs a message to the console.
- Prompts the user to enter their name.
- Greets the user by displaying the name they entered.

Notice how simple and easy-to-read the code is. This makes VB.NET a perfect choice for beginners who want to get started with programming without being overwhelmed by complex syntax or structures.

1.2 The Evolution of Visual Basic

Visual Basic (VB) has undergone significant changes since its inception in the early 1990s, transforming from a simple event-driven language to a robust, object-oriented programming language. The evolution of VB closely mirrors changes in the software development landscape, particularly as programming paradigms and technologies advanced. Let's take a detailed look at the evolution of Visual Basic, from its humble beginnings to its current role in the modern .NET ecosystem.

The Early Days: Visual Basic 1.0 - 6.0

Visual Basic was first introduced by Microsoft in 1991 with **Visual Basic 1.0**. It was developed to allow easy creation of graphical user interface (GUI)-based Windows applications, which was a significant step forward at the time. Visual Basic was not a traditional programming language but rather an event-driven programming tool aimed at simplifying the development of desktop applications for Windows. The major characteristics of early versions of VB included:

1. **Event-Driven Programming**: VB was designed around an event-driven programming model, where the program execution is largely determined by user actions (like clicks and key presses) or system events. This made it an excellent choice for building interactive GUI applications.
2. **Rapid Application Development (RAD)**: One of VB's core strengths was its ability to help developers quickly design and prototype applications. With its intuitive drag-and-drop interface, developers could build forms and controls with minimal effort.
3. **Simplified Syntax**: VB was specifically designed to be easy for beginners to learn. Its syntax was simple and intuitive, making it accessible to non-programmers and those new to coding.
4. **Limited Object-Oriented Features**: Initially, VB was primarily procedural and did not support advanced features like inheritance or polymorphism. However, the language allowed developers to create modular code with reusable functions and subroutines.

Visual Basic 4.0 - 6.0 (1995-1998)

As the demand for more powerful features grew, VB underwent several updates. **VB 4.0** (released in 1995) was a major upgrade that introduced support for 32-bit applications and the ability to create Windows-based applications with multiple forms. This version also introduced the **ActiveX controls**, enabling greater customization and integration with web-based applications.

In subsequent versions (VB 5.0 and VB 6.0), VB continued to evolve, adding new features like:

- **Support for COM (Component Object Model)** components, allowing VB applications to interact with other software components and languages.
- **Improved support for database access** via technologies like ADO (ActiveX Data Objects), which allowed VB developers to connect to databases and work with data more efficiently.
- **Deployment and distribution tools** that made it easier to package and deploy applications.

While these versions of VB were incredibly popular, they also had limitations:

- **Lack of true object-oriented capabilities**: While VB could manage some level of object abstraction, it lacked essential OOP features such as inheritance, polymorphism, and encapsulation.
- **Limited scalability**: As applications grew in complexity, it became clear that VB's procedural nature and limited OOP capabilities hindered larger, enterprise-level applications.

The Major Leap: Visual Basic .NET (VB.NET)

The **turning point in the evolution of Visual Basic** came in **2002** with the introduction of **VB.NET** as part of the .NET framework. This release marked a dramatic shift in both the language and the development environment. Here are the key milestones of this transformation:

Introduction of .NET Framework

VB.NET was no longer just a standalone language; it was fully integrated into the **.NET framework**, a software development platform that provided a collection of libraries, runtime environments, and development tools for building various types of applications. This change allowed VB.NET to take advantage of the advanced features offered by the .NET ecosystem, including:

- **The Common Language Runtime (CLR)**, which provides memory management, garbage collection, and exception handling.
- **The .NET Framework Class Library (FCL)**, a vast library of pre-built code for common programming tasks (e.g., data access, file handling, networking, etc.).

Object-Oriented Programming (OOP)

One of the most significant changes in VB.NET was the introduction of **true object-oriented programming**. Unlike earlier versions of VB, VB.NET fully supported the core principles of OOP:

- **Inheritance**: VB.NET allowed classes to inherit from other classes, enabling the reuse of code and the creation of more modular applications.
- **Polymorphism**: Developers could create methods or properties that could behave differently depending on the object calling them.
- **Encapsulation**: VB.NET allowed for better data hiding and access control using access modifiers (e.g., `Public`, `Private`, `Protected`).

These features gave VB.NET greater flexibility and power, making it more suitable for complex and large-scale software development.

Modern Programming Features

VB.NET introduced several modern programming features that improved the language's performance, safety, and maintainability:

- **Exception Handling**: VB.NET introduced structured exception handling with `Try...Catch` blocks, which replaced VB6's error-handling model, improving the robustness of applications.
- **Type Safety**: VB.NET was a **strongly typed** language, meaning that variables had specific data types, and type mismatches would result in compile-time errors. This helped catch many potential bugs early in development.

- **Garbage Collection**: The CLR's garbage collection automatically managed memory, freeing developers from having to manually manage memory allocation and deallocation, thus reducing memory leaks and improving application performance.
- **Multi-threading Support**: VB.NET supported multi-threading, allowing developers to create applications that could execute multiple tasks simultaneously, improving performance and responsiveness.

Web and Enterprise Application Development

VB.NET was designed to be suitable not only for traditional desktop applications but also for **web-based applications** and **enterprise-level systems**. Developers could use **ASP.NET**, the web framework within the .NET ecosystem, to build dynamic web applications with VB.NET. This made VB.NET a major player in web development, alongside C#.

VB.NET also provided better support for **distributed systems** and **networked applications**, leveraging .NET's support for web services, XML, and databases.

Post-VB.NET Era: Ongoing Development and Updates

Since the introduction of VB.NET, Microsoft has continued to update and improve the language, with new versions introduced alongside updates to the .NET framework. Some key developments over the years include:

.NET Core and Cross-Platform Support

With the advent of **.NET Core** (now .NET 5 and beyond), Microsoft made significant strides toward making .NET a **cross-platform framework**, allowing applications written in VB.NET (and other .NET languages) to run on multiple operating systems, including Windows, macOS, and Linux. This opened up new possibilities for VB.NET developers, who could now target a wider range of platforms beyond just Windows.

Visual Basic and C#

Although **C#** has gained a larger share of the .NET programming community, **VB.NET** remains a popular choice, particularly for developers with a background in classic Visual Basic. VB.NET continues to evolve alongside C#, with both languages being supported equally within the .NET ecosystem. However, C# has become the primary language for many developers, partly due to its growing use in various Microsoft technologies and platforms.

Performance Improvements and New Features

VB.NET, like C#, has benefited from performance improvements in the .NET framework and ongoing language enhancements, such as:

- **Asynchronous programming** (introduced in VB 2015) to make it easier to work with asynchronous tasks (e.g., network requests, file I/O) without blocking the main thread.
- **Improvements in LINQ (Language Integrated Query)**, enabling easier querying of data collections directly in VB.NET.
- **New language features** such as pattern matching, tuples, and records in newer versions of .NET, making it more modern and capable of handling complex programming tasks.

1.3 Understanding Event-Driven Programming

Event-driven programming is a programming paradigm that centers around the concept of **events** — actions or occurrences that trigger specific responses in a program. The flow of execution in an event-driven program is determined by these events, which can come from a variety of sources such as user actions (like clicking a button or pressing a key), messages from other programs, or system-generated events (such as timers or network requests).

In event-driven programming, the application does not run through a fixed sequence of instructions. Instead, it **waits for events to occur**, and when an event is detected, it responds by executing a specific block of code, commonly referred to as an **event handler**.

Core Concepts of Event-Driven Programming

To understand event-driven programming better, let's break down some core concepts:

1. **Events**: An event is any action that occurs within the system that can trigger a response in the program. In a **graphical user interface (GUI)** application, events are usually caused by user interactions such as:
    - **Mouse clicks** (e.g., clicking a button or a checkbox)
    - **Key presses** (e.g., typing on the keyboard)
    - **Mouse movement** (e.g., moving the cursor over an element)
    - **Form resizing** or **window closing**

    Events can also come from external sources like timers, background processes, or network messages.

2. **Event Handlers**: An **event handler** is a block of code that is executed in response to a specific event. Each event has an associated handler that is activated when the event occurs. For example, if a user clicks a button, the event handler for that button's "click" event will execute.

    In VB.NET, event handlers are typically written as **subroutines (Subs)** that are associated with specific events. These handlers contain the code to perform an action, such as displaying a message, updating a label, or performing a calculation.

3. **Control Flow**: In traditional procedural programming, the flow of control is linear and predictable, with the program executing from top to bottom. In event-driven programming, however, the control flow is **interrupt-driven**. The program is often idle or waiting, and when an event is triggered, control is handed over to the appropriate event handler. The program is then "interrupted" to respond to the event before continuing its execution.
4. **Event Loop**: Most event-driven programs have an **event loop** (or message loop) at their core. This loop continuously listens for events and routes them to the appropriate event handlers. The event loop runs in the background, keeping the program responsive and ready to react to events. In GUI applications, the event loop constantly monitors for mouse clicks, keyboard input, and other events.

Event-Driven Programming in VB.NET

In VB.NET, event-driven programming is particularly prominent in the development of Windows Forms applications. **Forms** are the main windows or dialogs in a graphical user interface (GUI), and they contain **controls** such as buttons, textboxes, and labels. Each control is capable of raising events, and the program responds by defining event handlers for these events.

Example of Event-Driven Code in VB.NET:

Consider the example of a button that triggers an action when clicked:

```
' Declare the event handler for the Button click event
Private Sub Button_Click(sender As Object, e As EventArgs) Handles
Button.Click
    ' This code will execute when the button is clicked
    MessageBox.Show("Button was clicked!")
End Sub
```

In the code above:

- **Button.Click** is the event being monitored.
- The **Button_Click** subroutine is the event handler that responds to the "click" event.
- The `MessageBox.Show("Button was clicked!")` is the action performed when the event occurs — in this case, displaying a message box.

The event handler is associated with the **Button.Click** event using the `Handles` keyword. Whenever the user clicks the button, the program "responds" by executing the code inside the `Button_Click` subroutine.

Common Events and Their Handlers in VB.NET:

Here are a few common types of events in VB.NET and how event handlers work with them:

- **Button Click** (`Button.Click`): Occurs when a user clicks a button.
- **TextBox Text Changed** (`TextBox.TextChanged`): Fired whenever the text in a `TextBox` changes.
- **Form Load** (`Form.Load`): Triggered when a form is loaded or opened.
- **Timer Tick** (`Timer.Tick`): Fired at regular intervals set by a timer control.

Benefits of Event-Driven Programming

1. **Interactivity**: The most significant advantage of event-driven programming is that it allows the application to be **responsive to user actions**. For instance, a program can wait for the user to click a button, enter text, or select an option, and respond accordingly. This makes event-driven programming particularly useful for building **interactive applications** like graphical user interfaces (GUIs), games, and real-time systems.
2. **Modularity**: Event-driven programming promotes **modular code** because each event handler is typically focused on a single task. By isolating the code that responds to specific events, developers can write smaller, more focused functions. This makes the code easier to maintain and debug.

   For example, rather than having one long procedure that manages every part of the program, you can have separate event handlers for different user actions, making the program more organized and easier to manage.

3. **Asynchronous Processing**: Event-driven programming naturally supports asynchronous execution. For example, if an application is waiting for data from a server or performing time-consuming calculations, it doesn't need to freeze or block the user interface. The program can continue waiting for events while the background process completes, keeping the application responsive.
4. **Flexibility**: In event-driven programming, the flow of execution is **dynamic**. The program does not follow a linear sequence of instructions. Instead, it reacts to external stimuli (events) that may occur at any time. This flexibility is essential for building modern applications where the user's actions can trigger a wide variety of different processes.
5. **Real-time Interaction**: Event-driven programming allows for **real-time responses**, where actions and events are handled immediately after they occur. This is essential in interactive applications, such as games or chat applications, where the user expects an immediate response to their actions.

Challenges of Event-Driven Programming

While event-driven programming provides numerous benefits, it does have some challenges:

1. **Complexity in Large Applications**: In large applications with many events and event handlers, managing the flow of execution can become **complex**. Developers need to keep track of how various components and controls interact with each other, especially in applications with many different types of events.
2. **Debugging**: Since event-driven applications often don't follow a clear, linear flow, debugging can be more difficult. Tracking down the exact cause of an issue may require investigating several different event handlers and understanding how they interact.
3. **Event Handling Conflicts**: In some cases, multiple events may conflict or overlap, leading to unintended behavior. For example, if two different controls trigger similar actions simultaneously, the program may behave unpredictably unless handled carefully.

1.4 The .NET Framework: An Overview

The **.NET Framework** is a powerful software development platform developed by Microsoft to facilitate the creation and running of a wide range of applications, including desktop, web, mobile, and cloud-based solutions. Its primary aim is to provide a unified, efficient, and scalable environment for developers to build applications using various programming languages. The .NET framework is known for its rich set of libraries, powerful runtime features, and its ability to support multiple programming languages, making it a versatile tool for developers.

The .NET Framework is composed of two core components: **Common Language Runtime (CLR)** and the **.NET Framework Class Library (FCL)**. Together, these components provide everything a developer needs to write, test, and deploy applications.

Core Components of the .NET Framework

1. Common Language Runtime (CLR)

The **Common Language Runtime (CLR)** is the engine at the heart of the .NET framework. It is responsible for executing all .NET applications. The CLR abstracts the underlying operating system, providing developers with a common environment for running applications, regardless of the platform on which they are executed (Windows, in particular). The CLR is similar to the Java Virtual Machine (JVM), in that it allows code to be written once and run on different platforms.

Key features and services provided by the CLR include:

1. **Memory Management and Garbage Collection**: The CLR automatically handles memory allocation and deallocation, relieving developers from manually managing memory. This process, known as **garbage collection**, involves identifying unused objects in memory and releasing them for future use. This helps to prevent memory leaks and optimizes application performance.

2. **Exception Handling**: The CLR provides a structured mechanism for managing errors through **exception handling**. This allows developers to write more robust applications by anticipating and handling potential runtime errors (e.g., invalid input, network failure) with `Try`, `Catch`, and `Finally` blocks. The CLR ensures that exceptions are propagated and caught in a controlled manner.
3. **Just-In-Time (JIT) Compilation**: .NET code is initially written in **Intermediate Language (IL)**, a platform-independent bytecode. When an application is executed, the CLR uses the **Just-In-Time (JIT) compiler** to compile IL into native machine code that is specific to the architecture of the host machine (e.g., x86, x64). This ensures that .NET applications can run efficiently on different hardware platforms.
4. **Security**: The CLR also provides **security features** that help protect applications from malicious code. The **Code Access Security (CAS)** model ensures that the application can only perform actions allowed by the security policies set for it. Additionally, the **type safety** features prevent operations on uninitialized or incompatible data types, reducing the risk of errors and malicious exploits.
5. **Thread Management**: The CLR manages **multithreading** within applications, allowing developers to write concurrent code that can take advantage of multiple CPU cores. This improves performance for applications that require parallel processing or need to remain responsive to user interactions (e.g., games, complex calculations).
6. **Type Safety and Metadata**: The CLR ensures that the data types used in an application are valid and correctly initialized. All .NET code is **type-safe**, meaning it is designed to prevent type mismatches, which could lead to unexpected behavior. Additionally, CLR-enabled applications can include **metadata**, which provides information about the program's types, methods, and properties to make the program more reflective and reusable.

2. .NET Framework Class Library (FCL)

The **.NET Framework Class Library (FCL)** is a vast collection of pre-built, reusable code libraries that provide essential functionality for application development. The FCL is one of the primary reasons why .NET is such a powerful platform — it contains thousands of classes that handle various common programming tasks, allowing developers to focus on application-specific logic rather than writing code from scratch.

The FCL is organized into namespaces, and each namespace provides classes, interfaces, and data structures designed for a specific task. Some of the key areas covered by the FCL include:

1. **System Namespace**: This namespace contains fundamental classes like `System.String`, `System.Int32`, and `System.DateTime`, as well as utilities for basic operations, such as **input/output**, **data conversion**, and **date/time manipulation**.
2. **System.IO**: This namespace provides classes for **file and stream I/O** operations. Developers can use it to read from and write to files, manage directories, and interact with the file system. It includes classes like `FileStream`, `StreamReader`, and `StreamWriter`.
3. **System.Net**: The `System.Net` namespace includes classes for **network communication**, such as HTTP requests, web services, and socket programming. It simplifies operations

like sending and receiving data over the internet (e.g., `HttpWebRequest`, `TcpListener`, and `WebClient`).

4. **System.Data**: The `System.Data` namespace provides tools for working with **databases**. It includes the **ADO.NET** classes, which allow developers to interact with relational databases (SQL Server, MySQL, etc.) using objects like `DataTable`, `SqlCommand`, and `SqlDataReader`.
5. **System.Collections**: This namespace contains classes for **data structures** like lists, arrays, queues, stacks, and dictionaries. It helps developers store and manipulate collections of data efficiently. Key classes include `ArrayList`, `Dictionary`, `Queue`, and `SortedList`.
6. **System.Threading**: For multithreaded programming, the `System.Threading` namespace provides classes to manage threads, synchronization, and asynchronous operations. It includes classes like `Thread`, `Mutex`, and `Task`, making it easier for developers to create parallel applications that can perform multiple tasks simultaneously.
7. **System.Windows.Forms**: The `System.Windows.Forms` namespace is essential for creating **desktop applications** with graphical user interfaces (GUIs). It provides classes for forms, controls (e.g., buttons, textboxes), event handling, and user interaction.
8. **System.Linq**: **LINQ (Language Integrated Query)** is a powerful feature of the .NET framework that allows developers to query collections of data using SQL-like syntax directly in their code. The `System.Linq` namespace provides the `IEnumerable<T>` and `IQueryable<T>` interfaces, as well as LINQ methods like `Select`, `Where`, and `Aggregate`.
9. **System.Security**: The `System.Security` namespace provides classes for **encryption**, **authentication**, and **authorization**. It includes support for cryptography, digital signatures, and secure communication protocols, making it easier to build secure applications.
10. **System.Drawing**: This namespace contains classes for **drawing graphics**, handling images, and creating visual elements in an application. It includes classes like `Graphics`, `Image`, `Bitmap`, and `Pen`.

Key Features of the .NET Framework

1. **Multi-Language Support**: One of the major benefits of the .NET framework is its **language interoperability**. The framework supports multiple programming languages, including **C#**, **VB.NET**, and **F#**. Developers can use the language they are most comfortable with, and .NET allows code from different languages to interact seamlessly. The CLR ensures that all languages are compiled to a common intermediate language (IL), which is executed by the runtime.
2. **Cross-Platform Development**: Originally, the .NET framework was exclusive to Windows, but with the introduction of **.NET Core** (now simply referred to as **.NET 5 and beyond**), developers can build applications that run on multiple platforms, including **Windows**, **macOS**, and **Linux**. This makes .NET a truly **cross-platform framework**.
3. **Rich Ecosystem**: The .NET ecosystem includes a range of tools, libraries, and frameworks, such as **ASP.NET** for web development, **Entity Framework** for object-

relational mapping, and **Xamarin** for mobile app development. This enables developers to build a variety of applications using a single platform.

4. **Powerful Tools**: The .NET framework is backed by powerful **development tools** like **Visual Studio** — a fully integrated development environment (IDE) that provides features like IntelliSense, debugging, and code profiling. It helps developers build applications efficiently and with fewer errors.
5. **Integrated Deployment and Maintenance**: The .NET framework includes built-in tools for **deployment** and **versioning**, making it easier to distribute and update applications. **ClickOnce** is one such deployment technology that simplifies the installation and maintenance of applications.

.

1.5 Architecture of the .NET Framework

The architecture of the **.NET Framework** is designed to provide a consistent and efficient environment for building and running applications across various platforms, including desktop, web, mobile, and cloud-based systems. It offers a wide range of tools and services to developers, making the development process more streamlined, secure, and scalable. The core components of the .NET framework architecture work together to deliver a unified environment for both development and execution of applications.

The major components of the .NET Framework architecture include:

1. **Common Language Runtime (CLR)**
2. **Class Libraries (Framework Class Library - FCL)**
3. **ASP.NET, ADO.NET, and Windows Forms**
4. **Assemblies**
5. **Common Type System (CTS) and Common Language Specification (CLS)**

Let's explore each of these components in detail.

---

1. Common Language Runtime (CLR)

The **Common Language Runtime (CLR)** is the heart of the .NET Framework and is responsible for managing the execution of .NET applications. It provides essential services like memory management, exception handling, and type safety, ensuring that applications run smoothly and securely. The CLR is a key element in enabling the interoperability between different languages in the .NET ecosystem.

Key responsibilities of the CLR include:

1. **Memory Management and Garbage Collection**: The CLR automatically manages memory allocation and deallocation through a process called **garbage collection**. When an object is no longer in use, the garbage collector reclaims the memory to prevent memory leaks, making memory management easier for developers and improving performance.
2. **Exception Handling**: The CLR provides a structured model for handling exceptions (runtime errors). Developers can define **try-catch-finally** blocks to handle errors, and the CLR ensures that errors are caught, managed, and logged in a controlled way. This increases the robustness of the application.
3. **Security**: The CLR enforces **security policies** to protect applications from malicious code. It uses the **Code Access Security (CAS)** model, ensuring that code running within the framework only has access to resources that it is authorized to use, thus preventing unauthorized access and operations.
4. **Just-In-Time (JIT) Compilation**: Code written in .NET languages (like VB.NET, C#, or F#) is compiled into **Intermediate Language (IL)**, a platform-independent bytecode. The CLR uses a **Just-In-Time (JIT) compiler** to convert IL code into native machine code at runtime. This allows .NET applications to run on any hardware architecture, ensuring platform independence while maintaining high performance.
5. **Thread Management**: The CLR also manages **multithreading** and **synchronization**, allowing developers to write applications that take advantage of modern processors with multiple cores. This ensures efficient handling of tasks that require parallel processing, such as complex calculations or background operations.
6. **Type Safety**: The CLR enforces **type safety**, ensuring that the data types used in an application are valid and consistent. This reduces the chances of runtime errors caused by incorrect data types and enhances the stability of the application.

---

2. Class Libraries (FCL - Framework Class Library)

The **Framework Class Library (FCL)** is a vast collection of pre-built classes, methods, and APIs that developers can use to build their applications. It provides essential functionality for a wide range of tasks, from basic data handling to complex networking and graphical user interface (GUI) management.

The FCL is organized into namespaces, with each namespace providing functionality for a specific type of operation. Examples of FCL namespaces include:

- **System**: Basic types and utilities, such as `System.String`, `System.Int32`, and `System.DateTime`.
- **System.IO**: Classes for working with input and output, such as `FileStream`, `StreamReader`, and `StreamWriter`.
- **System.Net**: Classes for handling network communication, such as `HttpWebRequest`, `TcpListener`, and `WebClient`.
- **System.Data**: Classes for database access and manipulation, such as `SqlConnection`, `DataTable`, and `SqlCommand`.

- **System.Windows.Forms**: Classes for creating graphical user interfaces (GUIs) in desktop applications.
- **System.Threading**: Classes for working with threads and asynchronous tasks.

The **FCL** significantly reduces the amount of code developers need to write from scratch by providing well-tested, reusable components for common programming tasks.

---

3. ASP.NET, ADO.NET, and Windows Forms

The .NET Framework includes specialized application frameworks that provide powerful tools for specific types of application development. These frameworks are built on top of the core components of the .NET framework and are designed to simplify the development of certain types of applications:

1. **ASP.NET**: ASP.NET is a framework for building **web applications** and **web services**. It provides tools for creating dynamic web pages, handling HTTP requests, managing session states, and interacting with databases. ASP.NET supports **MVC (Model-View-Controller)** architecture, Web API services, and SignalR for real-time web applications.
2. **ADO.NET**: ADO.NET (Active Data Objects) is a framework for working with **databases** in the .NET environment. It provides classes for connecting to databases, executing SQL commands, and retrieving data from relational databases like SQL Server, Oracle, and MySQL. Key components of ADO.NET include `SqlConnection`, `SqlCommand`, `DataSet`, and `DataReader`.
3. **Windows Forms**: Windows Forms is a framework for building **desktop applications** with a graphical user interface (GUI) in Windows. It provides a rich set of controls (such as buttons, textboxes, and labels) and layout management tools to design interactive desktop applications. While newer frameworks like WPF (Windows Presentation Foundation) have gained popularity, Windows Forms remains a powerful option for developing traditional desktop applications.

---

4. Assemblies

An **Assembly** in .NET is the primary unit of deployment and versioning. It is a compiled code library that contains all the resources required to execute an application. Assemblies can be in the form of **DLLs (Dynamic Link Libraries)** or **EXEs (Executable Files)**.

Key points about assemblies:

- **Metadata**: Assemblies contain metadata that describes the types, methods, and properties of the code contained within. This metadata is crucial for reflection and enables dynamic code execution and discovery.

- **Versioning**: Assemblies provide **versioning** capabilities, allowing different versions of the same library to coexist on a system. This helps in avoiding compatibility issues when updating applications or libraries.
- **Self-Contained**: An assembly is a self-contained unit that may include both the code (IL) and other resources such as images, configuration files, or data.

Assemblies are crucial for .NET's **managed code** environment, enabling developers to create modular, reusable, and versioned software components.

---

5. Common Type System (CTS) and Common Language Specification (CLS)

The **Common Type System (CTS)** and the **Common Language Specification (CLS)** ensure that all .NET languages can interoperate effectively.

1. **Common Type System (CTS)**: The **CTS** defines a set of data types and rules for how they are used across different .NET languages. This ensures that regardless of whether the developer is using **C#**, **VB.NET**, **F#**, or any other .NET language, the types will be consistent and compatible. The CTS defines the basic types such as `int`, `float`, `string`, as well as more complex types such as classes, structures, and arrays. It also ensures type safety by enforcing rules about type usage.
2. **Common Language Specification (CLS)**: The **CLS** is a set of guidelines that defines how .NET languages should be designed to be **interoperable** with each other. It ensures that code written in one .NET language can be used in another without compatibility issues. The CLS provides a subset of CTS types that are guaranteed to be accessible across all compliant .NET languages. By following the CLS, developers can ensure that their code can be used by others, even if they are working in a different programming language.

Together, the **CTS** and **CLS** ensure that .NET applications are language-agnostic, enabling seamless interoperability between different .NET languages.

1.6 Just-In-Time Compiler and Its Role

The **Just-In-Time (JIT) Compiler** is a critical component of the .NET framework's **Common Language Runtime (CLR)** that plays a key role in executing .NET applications. The JIT compiler is responsible for converting the **Intermediate Language (IL)** code, produced when the application is first compiled, into **native machine code** that the computer's processor can execute directly. This process is essential for enabling the application to run efficiently across different hardware environments.

Let's break down the process of how the JIT compiler works and explore its significance in the .NET ecosystem.

How the JIT Compiler Works

When a .NET application is developed, it is typically written in a language such as **C#**, **VB.NET**, or **F#**. The application source code is then compiled by the **compiler** (e.g., the C# compiler) into **Intermediate Language (IL)**, which is an intermediate form of code that is platform-independent. IL is not directly executable by the computer's processor.

However, the application cannot run as-is because the machine (CPU) only understands native machine code specific to its architecture (e.g., x86, ARM, x64). This is where the **JIT compiler** comes in.

The **JIT compiler** works as follows:

1. **IL to Native Code**: When the application is run, the CLR takes the IL code and passes it to the JIT compiler. The JIT compiler then converts the IL into **native machine code** specific to the hardware on which the application is running.
2. **Compilation at Runtime**: The JIT compiler does this conversion at **runtime**, which means that the code is compiled as it is being executed, rather than beforehand (as is the case with traditional ahead-of-time compilation).
3. **Execution of Native Code**: Once the JIT compiler has translated the IL into native machine code, it can be executed by the computer's processor. The CLR manages the interaction between the native code and the operating system, ensuring that the application runs as expected.

Role of the JIT Compiler in .NET

The JIT compiler plays a fundamental role in optimizing the performance, flexibility, and platform independence of .NET applications. Let's look at its key functions and contributions:

1. Performance Optimization

One of the most significant advantages of the JIT compiler is its ability to optimize code during runtime. Traditional compilation processes are static and produce a fixed output, which may not be able to take full advantage of the specific hardware features available at runtime. The JIT compiler, however, has the flexibility to perform optimizations based on the runtime environment, leading to more efficient execution of the code.

Key performance optimizations performed by the JIT compiler include:

- **In-lining of Methods**: The JIT compiler can replace method calls with the body of the method itself, which reduces the overhead of calling the method and can improve performance.
- **Loop Unrolling**: The JIT can optimize loops by unrolling them, thereby reducing the number of iterations and improving performance for certain types of loops.

- **Dead Code Elimination**: The JIT compiler can identify and eliminate code that does not contribute to the final result, such as code that is never executed.
- **Register Allocation**: The JIT compiler can optimize the use of CPU registers, which are faster than memory, to speed up computations.

By compiling code at runtime, the JIT compiler can make decisions based on the specific environment, such as the number of processors, available memory, and the architecture of the CPU, which leads to more efficient code execution.

2. Platform Independence

A key feature of the .NET framework is its **platform independence**. The **Intermediate Language (IL)** is platform-agnostic, meaning that the same IL code can be executed on different systems (e.g., Windows, Linux, macOS) without modification. The **JIT compiler** ensures this platform independence by translating the IL code into native machine code specific to the underlying operating system and hardware at runtime.

For example, if a .NET application is written on a machine running Windows on an x64 architecture, the application will first be compiled to IL. If the application is then moved to a Linux machine running on an ARM architecture, the same IL code can be executed by the CLR and JIT compiler, which will translate it into machine code suited for the ARM processor.

This means that developers can write code once in any .NET-supported language, and the JIT compiler ensures that the application can run on any platform that supports the .NET runtime, without the need for recompiling the code.

3. Adaptive Compilation

Because the JIT compiler compiles code at runtime, it has the flexibility to make decisions based on the **current state of the system**. This is known as **adaptive compilation**. The JIT compiler can monitor the application's execution and make changes to the compiled code to improve performance or address issues that arise during execution.

For instance, the JIT compiler can:

- Optimize code differently based on which methods are being called most frequently (this is known as **hot code paths**).
- Use **profile-guided optimizations** based on how the application is running on a specific machine (e.g., adjusting for available memory or processor cores).

This dynamic approach allows the application to continuously optimize itself, improving overall performance as it runs.

4. Memory Efficiency

The JIT compiler also plays an important role in memory efficiency. It compiles only the parts of the code that are actually used during runtime. This **lazy compilation** ensures that unnecessary code is not compiled, saving both time and memory. This is in contrast to **ahead-of-time (AOT)** compilation, where the entire application is compiled before execution, even if only certain portions are needed at runtime.

The JIT compiler can also take advantage of **locality of reference**, meaning it can optimize memory access patterns based on how the application is actually using memory, improving both speed and memory usage.

Benefits of JIT Compilation

The JIT compiler provides several benefits for .NET developers and users:

1. **Performance Optimization**: The ability to optimize code at runtime based on the current environment leads to better performance, especially when compared to static compilation approaches.
2. **Platform Independence**: The .NET runtime allows code to be written once and run anywhere. The JIT compiler adapts the IL code for execution on different platforms and hardware, ensuring that the same application can run seamlessly across different devices.
3. **Flexibility and Adaptation**: The JIT compiler allows the application to optimize and adapt during execution, providing a level of flexibility not possible with traditional ahead-of-time compiled languages.
4. **Reduced Memory Usage**: By compiling only the necessary parts of the application at runtime, the JIT compiler reduces memory consumption, which is especially important in resource-constrained environments.
5. **Security**: The JIT compiler helps the CLR enforce **type safety** and **security** by ensuring that only valid code is executed. This reduces the chances of vulnerabilities in the application.

1.7 Introduction to the .NET Framework Class Library

The **.NET Framework Class Library (FCL)** is an extensive, pre-built set of libraries, classes, and interfaces that are part of the .NET framework. It provides a vast collection of functionality that simplifies the development of applications across a wide range of domains, from basic file manipulation to complex network communication, user interface development, and security management. The FCL enables developers to avoid writing code for common tasks by providing robust, reusable components for almost every aspect of application development.

The **FCL** is a cornerstone of the **.NET framework**, offering a rich ecosystem of classes that help developers write efficient, secure, and maintainable code. By utilizing the FCL, developers can build applications more quickly, with less effort, and fewer bugs. The FCL is part of the **Framework Class Library**, which is accessible in various .NET-based languages, such as C#, VB.NET, and F#.

Key Features of the .NET Framework Class Library

The FCL covers a wide range of programming tasks, and it is organized into **namespaces**, which are logical groupings of related classes. These namespaces provide predefined classes that solve specific problems. Below, we explore some of the most important categories of functionality provided by the FCL:

---

1. Data Access

The **data access** portion of the FCL provides powerful tools to interact with databases and other data sources. The **ADO.NET** library is one of the most widely used parts of the FCL for accessing and manipulating data.

Key classes and namespaces for data access include:

- **ADO.NET** (`System.Data`): ADO.NET is the primary library for interacting with relational databases (e.g., SQL Server, MySQL, Oracle). It provides classes such as `SqlConnection`, `SqlCommand`, and `DataReader` to connect to databases, execute commands, and retrieve data.
- **Entity Framework**: For object-relational mapping (ORM), the **Entity Framework** allows developers to interact with a database using object-oriented classes, reducing the need for writing raw SQL queries.
- **LINQ to SQL**: Another important tool for working with data in .NET, **Language Integrated Query (LINQ)** allows developers to write queries directly in C# or VB.NET syntax, making data manipulation easier and more intuitive.

These classes enable developers to interact with various data sources, perform queries, and manage data in a highly efficient way.

---

2. File Handling

File handling is an essential part of any application. The **System.IO** namespace in the FCL provides a rich set of classes for working with files and directories.

Key classes and functions include:

- **File and Directory Management**: Classes like `File`, `FileInfo`, `Directory`, and `DirectoryInfo` help you manage files and directories (e.g., create, delete, copy, move, and manipulate).
- **Streams**: The **Stream** class hierarchy, including classes like `FileStream`, `MemoryStream`, and `BufferedStream`, allows for efficient reading and writing of data to files or memory. Streams are particularly useful for handling large amounts of data.
- **File I/O Operations**: Classes like `StreamReader` and `StreamWriter` make it easy to read from and write to text files, while `BinaryReader` and `BinaryWriter` are designed for reading and writing binary data.

These built-in file-handling features significantly reduce the amount of custom code developers need to write when working with files, making the process more reliable and efficient.

---

3. User Interface (UI) Development

For building graphical user interfaces (GUIs), the FCL provides a variety of libraries to help create desktop applications and web interfaces.

- **Windows Forms** (`System.Windows.Forms`): Windows Forms is one of the oldest and most commonly used libraries for building desktop applications in .NET. It provides a rich set of controls, such as buttons, text boxes, and labels, that are used to create Windows-based applications with interactive GUIs.
- **Windows Presentation Foundation (WPF)** (`System.Windows`): WPF is a more modern UI framework that enables the creation of visually rich desktop applications. It allows for a separation between user interface design and logic using **XAML** (Extensible Application Markup Language) for layout and styles, and it supports advanced features such as animations, 3D graphics, and data binding.
- **ASP.NET** (`System.Web`): For web applications, **ASP.NET** provides the tools and controls needed to create dynamic web pages, handle HTTP requests, and manage session states. It supports the **Model-View-Controller (MVC)** architecture and other web technologies like **Web API** and **SignalR**.

These UI frameworks save developers significant time by providing all the components necessary for building applications with interactive and visually appealing interfaces.

---

4. Networking

The **System.Net** namespace provides a comprehensive set of tools for building networked applications, handling internet protocols, and working with web services.

Key classes for networking include:

- **HttpWebRequest and HttpWebResponse**: These classes enable sending and receiving HTTP requests and responses, which is essential for working with web APIs, websites, and cloud services.
- **Sockets**: The **Socket** class and related classes allow for lower-level network communication. Sockets are used to create networked applications that communicate over TCP/IP or UDP protocols, such as chat applications or client-server software.
- **WebClient and WebRequest**: These classes provide simplified methods for downloading and uploading data over HTTP, making it easier to work with web resources like files, images, and other content.

These libraries significantly simplify networking tasks by abstracting the complex details of communication protocols, allowing developers to focus on higher-level application logic.

---

5. Security

The **System.Security** namespace in the FCL provides tools to ensure the security of .NET applications by offering classes for encryption, authentication, and authorization.

Some key features include:

- **Cryptography**: Classes such as `AesManaged`, `RijndaelManaged`, and `RSA` provide strong encryption and decryption capabilities, ensuring data confidentiality.
- **Authentication and Authorization**: The FCL includes classes like `WindowsIdentity` and `Principal` to manage user identities and permissions. It also supports **role-based security**, enabling applications to restrict access to certain resources based on user roles.
- **Secure Socket Layer (SSL)**: The `SslStream` class provides secure communication over networks, ensuring that data transferred over the internet is encrypted.

These classes make it easy to implement security features such as encryption, authentication, and secure communication in applications, helping developers protect sensitive data and prevent unauthorized access.

---

6. Threading and Parallelism

The FCL includes powerful tools for working with **multi-threading** and **parallelism**, making it easier to write applications that can take advantage of multi-core processors.

Key classes and namespaces include:

- **System.Threading**: The `Thread` class and other related classes (like `Mutex`, `Semaphore`, and `Monitor`) allow developers to work with threads directly. These classes enable concurrent operations, where different parts of an application can run in parallel.

- **Task Parallel Library (TPL)** (`System.Threading.Tasks`): The TPL simplifies parallel programming by providing classes such as `Task` and `Parallel` to run code concurrently across multiple threads without managing low-level details. The TPL automatically schedules tasks to take advantage of multi-core processors, making applications more efficient.
- **Asynchronous Programming**: The FCL provides **async** and **await** keywords, which, when used with classes like `Task`, simplify the development of asynchronous applications. Asynchronous programming allows the application to remain responsive while performing lengthy operations, such as file I/O or network communication.

With these classes, developers can easily write applications that perform multiple operations at once, improving responsiveness and performance.

Benefits of the .NET Framework Class Library

The **.NET Framework Class Library (FCL)** offers several key benefits for developers:

- **Time Savings**: By using the pre-built, reusable classes in the FCL, developers save time and effort by not having to reinvent the wheel for common programming tasks.
- **Consistency and Reliability**: The FCL is extensively tested and optimized by Microsoft, ensuring that the components you use are reliable and high-performing.
- **Rich Ecosystem**: The FCL provides a vast array of functionality for virtually every aspect of application development, from data access to security and networking, reducing the need for third-party libraries.
- **Cross-Language Support**: The FCL can be used with all .NET languages, including C#, VB.NET, F#, and more, enabling developers to work with a common set of tools across different programming languages.

1.8 Setting Up the Development Environment

Before diving into VB.NET programming, it's important to set up the appropriate development environment on your machine. A development environment typically consists of the **IDE** (Integrated Development Environment), required tools, and necessary configurations to ensure you can write, test, and debug your VB.NET applications. In this section, we'll walk through the steps to set up **Visual Studio**, the most commonly used IDE for VB.NET development, as well as how to create your first VB.NET program.

Installing Visual Studio

Visual Studio is the official IDE for .NET development, offering all the necessary features for creating applications in languages like **C#**, **F#**, and **VB.NET**. Here's how to install Visual Studio:

Steps to Install Visual Studio:

1. **Download Visual Studio:**
   - Go to the official Visual Studio download page.
   - Choose the appropriate edition. Microsoft offers a **Community edition** for free, which is ideal for individual developers, students, and small teams. The **Professional** and **Enterprise** editions are paid versions with additional features.
2. **Run the Visual Studio Installer:**
   - After downloading the installer, run it to begin the installation process.
3. **Select the Workload:**
   - When the installer starts, you'll be asked to select workloads (groups of related tools and features).
   - To develop VB.NET applications, choose the **"Desktop development with .NET"** workload. This workload includes everything necessary for creating **Windows desktop applications** using VB.NET.
4. **Installation:**
   - Click **Install** to start the installation process. The installer will download and install the selected components, which may take some time depending on your internet speed and computer specifications.
5. **Complete the Installation:**
   - Once installation is complete, Visual Studio will open, and you'll be ready to start developing applications in VB.NET.

Configuring the IDE for VB.NET

Now that Visual Studio is installed, you need to configure it to work with VB.NET and start developing your first application. The default installation of Visual Studio will have the **VB.NET** tools already installed, but here's how to create and configure a project.

Steps to Configure Visual Studio:

1. **Open Visual Studio:**
   - Start Visual Studio by double-clicking its shortcut or launching it from the Start menu.
2. **Create a New Project:**
   - Once Visual Studio opens, select **"Create a new project"** from the main screen.
3. **Select a VB.NET Project Template:**
   - In the **Create a new project** window, you can search for project templates. Type "VB.NET" into the search bar.
   - If you want to create a **Windows Forms App** (a graphical desktop application), type **"Windows Forms App"** and select it. If you want to create a **Console Application** (a text-based program), choose **"Console App"** instead.

4. **Set Project Details:**
   - Choose a **Project Name**, and set the **Location** where your project files will be saved.
   - Click **Create** to initialize the project.
5. **Customizing the IDE (Optional):**
   - Visual Studio offers customization options such as changing the theme (e.g., light or dark mode) and adjusting key bindings for shortcuts.
   - You can also install extensions or tools that may help with specific tasks (e.g., code analysis, version control integration).

After completing these steps, your Visual Studio IDE will be configured to create and run **VB.NET** projects. You can start adding code to your project and experiment with the various built-in features Visual Studio provides.

Creating Your First VB.NET Program

With Visual Studio set up and configured, you're ready to create your first VB.NET program. Below are steps for creating both a **Console Application** and a **Windows Forms Application**.

1. Creating a Console Application (Text-Based Program):

1. **Open Visual Studio and Create a New Project:**
   - Follow the steps above to create a new **Console App** in Visual Studio.
2. **Write the Code:**
   - Once the project is created, the **Code Editor** window will open with a default template. For a simple program, replace the default code with the following code:

```
Module Program
    Sub Main()
        Console.WriteLine("Hello, World!")
    End Sub
End Module
```

3. **Run the Program:**
   - Press **F5** on your keyboard or click the **Start** button in the toolbar to run your application.
   - A console window will appear displaying the message: **Hello, World!**.

Congratulations! You've just written your first **Console Application** in VB.NET!

---

2. Creating a Windows Forms Application (Graphical User Interface):

1. **Open Visual Studio and Create a New Project:**
   - Follow the same steps to create a new **Windows Forms App** (VB.NET).
2. **Add a Button Control:**

- After the project is created, you will see the **Form Designer** window. From the **Toolbox** (on the left), drag a **Button** control onto the form.

3. **Write the Code for the Button Click Event:**
   - Double-click the **Button** on the form. This will open the **Code Editor** and automatically generate an event handler for the button's **Click** event.
   - Inside the event handler, add the following code:

```
Private Sub Button1_Click(sender As Object, e As EventArgs) Handles
Button1.Click
    MessageBox.Show("Hello, World!")
End Sub
```

   This code will display a **MessageBox** with the message **"Hello, World!"** when the user clicks the button.

4. **Run the Program:**
   - Press **F5** or click the **Start** button to run your program.
   - A window will appear with a button. When you click the button, a **MessageBox** will pop up showing **"Hello, World!"**.

Congratulations! You've just created your first **Windows Forms Application** with a **button** and an event handler!

30 multiple-choice questions (MCQs)

1.1 What is Visual Basic .NET?

1. **What is Visual Basic .NET?**
   - A) A web development framework
   - B) An object-oriented programming language
   - C) A data manipulation tool
   - D) A database management system
   - **Answer**: B) An object-oriented programming language
2. **Which of the following is a feature of VB.NET?**
   - A) Non-Object-Oriented
   - B) Incompatible with .NET Framework
   - C) Supports event-driven programming
   - D) Only used for web applications
   - **Answer**: C) Supports event-driven programming
3. **VB.NET is a successor to which programming language?**
   - A) C#
   - B) C++
   - C) Visual Basic
   - D) JavaScript
   - **Answer**: C) Visual Basic

4. **VB.NET is integrated into which software platform?**
   - A) Java Platform
   - B) .NET Framework
   - C) Eclipse IDE
   - D) Android Studio
   - **Answer**: B) .NET Framework

1.2 The Evolution of Visual Basic

5. **The first version of Visual Basic was introduced in which decade?**
   - A) 1980s
   - B) 1990s
   - C) 2000s
   - D) 2010s
   - **Answer**: A) 1980s
6. **What was a major improvement introduced in VB.NET compared to earlier versions of Visual Basic?**
   - A) Object-Oriented Programming (OOP) support
   - B) No GUI support
   - C) Only command-line interface
   - D) Incompatibility with Windows
   - **Answer**: A) Object-Oriented Programming (OOP) support
7. **Which year was VB.NET released?**
   - A) 2000
   - B) 2001
   - C) 2002
   - D) 2005
   - **Answer**: C) 2002
8. **VB.NET was fully integrated into which framework?**
   - A) Java
   - B) .NET Framework
   - C) Spring Framework
   - D) Node.js
   - **Answer**: B) .NET Framework

1.3 Understanding Event-Driven Programming

9. **In event-driven programming, the program flow is determined by:**
   - A) User-defined loops
   - B) Data processing
   - C) Events such as user actions
   - D) The system clock

- **Answer**: C) Events such as user actions

10. **Which of the following is NOT an example of an event in event-driven programming?**
    - A) Button click
    - B) Timer tick
    - C) Mouse hover
    - D) Mathematical operation
    - **Answer**: D) Mathematical operation
11. **What does an event handler do in event-driven programming?**
    - A) Starts the program
    - B) Sends data to a database
    - C) Responds to an event by executing code
    - D) Draws the user interface
    - **Answer**: C) Responds to an event by executing code
12. **Which of the following languages supports event-driven programming?**
    - A) C#
    - B) VB.NET
    - C) JavaScript
    - D) All of the above
    - **Answer**: D) All of the above

1.4 The .NET Framework: An Overview

13. **The .NET Framework was developed by which company?**
    - A) Google
    - B) Apple
    - C) Microsoft
    - D) IBM
    - **Answer**: C) Microsoft
14. **Which component of the .NET Framework executes applications?**
    - A) Common Language Runtime (CLR)
    - B) Visual Studio
    - C) Framework Class Library (FCL)
    - D) System.IO
    - **Answer**: A) Common Language Runtime (CLR)
15. **Which language is NOT supported by the .NET Framework?**
    - A) VB.NET
    - B) C#
    - C) Python
    - D) F#
    - **Answer**: C) Python
16. **The .NET Framework Class Library (FCL) provides pre-built functionality for:**
    - A) Only database connections
    - B) Common programming tasks

- C) Web development only
- D) Low-level hardware programming
- **Answer**: B) Common programming tasks

1.5 Architecture of the .NET Framework

17. **Which component of the .NET framework handles memory management and garbage collection?**
    - A) Common Type System (CTS)
    - B) Common Language Runtime (CLR)
    - C) Framework Class Library (FCL)
    - D) Visual Studio
    - **Answer**: B) Common Language Runtime (CLR)
18. **What is the role of assemblies in the .NET Framework?**
    - A) Store data in databases
    - B) Store compiled code and resources for applications
    - C) Provide network communication
    - D) Manage user interfaces
    - **Answer**: B) Store compiled code and resources for applications
19. **What is the purpose of the Common Language Specification (CLS)?**
    - A) Define guidelines for code formatting
    - B) Ensure language interoperability
    - C) Manage memory allocation
    - D) Define security policies
    - **Answer**: B) Ensure language interoperability
20. **Which application framework is used to build web applications in the .NET Framework?**
    - A) ADO.NET
    - B) Windows Forms
    - C) ASP.NET
    - D) WPF
    - **Answer**: C) ASP.NET

1.6 Just-In-Time Compiler and Its Role

21. **What does the Just-In-Time (JIT) compiler do in the .NET framework?**
    - A) Compiles code during the development phase
    - B) Translates Intermediate Language (IL) to native machine code at runtime
    - C) Writes code to a file
    - D) Ensures code security
    - **Answer**: B) Translates Intermediate Language (IL) to native machine code at runtime

22. **Which of the following is a benefit of JIT compilation?**
    - A) Slower performance compared to ahead-of-time compilation
    - B) Platform independence and optimizations at runtime
    - C) Does not support multiple languages
    - D) Limited to only Windows operating systems
    - **Answer**: B) Platform independence and optimizations at runtime
23. **Which type of code does the JIT compiler work with in .NET?**
    - A) Source code
    - B) Intermediate Language (IL) code
    - C) Machine code
    - D) Assembly language code
    - **Answer**: B) Intermediate Language (IL) code
24. **JIT compilation enables .NET applications to run on different platforms by:**
    - A) Compiling code before runtime
    - B) Converting to machine code at runtime
    - C) Generating platform-specific code during development
    - D) Using platform-dependent libraries
    - **Answer**: B) Converting to machine code at runtime

1.7 Introduction to the .NET Framework Class Library

25. **Which of the following namespaces is part of the .NET Framework Class Library (FCL)?**
    - A) System.Data
    - B) System.Console
    - C) System.IO
    - D) All of the above
    - **Answer**: D) All of the above
26. **The System.IO namespace in the FCL is used for:**
    - A) Networking
    - B) File operations like reading and writing
    - C) Database connectivity
    - D) User Interface creation
    - **Answer**: B) File operations like reading and writing
27. **Which FCL namespace is used for security-related functions?**
    - A) System.Security
    - B) System.IO
    - C) System.Data
    - D) System.Net
    - **Answer**: A) System.Security
28. **Which of the following is NOT a task that the .NET Framework Class Library (FCL) helps with?**
    - A) Threading
    - B) Network communication

- C) Memory management
- D) Code versioning
- **Answer**: D) Code versioning

1.8 Setting Up the Development Environment

29. **Which IDE is most commonly used for VB.NET development?**
    - A) Eclipse
    - B) Visual Studio
    - C) IntelliJ IDEA
    - D) Xcode
    - **Answer**: B) Visual Studio
30. **Which of the following steps is essential when creating a new VB.NET project in Visual Studio?**
    - A) Selecting the correct project template
    - B) Installing third-party plugins
    - C) Writing code in C#
    - D) Manually compiling the project
    - **Answer**: A) Selecting the correct project template

CHAPTER 2: ELEMENTS OF USER INTERFACE IN VB.NET

2.1 Introduction to Windows Forms

Windows Forms (WinForms) is one of the primary graphical user interface (GUI) toolkits provided by the .NET framework for building desktop applications for the Windows operating system. It offers a powerful and flexible environment for creating rich, interactive, and user-friendly applications that can run on any Windows-based machine.

In Windows Forms, you design your application by creating *forms*, which are windows or screens that contain user interface elements (such as buttons, textboxes, labels, and more). These forms act as containers for various controls that make up the user interface. The WinForms platform provides a rich set of pre-built controls and components that you can use to build your application's interface without needing to worry about low-level drawing operations.

Key Characteristics of Windows Forms:

1. **Drag-and-Drop UI Design**: One of the most significant features of Windows Forms is the ability to design user interfaces visually. In Visual Studio, the integrated development environment (IDE) for .NET, you can simply drag and drop controls from the toolbox onto a form. This allows developers to quickly and intuitively arrange the elements on the screen. For example, you can drag a Button control to your form and resize it or position it exactly where you want it. This eliminates the need for writing code to manually place or configure each control.
2. **Event-Driven Programming**: WinForms applications are typically event-driven, meaning that the flow of the application is determined by user actions or other events that occur while the program is running. Common events include actions like mouse clicks, key presses, form loading, and control interactions. For example, when a user clicks a button, the corresponding event handler (written in code) is executed. This event-driven model is fundamental to the WinForms approach because it allows applications to respond dynamically to user input in real time.

   Example: If you create a `Button` control, you can write an event handler method to define what happens when the button is clicked. This method might display a message, perform calculations, or navigate to another form.

3. **Customizable Controls**: Windows Forms comes with a broad range of built-in controls such as labels, buttons, checkboxes, textboxes, listboxes, and more. Each control has a set of properties that can be customized to meet the design requirements. These properties allow you to change the appearance, size, color, font, and behavior of each control.

   For example:

   - A `TextBox` can be set to multiline mode, allowing users to type multiple lines of text.
   - A `Button` can have its color and text changed dynamically.

    - A `ComboBox` can be populated with items either statically or programmatically.

   This flexibility makes Windows Forms a versatile toolkit for creating various types of user interfaces, from simple forms to complex applications.

4. **Integration with .NET Framework**: Windows Forms is deeply integrated with the .NET Framework, which means it can take advantage of the extensive libraries and features available in .NET. Controls in WinForms can work seamlessly with other .NET components, such as ADO.NET for database access, LINQ for data queries, and other APIs for networking, security, and more.

   This integration provides the advantage of not needing to worry about low-level system details or interoperability between components. For example, a `TextBox` control in a WinForms application can easily be bound to data from a database or interact with other parts of the application.

Structure of a Windows Forms Application

A Windows Forms application typically consists of one or more forms. The forms are the main windows that users interact with. Each form is an instance of the `Form` class, which is a container for other controls. A basic form could be something like a login screen, while a more complex application might have multiple forms representing different screens or windows within the application.

Example: Consider a simple form with the following controls:

- A `TextBox` to accept user input (e.g., a username).
- A `Button` to submit the input.
- A `Label` to display messages (e.g., "Welcome, user!").

The user would interact with the `TextBox` to enter their username, click the `Button`, and the `Label` would update to show a greeting message. This interaction is controlled by event handlers that define the actions to take when events like clicks occur.

Benefits of Windows Forms:

1. **Rapid Development**: The ability to drag and drop controls onto a form simplifies the UI design process. Developers don't need to manually position or render controls, which accelerates development time.
2. **Wide Range of Controls**: WinForms offers an extensive collection of controls that cover most common needs in desktop applications, making it easier to design professional-looking UIs.
3. **Event-Handling Mechanism**: Since WinForms is event-driven, developers can define responses to specific actions such as button clicks, key presses, mouse movements, and more, allowing for interactive user experiences.

4. **Strong Integration with .NET Libraries**: The seamless integration with the broader .NET ecosystem means that WinForms applications can take full advantage of all the features provided by the .NET Framework, including libraries for data access, security, network communication, and more.
5. **Customizable Appearance and Behavior**: You can easily adjust the appearance and behavior of WinForms controls to meet your application's needs, creating a tailored user experience.

2.2 Working with Basic Controls

In Windows Forms (WinForms) applications, basic controls are essential building blocks that make up the user interface (UI). These controls allow the user to interact with the application, input data, and trigger actions. The following are some of the most commonly used basic controls in WinForms:

TextBox

The `TextBox` control is one of the most widely used controls in WinForms. It allows users to input text or display text that can be edited. TextBoxes are highly customizable, making them suitable for a variety of input tasks.

Key Features:

- **Input**: Users can type text into the TextBox, making it ideal for capturing data such as names, addresses, and search queries.
- **Multiline Support**: A TextBox can be set to allow multiple lines of text (i.e., a multiline mode), which is useful for comments, descriptions, or notes.
- **Password Mode**: You can set a TextBox to hide the input characters, making it ideal for capturing sensitive data like passwords.

Common Events:

- **TextChanged**: Triggered when the text in the TextBox changes. For example, if a user types or deletes characters, this event will fire.
- **KeyPress**: Fires when a key is pressed in the TextBox. It can be used for input validation or to perform an action when the user hits a specific key, such as "Enter."

Example Use Case:

```
' A TextBox used to collect a user's name:
TextBox1.Text = "Enter your name here"
```

In this example, the `TextBox1.Text` property is used to access or set the text displayed inside the TextBox.

Button

The `Button` control is essential in any WinForms application, as it triggers actions or commands when clicked. Buttons are interactive controls, and they can be used to initiate a variety of tasks, such as submitting data, opening new forms, or running a function.

Key Features:

- **Action-Triggering**: The primary purpose of a Button is to invoke an action when the user clicks it.
- **Text and Image**: Buttons can display both text and images, allowing you to customize their appearance to fit the design of your application.

Common Events:

- **Click**: Fired when the user clicks the button. You can write a method to define what happens when the button is clicked.

Example Use Case:

```
' A Button that, when clicked, shows a message box:
Private Sub Button1_Click(sender As Object, e As EventArgs) Handles
Button1.Click
    MessageBox.Show("Button clicked!")
End Sub
```

In this example, the `Button1_Click` event handler displays a message box when the button is clicked.

Label

The `Label` control is used to display text on the form, but unlike TextBoxes, Labels are not interactive. Labels are useful for providing instructions, titles, or other non-editable information to the user.

Key Features:

- **Display Text**: Labels can display static text to inform or guide users.
- **No User Interaction**: Unlike TextBoxes or Buttons, Labels are not interactive; they simply present information.

Common Uses:

- Instructions: "Enter your name below."
- Titles or Headers: "Welcome to the Application!"
- Results: Displaying the result of a calculation or action, such as "Your balance is $100."

Example Use Case:

```
' A Label displaying instructions to the user:
Label1.Text = "Please enter your username"
```

Here, the `Label1.Text` property is set to display instructions to the user.

CheckBox

The `CheckBox` control is used when you need the user to make a binary (yes/no) choice. It has two states: checked and unchecked. When a CheckBox is checked, it indicates the user has selected an option; when unchecked, it means the user has deselected that option.

Key Features:

- **Binary Choice**: Users can select or deselect a CheckBox to make a decision. This is particularly useful for settings or preferences.
- **Visibility of State**: The state (checked or unchecked) is always visible to the user.

Common Uses:

- Terms and conditions agreement: "I agree to the terms and conditions."
- Preferences: "Enable notifications."
- Selections: "Subscribe to the newsletter."

Common Events:

- **CheckedChanged**: Fired when the state of the CheckBox changes (checked to unchecked, or vice versa).

Example Use Case:

```
' A CheckBox for accepting terms and conditions:
If CheckBox1.Checked Then
    MessageBox.Show("You accepted the terms.")
Else
    MessageBox.Show("You did not accept the terms.")
End If
```

In this example, when the CheckBox is checked or unchecked, the event triggers a message box to inform the user of their choice.

RadioButton

The `RadioButton` control is used when you want the user to choose only one option from a group of options. A group of RadioButtons works together, meaning that when one RadioButton is selected, the others in the group are automatically deselected. This is perfect for scenarios where the user needs to select a single option, such as choosing a payment method or selecting a preferred language.

Key Features:

- **Single Selection**: Only one RadioButton can be selected at a time in a group.
- **Grouped Behavior**: You can group multiple RadioButtons together by placing them in the same container, such as a GroupBox or Panel, so that when one is selected, the others are automatically deselected.

Common Uses:

- Selecting a preferred language: "English", "Spanish", "French"
- Choosing a payment method: "Credit Card", "PayPal", "Bank Transfer"

Common Events:

- **CheckedChanged**: Fires when a RadioButton is checked or unchecked. Typically, you use this event to handle actions when the user selects a particular option.

Example Use Case:

```
' A RadioButton group for choosing a payment method:
If RadioButton1.Checked Then
    MessageBox.Show("You selected Credit Card")
ElseIf RadioButton2.Checked Then
    MessageBox.Show("You selected PayPal")
End If
```

In this example, based on which RadioButton is checked, a corresponding message is displayed.

2.3 Advanced Controls

Advanced controls in Windows Forms (WinForms) allow developers to create more complex and interactive user interfaces. These controls extend the functionality of basic controls by providing options for richer user interactions and more flexible layouts. Here are some key advanced controls in WinForms:

ListBox

The `ListBox` control is used to display a list of items from which the user can select one or more options. This control is ideal for situations where a list of choices is needed, and you want to display a set of options in a scrollable area.

Key Features:

- **Multiple Selection**: You can configure the ListBox to allow the user to select one item (Single) or multiple items (MultiSimple or MultiExtended).
- **Dynamic Items**: Items can be added or removed from the ListBox at runtime, making it highly flexible.
- **Scrolling**: When there are more items than can fit in the ListBox's visible area, it will automatically display a vertical scrollbar.

Common Uses:

- Displaying a list of available products, users, or options.
- Allowing users to select items from a list for further processing (e.g., selection of categories or files).

Example Use Case:

```
' Adding items to a ListBox:
ListBox1.Items.Add("Item 1")
ListBox1.Items.Add("Item 2")
ListBox1.Items.Add("Item 3")

' Retrieving selected item:
Dim selectedItem As String = ListBox1.SelectedItem.ToString()
MessageBox.Show("You selected: " & selectedItem)
```

In this example, items are added to the `ListBox1`, and when an item is selected, its value is retrieved and displayed in a message box.

ComboBox

The `ComboBox` control is similar to a `ListBox`, but it provides a more compact, drop-down list of items. It combines the functionality of a TextBox and a ListBox, allowing the user to either select an item from a list or type their own input. ComboBoxes are highly useful when you want to provide a smaller space for selections but still give users a list of choices.

Key Features:

- **Drop-Down List**: By default, a ComboBox shows only one selected item and can be expanded to reveal a list of choices when clicked.
- **Editable**: Users can either select a predefined option or type their own custom input, depending on whether the ComboBox is set to be editable.
- **AutoComplete**: The ComboBox can be configured to automatically suggest options as the user types, improving usability.

Common Uses:

- Selecting an item from a long list, such as a list of countries or products.
- Allowing users to enter a custom value or select from a list of predefined options.

Example Use Case:

```
' Adding items to a ComboBox:
ComboBox1.Items.Add("USA")
ComboBox1.Items.Add("Canada")
ComboBox1.Items.Add("Mexico")

' Setting the selected item:
ComboBox1.SelectedItem = "Canada"

' Retrieving selected item:
Dim selectedCountry As String = ComboBox1.SelectedItem.ToString()
MessageBox.Show("You selected: " & selectedCountry)
```

In this example, items are added to the `ComboBox1`, and the user can either select an item or type in their own value.

PictureBox

The `PictureBox` control is used to display images, making it an essential control for any application that requires graphical content. It supports various image formats, such as JPEG, PNG, and GIF, and allows for advanced features like stretching and alignment of images.

Key Features:

- **Display Images**: The PictureBox allows you to display images from local files, embedded resources, or web sources.
- **Image Sizing**: You can control how the image fits into the PictureBox using properties like `SizeMode`, which determines whether the image is stretched, centered, or tiled.

- **Image Loading**: Images can be loaded from disk, memory, or external resources.

Common Uses:

- Displaying profile pictures, logos, or product images in an application.
- Visualizing dynamic content like charts, graphs, or status icons.

Example Use Case:

```
' Setting an image in a PictureBox:
PictureBox1.Image = Image.FromFile("C:\Images\logo.png")

' Adjusting the display mode:
PictureBox1.SizeMode = PictureBoxSizeMode.StretchImage
```

In this example, an image file is loaded into the `PictureBox1`, and the `SizeMode` property is set to stretch the image to fit the control's dimensions.

ScrollBar

The `ScrollBar` control is used to allow users to navigate through content that is too large to fit within the visible area of the form or container. It provides horizontal or vertical scrolling functionality.

Key Features:

- **Horizontal and Vertical**: You can add either a horizontal or vertical scrollbar, depending on the layout of your content.
- **Scrolling Content**: When a user interacts with the scrollbar, the content (like a large image or text) can be scrolled, making it viewable without resizing the window.

Common Uses:

- Scrolling through a large dataset, image, or text block that does not fit within the screen.
- Navigating through content such as text in a text box or data in a table.

Example Use Case:

```
' Setting the ScrollBar's range:
HScrollBar1.Minimum = 0
HScrollBar1.Maximum = 100
HScrollBar1.LargeChange = 10
HScrollBar1.SmallChange = 1

' Handling the Scroll event:
Private Sub HScrollBar1_Scroll(sender As Object, e As ScrollEventArgs)
Handles HScrollBar1.Scroll
```

```
    Label1.Text = "Scroll Position: " & e.NewValue
End Sub
```

In this example, a horizontal scrollbar is set up with a range from 0 to 100. The `Scroll` event updates the `Label1` to display the current position of the scrollbar.

Splitter

The `Splitter` control is used to create resizable panes in an application, allowing users to adjust the size of multiple panels. Splitters are commonly used in applications with complex layouts, such as email clients or file explorers.

Key Features:

- **Resizable Panels**: Splitters allow users to resize adjacent panels by dragging the splitter bar between them.
- **Vertical and Horizontal**: Splitters can be used vertically or horizontally, depending on the layout of the panels.
- **Adjustable Size**: Splitter controls can be configured to specify a minimum and maximum size for each panel.

Common Uses:

- Creating applications where users need to adjust the layout of the screen, such as resizing a navigation pane and content pane.
- Building custom layouts for dashboards, file explorers, or chat applications.

Example Use Case:

```
' A Splitter is added between two panels, allowing users to adjust the panel
size:
Splitter1.SplitPosition = 200 ' Set initial position of the splitter
```

In this example, a `Splitter` control is used to resize the panels, and its position is initially set to 200 pixels.

2.4 Working with Menus and Toolbars

Menus and toolbars play a crucial role in creating an organized and intuitive user interface. They provide users with easy access to various commands and features, allowing for efficient interaction with the application. In WinForms, there are several controls that facilitate the creation of menus and toolbars, including the `MenuStrip`, `ContextMenuStrip`, and `ToolStrip`. Let's dive into each of these components:

MenuStrip

The `MenuStrip` is used to create a horizontal menu bar at the top of a Windows Form. It contains multiple menu items (e.g., "File", "Edit", "Help"), each of which can have sub-items (e.g., "Open", "Save", "Exit"). MenuStrip is ideal for implementing traditional menus, such as the ones commonly found in desktop applications.

Key Features:

- **Menu Items**: A `MenuStrip` can contain multiple menus, each with its own set of commands or actions.
- **Drop-down Behavior**: When a menu item is clicked, it reveals a list of options that the user can select.
- **Multiple Levels of Menu Items**: You can add submenus under each menu item for further organization (e.g., a "File" menu with submenus for "New", "Open", "Save").

Common Uses:

- Creating a typical application menu bar (File, Edit, View, etc.).
- Providing users with actions such as opening files, saving, or quitting the application.

Example Use Case:

```
' Adding a MenuStrip to a form:
Dim menuStrip As New MenuStrip()
Me.Controls.Add(menuStrip)

' Adding MenuItems to the MenuStrip:
Dim fileMenu As New ToolStripMenuItem("File")
menuStrip.Items.Add(fileMenu)

' Adding SubItems to the "File" menu:
fileMenu.DropDownItems.Add("New")
fileMenu.DropDownItems.Add("Open")
fileMenu.DropDownItems.Add("Save")
fileMenu.DropDownItems.Add("Exit")

' Handling menu item click events:
AddHandler fileMenu.DropDownItems("Exit").Click, AddressOf ExitMenuItem_Click

' Exit action:
Private Sub ExitMenuItem_Click(sender As Object, e As EventArgs)
    Me.Close()
End Sub
```

In this example, a `MenuStrip` is added to a form with a "File" menu and several sub-items. The "Exit" item closes the form when clicked.

ContextMenuStrip

A `ContextMenuStrip` provides a pop-up menu that appears when a user right-clicks on a control or form. This is typically used for providing additional, context-specific actions related to the selected item or area of the application.

Key Features:

- **Right-click Activation**: The `ContextMenuStrip` appears when the user right-clicks on a specific control, allowing for actions relevant to that control (e.g., right-clicking on a list box to delete an item).
- **Customizable**: You can add items to the `ContextMenuStrip` dynamically based on the user's selection or the application's state.
- **User Interaction**: It enhances the user experience by offering actions that are closely related to the current context.

Common Uses:

- Providing options like "Cut", "Copy", "Paste" on a right-click in text fields or lists.
- Displaying specific actions for a list or grid, such as "Delete" or "Edit" for individual items.

Example Use Case:

```
' Create a ContextMenuStrip:
Dim contextMenu As New ContextMenuStrip()

' Add items to the context menu:
contextMenu.Items.Add("Delete")
contextMenu.Items.Add("Copy")

' Bind the context menu to a control (e.g., ListBox):
ListBox1.ContextMenuStrip = contextMenu

' Handling item click event:
AddHandler contextMenu.Items("Delete").Click, AddressOf DeleteItem_Click

' Deleting an item from the ListBox:
Private Sub DeleteItem_Click(sender As Object, e As EventArgs)
    If ListBox1.SelectedIndex >= 0 Then
        ListBox1.Items.RemoveAt(ListBox1.SelectedIndex)
    End If
End Sub
```

In this example, a `ContextMenuStrip` is created with "Delete" and "Copy" options. When a user right-clicks on a `ListBox`, the context menu appears, and the "Delete" option removes the selected item.

ToolStrip

The `ToolStrip` is a container for buttons, labels, and other controls that provide quick access to common actions, typically displayed as a toolbar. It is often used to create a set of icons or buttons for frequently used functions, such as opening a file, saving a document, or printing.

Key Features:

- **Customizable Controls**: The `ToolStrip` can contain buttons, drop-down buttons, text boxes, labels, and other controls that allow for flexible toolbars.
- **Quick Access**: ToolStrips are designed for actions that are commonly performed, providing a way to execute commands with a single click.
- **Icons and Text**: You can add icons or text to buttons in a `ToolStrip` to make the toolbar more user-friendly.

Common Uses:

- Creating a toolbar with buttons for actions like "Save", "Print", "Undo", and "Redo".
- Providing quick access to settings, tools, or custom actions in an application.

Example Use Case:

```
' Create a ToolStrip:
Dim toolStrip As New ToolStrip()
Me.Controls.Add(toolStrip)

' Add buttons to the ToolStrip:
Dim saveButton As New ToolStripButton("Save")
Dim printButton As New ToolStripButton("Print")
toolStrip.Items.Add(saveButton)
toolStrip.Items.Add(printButton)

' Add icons to the buttons:
saveButton.Image = Image.FromFile("save_icon.png")
printButton.Image = Image.FromFile("print_icon.png")

' Handling button click events:
AddHandler saveButton.Click, AddressOf SaveButton_Click
AddHandler printButton.Click, AddressOf PrintButton_Click

' Save action:
Private Sub SaveButton_Click(sender As Object, e As EventArgs)
    ' Code to save the document
    MessageBox.Show("Document saved.")
End Sub

' Print action:
Private Sub PrintButton_Click(sender As Object, e As EventArgs)
    ' Code to print the document
    MessageBox.Show("Document printed.")
End Sub
```

In this example, a `ToolStrip` is added to a form with two buttons: "Save" and "Print". Each button has an icon and a click event that triggers the corresponding action.

2.5 Dialogs and Message Boxes

Dialogs and message boxes are integral components of any application that allows interaction with the user, either by displaying information, requesting input, or confirming actions. In WinForms applications, these components enhance the user experience by providing simple and effective ways to communicate with the user.

Built-In Dialogs in VB.NET

VB.NET provides several built-in dialogs that make it easy to interact with the user without having to manually code complex UI components. Some common dialog controls include:

OpenFileDialog

The `OpenFileDialog` control allows the user to browse and select a file from their computer. It provides functionality such as file type filtering, previewing files, and supporting multiple file selections. This dialog is commonly used when the application needs to open an existing file.

Key Features:

- Filters file types (e.g., .txt, .jpg, .pdf).
- Lets the user browse directories and select a file.
- Allows setting a default directory and file extension.
- Can support multiple file selection (if configured).

Example Use Case:

```
Dim openFileDialog As New OpenFileDialog()
openFileDialog.Filter = "Text Files (*.txt)|*.txt|All Files (*.*)|*.*" '
Filter for text files
openFileDialog.Title = "Select a File"

If openFileDialog.ShowDialog() = DialogResult.OK Then
    Dim filePath As String = openFileDialog.FileName
    ' Use the selected file path (e.g., open the file)
    MessageBox.Show("File selected: " & filePath)
End If
```

In this example, an `OpenFileDialog` allows the user to select a `.txt` file. After selecting the file, the file path is displayed in a message box.

SaveFileDialog

The `SaveFileDialog` control is used when the user wants to save a file. It provides similar functionality as the `OpenFileDialog` but with the primary goal of specifying the location and filename where the file should be saved.

Key Features:

- Lets the user choose where to save the file and under what name.
- Can filter by file type.
- Supports file extension validation.

Example Use Case:

```
Dim saveFileDialog As New SaveFileDialog()
saveFileDialog.Filter = "Text Files (*.txt)|*.txt|All Files (*.*)|*.*" '
Filter for text files
saveFileDialog.Title = "Save Your File"

If saveFileDialog.ShowDialog() = DialogResult.OK Then
    Dim filePath As String = saveFileDialog.FileName
    ' Code to save the file
    MessageBox.Show("File saved at: " & filePath)
End If
```

In this example, a `SaveFileDialog` is used to save a `.txt` file. The user is prompted to specify the file name and location. After the file is saved, the location is displayed in a message box.

FolderBrowserDialog

The `FolderBrowserDialog` control is used when the user needs to select a folder rather than a file. It's commonly used when you want the user to pick a destination folder, like when choosing where to save data or backup files.

Key Features:

- Allows the user to browse the file system and select a folder.
- Can set the initial folder path.
- Supports browsing for both local and network folders.

Example Use Case:

```
Dim folderBrowserDialog As New FolderBrowserDialog()
folderBrowserDialog.Description = "Select a Folder to Save Your Files"

If folderBrowserDialog.ShowDialog() = DialogResult.OK Then
    Dim folderPath As String = folderBrowserDialog.SelectedPath
    ' Use the selected folder path (e.g., save data in the folder)
    MessageBox.Show("Selected folder: " & folderPath)
End If
```

In this example, a `FolderBrowserDialog` allows the user to select a folder. The selected folder path is then displayed in a message box.

MessageBox

A `MessageBox` is a pop-up window that can display a message to the user, often used for notifications, warnings, or confirmations. The user can interact with the message box through buttons, such as "OK", "Cancel", "Yes", "No", etc. It is one of the most common ways to communicate with the user in Windows Forms applications.

Key Features:

- **Message Content**: Displays text, typically a notification, error message, or question.
- **Buttons**: You can customize the buttons displayed (e.g., "OK", "Cancel", "Yes", "No").
- **Icons**: You can set an icon to show the nature of the message (e.g., Information, Warning, Error).
- **Title**: You can specify the title of the message box.

Common Uses:

- Displaying simple messages like success, error, or information.
- Asking users to confirm actions (e.g., "Are you sure you want to delete this file?").
- Providing feedback after an operation (e.g., "File saved successfully").

Example Use Case:

```
MessageBox.Show("Your file has been saved successfully.", "Success",
MessageBoxButtons.OK, MessageBoxIcon.Information)
```

In this example, a simple `MessageBox` displays a success message with an "OK" button and an information icon.

Customizing Message Boxes

You can customize the behavior and appearance of a `MessageBox` by using different combinations of buttons, icons, and titles.

Customizing Buttons: The buttons that appear in the message box can be set using the `MessageBoxButtons` enumeration, which includes options such as:

- `MessageBoxButtons.OK`
- `MessageBoxButtons.OKCancel`
- `MessageBoxButtons.YesNo`
- `MessageBoxButtons.YesNoCancel`

Customizing Icons: The icons displayed in the message box can be set using the `MessageBoxIcon` enumeration, which includes options such as:

- `MessageBoxIcon.Information`
- `MessageBoxIcon.Warning`
- `MessageBoxIcon.Error`
- `MessageBoxIcon.Question`

Example with Custom Buttons and Icon:

```
Dim result As DialogResult = MessageBox.Show("Are you sure you want to delete
this file?", "Confirm Delete", MessageBoxButtons.YesNo,
MessageBoxIcon.Question)

If result = DialogResult.Yes Then
    ' Perform the delete action
    MessageBox.Show("File deleted successfully.", "Success",
MessageBoxButtons.OK, MessageBoxIcon.Information)
Else
    ' Do nothing if user clicks No
    MessageBox.Show("File deletion canceled.", "Canceled",
MessageBoxButtons.OK, MessageBoxIcon.Information)
End If
```

In this example:

- The `MessageBox` asks the user to confirm a delete action with "Yes" and "No" options.
- Depending on the user's choice, a different message box appears to confirm the action.

2.6 Working with Images and Icons

Images and icons are vital for enhancing the visual appearance and usability of applications. They are frequently used in graphical user interfaces (GUIs) to represent actions, items, and branding, providing users with a more engaging and interactive experience. In Windows Forms (WinForms) development, handling images and icons involves utilizing controls like `ImageList`, working with different image formats such as icons and bitmaps, and displaying these images in various UI components.

Using the Image List

An `ImageList` in VB.NET is a control that stores a collection of images (icons or bitmaps) which can be used in other UI elements like `ListView`, `TreeView`, or `ToolStrip`. The `ImageList` allows developers to easily manage and reuse images, ensuring that images are not duplicated in memory and are accessible across different controls in the application.

Key Features of the ImageList:

- **Storage**: It stores images in a collection that can be accessed by an index.
- **Reusable**: The images can be reused in multiple controls without needing to load them repeatedly.
- **Organization**: Images can be organized and indexed for easy reference.
- **Automatic Scaling**: It supports automatic scaling of images to fit the size of controls.

Example: Using ImageList to Display Icons in ListView

Here's how you can use an `ImageList` to display different icons in a `ListView` control. Let's assume we want to display file type icons (e.g., document icon, image icon) next to items in a list:

1. **Add an ImageList to your form**:
   - Drag an `ImageList` from the toolbox onto your form.
   - Add images to the `ImageList` (you can add icons for documents, images, etc.).
2. **Assign the ImageList to the ListView**:
   - Set the `ListView`'s `LargeImageList` or `SmallImageList` property to the `ImageList`.
3. **Display items with images**:
   - Add items to the `ListView`, assigning each item an image from the `ImageList` using its index.

Example Code:

```
' Create and populate the ImageList with images
Dim imageList As New ImageList()
imageList.Images.Add("document", Image.FromFile("document_icon.png"))
imageList.Images.Add("image", Image.FromFile("image_icon.png"))

' Assign the ImageList to the ListView
ListView1.LargeImageList = imageList

' Add items to the ListView with associated images
Dim item1 As New ListViewItem("Document 1")
item1.ImageIndex = 0 ' Using the "document" icon
ListView1.Items.Add(item1)
```

```
Dim item2 As New ListViewItem("Image 1")
item2.ImageIndex = 1 ' Using the "image" icon
ListView1.Items.Add(item2)
```

In this example:

- We create an `ImageList` and add images to it.
- The `ListView` control displays the images next to the corresponding items by setting the `ImageIndex`.

Handling Icons and Bitmaps

In VB.NET, icons and bitmaps are two types of image formats that are frequently used in GUI development. They are essential for adding visual cues and making applications more user-friendly.

Icons:

An **Icon** is a small image (typically 16x16, 32x32, or 48x48 pixels) used to represent an application, file, or a UI element. Icons are usually designed to be visually distinct and clear at small sizes. They are used in many parts of the operating system and application, including the taskbar, buttons, menus, and file associations.

Key Features of Icons:

- **File Representations**: Often used to represent file types (e.g., text file, image file, executable file).
- **Size and Resolution**: Icons typically come in multiple sizes (16x16, 32x32, 48x48) to adapt to different display contexts.
- **File Format:** Icons are stored in `.ico` or `.png` formats.

Example Use of an Icon in a Button:

```
' Assign an icon to a Button
Button1.Image = Icon.ExtractAssociatedIcon("C:\path\to\file.exe").ToBitmap()
```

In this example:

- The `ExtractAssociatedIcon` method retrieves the icon associated with a file (e.g., executable or document), and then it is displayed on a button.

Bitmaps:

A **Bitmap** is an image format that stores pixel-based images, commonly used for photos, graphics, or other non-vector images. Bitmaps are ideal for handling raster images where each pixel is individually defined. They are usually stored in `.bmp`, `.jpg`, `.png`, `.gif`, and other common image formats.

Key Features of Bitmaps:

- **Pixel-Based**: Each image is represented as a grid of pixels, where each pixel is defined by a color value.
- **Flexible Formats**: Bitmaps can be saved in various formats, including lossless formats (e.g., PNG) and lossy formats (e.g., JPEG).
- **Resolution**: Bitmaps can be of any size, but the quality of the image is heavily dependent on the resolution (number of pixels).

Example Use of Bitmap for Displaying an Image in a PictureBox:

```
' Display a bitmap image in a PictureBox
PictureBox1.Image = New Bitmap("C:\path\to\image.jpg")
```

In this example:

- The `Bitmap` class is used to load an image from a file, which is then displayed in a `PictureBox` control.

Handling Icons and Bitmaps Together

Often, you may need to handle both icons and bitmaps in your application. For instance, you may want to display an icon for a file and a bitmap for a larger image like a profile picture or a product image. While icons are great for small representations of files and applications, bitmaps are better suited for larger, detailed images.

Example: Using Icons and Bitmaps in a ToolStrip

Suppose you want to create a `ToolStrip` with both icons and bitmaps. You can use `ImageList` to store icons for tool buttons, while using bitmaps for larger images or more detailed icons.

```
Dim toolStrip As New ToolStrip()

' Add a button with an icon
Dim button1 As New ToolStripButton("Open", ImageList1.Images(0))
toolStrip.Items.Add(button1)

' Add a button with a bitmap
```

```
Dim button2 As New ToolStripButton("Save", New
Bitmap("C:\path\to\save_icon.png"))
toolStrip.Items.Add(button2)

' Add the ToolStrip to the form
Me.Controls.Add(toolStrip)
```

In this example:

- The first button uses an icon from an `ImageList` to represent the "Open" action.
- The second button uses a bitmap to represent the "Save" action, offering more detailed visuals.

2.7 Creating Status Bars and Progress Bars

Status bars and progress bars are essential UI elements that provide real-time feedback to users, enhancing the overall user experience. They help users understand the current state of an application and track ongoing tasks. In VB.NET, both of these controls are easily implemented using the `StatusStrip` and `ProgressBar` controls.

Adding and Configuring a Status Bar

A **StatusStrip** is a control that allows you to display information at the bottom of a form. It's commonly used for showing status messages, such as "Ready", "Saving Data", or "Operation Complete". It can also display the current time, application status, or any other helpful information. The `StatusStrip` can contain multiple status labels or other controls that are dynamically updated based on the application's state.

Key Features of a StatusStrip:

- **Position**: It appears at the bottom of the form, making it a non-intrusive way to display information.
- **Dynamic Updates**: You can update the content of the `StatusStrip` at runtime to reflect changes in the application's state.
- **Customizable**: It allows you to add multiple `ToolStripStatusLabel` controls or other controls (like buttons or progress bars) within the status strip.

Steps to Add and Configure a StatusStrip:

1. **Add a StatusStrip to the Form**:

   - In Visual Studio, drag the `StatusStrip` control from the toolbox and place it on your form.
   - By default, it will appear at the bottom of the form.
2. **Add ToolStripStatusLabel(s)**:
   - ToolStripStatusLabels are used to display static or dynamic text within the `StatusStrip`.
   - You can add multiple labels to show different status messages.
3. **Update the Status**:
   - You can programmatically update the text of the `ToolStripStatusLabel` to reflect changes in the application state.

Example: Configuring a Simple StatusStrip:

```
' Create a new StatusStrip
Dim statusStrip As New StatusStrip()

' Create a ToolStripStatusLabel to show status messages
Dim statusLabel As New ToolStripStatusLabel()
statusLabel.Text = "Ready" ' Initial message

' Add the label to the StatusStrip
statusStrip.Items.Add(statusLabel)

' Add the StatusStrip to the form
Me.Controls.Add(statusStrip)

' Dynamically update the status message
statusLabel.Text = "Saving Data..."
```

In this example:

- A `StatusStrip` with a `ToolStripStatusLabel` is created.
- Initially, the label shows "Ready", and it is updated to "Saving Data..." when a task begins.

Visualizing Progress with Progress Bars

A **ProgressBar** is a control that visually represents the progress of a task. It is commonly used for operations that take a noticeable amount of time, such as file downloads, data processing, or long-running background tasks. It provides users with a way to track how much of the task is completed and how much is remaining.

Key Features of a ProgressBar:

- **Appearance**: The progress is shown as a bar that fills as the task progresses. The bar can be set to either a smooth progression or a determinate mode, where you define the exact percentage of completion.
- **Determinate vs. Indeterminate**:
    - **Determinate Progress**: When the total progress is known, the `ProgressBar` will fill based on a specific percentage (e.g., 50% complete).
    - **Indeterminate Progress**: When the total progress is not known, the `ProgressBar` will show an animated bar to indicate that something is happening but won't show an exact percentage.
- **Customizable**: You can customize the color, style, and maximum value of the progress bar.

Steps to Add and Configure a ProgressBar:

1. **Add a ProgressBar to the Form**:
    - Drag the `ProgressBar` control from the toolbox to your form.
    - Set the `Maximum` property to define the total value for the progress (e.g., 100 for 100% completion).
    - Set the `Minimum` property to 0 (default value) to represent the start of the progress.
2. **Update Progress**:
    - You can update the `ProgressBar`'s value programmatically to reflect the current progress.
    - The value should be between the `Minimum` and `Maximum` values.
3. **Handle Background Tasks**:
    - For long-running tasks, it's a good practice to use a background thread or the `BackgroundWorker` to update the progress bar without freezing the UI.

Example: Using a ProgressBar for File Download:

```
' Create and configure the ProgressBar
Dim progressBar As New ProgressBar()
progressBar.Maximum = 100
progressBar.Minimum = 0
progressBar.Step = 1
progressBar.Value = 0
progressBar.Width = 200
Me.Controls.Add(progressBar)

' Simulate a file download
For i As Integer = 0 To 100
    ' Simulate a time-consuming task
    Threading.Thread.Sleep(50) ' Sleep to simulate download time

    ' Update the progress bar
    progressBar.Value = i
Next
```

In this example:

- A `ProgressBar` is created and configured with a maximum value of 100 (representing 100%).
- The progress bar's value is updated incrementally in a loop to simulate the download process, with each iteration reflecting progress.

Combining StatusStrip and ProgressBar

You can combine both the `StatusStrip` and `ProgressBar` to provide both status messages and a visual representation of progress. For example, you could display "Saving Data..." in the status bar while also filling a progress bar to show the task's progress.

Example: Status Bar with ProgressBar:

```
' Create StatusStrip and add a ToolStripStatusLabel
Dim statusStrip As New StatusStrip()
Dim statusLabel As New ToolStripStatusLabel("Ready")
statusStrip.Items.Add(statusLabel)
Me.Controls.Add(statusStrip)

' Create a ProgressBar and set its properties
Dim progressBar As New ProgressBar()
progressBar.Maximum = 100
progressBar.Minimum = 0
progressBar.Width = 200
Me.Controls.Add(progressBar)

' Simulate a task and update the progress bar
For i As Integer = 0 To 100
    ' Update the status message
    statusLabel.Text = "Processing... " & i & "%"

    ' Update the progress bar
    progressBar.Value = i

    ' Simulate work
    Threading.Thread.Sleep(50)
Next

' Once complete, update the status label
statusLabel.Text = "Task Complete!"
```

In this example:

- The `StatusStrip` is used to show the status message, which updates as the task progresses.
- The `ProgressBar` fills as the task progresses, giving the user a visual cue of the current completion status.

30 multiple-choice questions (MCQs)

2.1 Introduction to Windows Forms

1. **What is the primary purpose of Windows Forms in VB.NET?**
   - A) To create web applications
   - B) To design graphical user interfaces for desktop applications
   - C) To connect to databases
   - D) To create mobile applications

   Answer: B) To design graphical user interfaces for desktop applications

2. **Which of the following is used to design the layout of Windows Forms in Visual Studio?**
   - A) Code editor
   - B) Form Designer
   - C) Server Explorer
   - D) Toolbox

   Answer: B) Form Designer

3. **What feature does Windows Forms provide for user interaction?**
   - A) Command-line interface
   - B) Graphical user interface (GUI) controls
   - C) Machine learning algorithms
   - D) Database management systems

   Answer: B) Graphical user interface (GUI) controls

4. **Which of the following is a key advantage of Windows Forms?**
   - A) It is used for creating mobile apps.
   - B) It supports interactive user interfaces.
   - C) It supports command-line interfaces.
   - D) It does not support event-driven programming.

   Answer: B) It supports interactive user interfaces.

2.2 Working with Basic Controls

TextBoxes, Buttons, Labels

5. **Which control is used to allow users to enter text in a Windows Forms application?**
   - A) Label
   - B) TextBox

- C) Button
- D) CheckBox

Answer: B) TextBox

6. **What is the main function of a Button control in Windows Forms?**
   - A) To display text
   - B) To trigger an action when clicked
   - C) To show images
   - D) To accept user input

   Answer: B) To trigger an action when clicked

7. **Which control in Windows Forms is typically used to display static text?**
   - A) TextBox
   - B) Button
   - C) Label
   - D) RadioButton

   Answer: C) Label

CheckBoxes and RadioButtons

8. **Which of the following controls is used for selecting a single option from a group of options?**
   - A) CheckBox
   - B) ComboBox
   - C) RadioButton
   - D) ListBox

   Answer: C) RadioButton

9. **What is the main purpose of a CheckBox in Windows Forms?**
   - A) To allow the user to select one option from a list
   - B) To display text
   - C) To toggle between two options (checked or unchecked)
   - D) To execute a command when clicked

   Answer: C) To toggle between two options (checked or unchecked)

10. **Which of the following properties would you use to check if a CheckBox is selected?**
    - A) CheckBox.Checked
    - B) Button.Enabled
    - C) TextBox.Text
    - D) Label.Text

    Answer: A) CheckBox.Checked

2.3 Advanced Controls

ListBoxes and ComboBoxes

11. **Which control is used to display a list of items from which the user can select?**
    - A) RadioButton
    - B) ListBox
    - C) TextBox
    - D) Button

    Answer: B) ListBox

12. **What is a key difference between a ComboBox and a ListBox?**
    - A) ComboBox allows multi-selection, ListBox does not.
    - B) ComboBox is used for displaying images, ListBox is used for text.
    - C) ComboBox allows the user to select from a dropdown or enter custom input, while ListBox does not.
    - D) ComboBox does not support events, while ListBox does.

    Answer: C) ComboBox allows the user to select from a dropdown or enter custom input, while ListBox does not.

PictureBox, ScrollBars, and Splitters

13. **What is the purpose of the PictureBox control in Windows Forms?**
    - A) To display text
    - B) To display images or graphics
    - C) To create dropdown menus
    - D) To manage files

    Answer: B) To display images or graphics

14. **Which control allows users to scroll through content larger than the visible area?**
    - A) PictureBox
    - B) ProgressBar
    - C) ScrollBar
    - D) Button

    Answer: C) ScrollBar

15. **What is the function of a Splitter control in Windows Forms?**
    - A) To allow resizing of panels within a form
    - B) To create menus
    - C) To display images
    - D) To handle database operations

    Answer: A) To allow resizing of panels within a form

2.4 Working with Menus and Toolbars

16. **Which control is used to create menus in Windows Forms?**
    - A) ToolStrip
    - B) ContextMenuStrip
    - C) MenuStrip
    - D) StatusStrip

    Answer: C) MenuStrip

17. **What does a ContextMenuStrip display?**
    - A) A drop-down list at the top of the form
    - B) A pop-up menu when the user right-clicks on a control or form
    - C) A series of buttons for quick actions
    - D) A menu displayed at the bottom of the form

    Answer: B) A pop-up menu when the user right-clicks on a control or form

18. **Which of the following is commonly found in a ToolStrip control?**
    - A) Buttons for quick actions
    - B) A list of options
    - C) A progress bar
    - D) A text input field

    Answer: A) Buttons for quick actions

2.5 Dialogs and Message Boxes

Built-In Dialogs in VB.NET

19. **Which dialog is used to allow a user to select a file to open?**
    - A) SaveFileDialog
    - B) OpenFileDialog
    - C) FolderBrowserDialog
    - D) ColorDialog

    Answer: B) OpenFileDialog

20. **What is the purpose of the SaveFileDialog control?**
    - A) To select a file to delete
    - B) To select a folder for saving files
    - C) To allow the user to choose a file to open

- D) To save files with specific names and locations

Answer: D) To save files with specific names and locations

21. **Which dialog allows users to select a folder rather than a file?**
    - A) OpenFileDialog
    - B) FolderBrowserDialog
    - C) PrintDialog
    - D) SaveFileDialog

    Answer: B) FolderBrowserDialog

Customizing Message Boxes

22. **Which property allows you to customize the buttons displayed in a MessageBox?**
    - A) MessageBoxIcon
    - B) MessageBoxButtons
    - C) MessageBoxText
    - D) MessageBoxForm

    Answer: B) MessageBoxButtons

23. **Which of the following code will display a MessageBox with a "Yes" and "No" button?**
    - A) `MessageBox.Show("Confirm?", "Confirm", MessageBoxButtons.YesNo)`
    - B) `MessageBox.Show("Alert!", "Error", MessageBoxButtons.OKCancel)`
    - C) `MessageBox.Show("Success", "Message", MessageBoxButtons.OK)`
    - D) `MessageBox.Show("Warning", "Caution", MessageBoxButtons.AbortRetryIgnore)`

    Answer: A) `MessageBox.Show("Confirm?", "Confirm", MessageBoxButtons.YesNo)`

2.6 Working with Images and Icons

Using the Image List

24. **What control can you use to store and manage images for use in other controls like ListView or TreeView?**
    - A) PictureBox
    - B) ToolStrip
    - C) ImageList
    - D) Label

    Answer: C) ImageList

25. **What is the primary use of icons in Windows Forms applications?**
    - A) To display error messages
    - B) To represent application or file types visually
    - C) To handle user input
    - D) To store text data

    Answer: B) To represent application or file types visually

26. **Which image format is typically used for pixel-based images such as photos or graphics?**
    - A) Icon
    - B) Bitmap
    - C) JPEG
    - D) GIF

    Answer: B) Bitmap

2.7 Creating Status Bars and Progress Bars

Adding and Configuring a Status Bar

27. **Which control is used to display status messages at the bottom of a Windows Form?**
    - A) ProgressBar
    - B) StatusStrip
    - C) ToolStrip
    - D) Label

    Answer: B) StatusStrip

28. **Which of the following is commonly displayed in a StatusStrip?**
    - A) Input fields for user data
    - B) Information about the current task or application state
    - C) Buttons for performing actions
    - D) A drop-down menu

    Answer: B) Information about the current task or application state

Visualizing Progress with Progress Bars

29. **Which control would you use to show the progress of a long-running task in a VB.NET application?**
    - A) ProgressBar
    - B) TextBox
    - C) ComboBox
    - D) ListBox

Answer: A) ProgressBar

30. **What is the default behavior of a ProgressBar in determinate mode?**
    - A) It displays an animated bar without showing specific progress.
    - B) It fills according to a percentage or value set by the program.
    - C) It only displays a text message.
    - D) It is invisible until the task is completed.

Answer: B) It fills according to a percentage or value set by the program.

2.1 Introduction to Windows Forms

1. **Create a simple Windows Forms application with a button. When the button is clicked, display a message box that says "Hello, World!"**

Answer:

```
Public Class Form1
    Private Sub Button1_Click(sender As Object, e As EventArgs) Handles
Button1.Click
        MessageBox.Show("Hello, World!")
    End Sub
End Class
```

2.2 Working with Basic Controls

2. **Write a program that takes user input from a TextBox and displays it in a Label when a Button is clicked.**

Answer:

```
Public Class Form1
    Private Sub Button1_Click(sender As Object, e As EventArgs) Handles
Button1.Click
        Label1.Text = TextBox1.Text
    End Sub
End Class
```

3. **Create a form with a CheckBox. When the CheckBox is checked, display "Checked" in a Label; when unchecked, display "Unchecked".**

Answer:

```
Public Class Form1
    Private Sub CheckBox1_CheckedChanged(sender As Object, e As
EventArgs) Handles CheckBox1.CheckedChanged
        If CheckBox1.Checked Then
            Label1.Text = "Checked"
```

```
        Else
            Label1.Text = "Unchecked"
        End If
    End Sub
End Class
```

4. **Write a program that uses a RadioButton to let the user choose between "Male" and "Female". When the user selects one, display the chosen gender in a Label.**

   Answer:

```
Public Class Form1
    Private Sub RadioButton_CheckedChanged(sender As Object, e As
EventArgs) Handles RadioButton1.CheckedChanged,
RadioButton2.CheckedChanged
        If RadioButton1.Checked Then
            Label1.Text = "Male"
        ElseIf RadioButton2.Checked Then
            Label1.Text = "Female"
        End If
    End Sub
End Class
```

2.3 Advanced Controls

5. **Create a ListBox that allows the user to select multiple items. Add items to the ListBox at runtime.**

   Answer:

```
Public Class Form1
    Private Sub Button1_Click(sender As Object, e As EventArgs) Handles
Button1.Click
        ListBox1.Items.Add("Item 1")
        ListBox1.Items.Add("Item 2")
        ListBox1.Items.Add("Item 3")
    End Sub
End Class
```

6. **Write a program with a ComboBox that allows the user to select their country from a pre-populated list. Display the selected country in a Label.**

   Answer:

```
Public Class Form1
    Private Sub Form1_Load(sender As Object, e As EventArgs) Handles
MyBase.Load
        ComboBox1.Items.Add("USA")
        ComboBox1.Items.Add("Canada")
        ComboBox1.Items.Add("Mexico")
    End Sub
```

```
    Private Sub ComboBox1_SelectedIndexChanged(sender As Object, e As
EventArgs) Handles ComboBox1.SelectedIndexChanged
        Label1.Text = "Selected country: " &
ComboBox1.SelectedItem.ToString()
    End Sub
End Class
```

7. **Create a program where a PictureBox displays an image when a Button is clicked.**

   Answer:

```
Public Class Form1
    Private Sub Button1_Click(sender As Object, e As EventArgs) Handles
Button1.Click
        PictureBox1.Image = Image.FromFile("path_to_image.jpg")
    End Sub
End Class
```

8. **Write a program with a ScrollBar. When the user scrolls, the value of the ScrollBar should be displayed in a Label.**

   Answer:

```
Public Class Form1
    Private Sub HScrollBar1_Scroll(sender As Object, e As
ScrollEventArgs) Handles HScrollBar1.Scroll
        Label1.Text = "Scroll Value: " & HScrollBar1.Value.ToString()
    End Sub
End Class
```

2.4 Working with Menus and Toolbars

9. **Create a form with a MenuStrip containing "File" and "Edit" menus. Under "File", add "New" and "Open" options. When "New" is clicked, display a message box saying "New File".**

   Answer:

```
Public Class Form1
    Private Sub NewToolStripMenuItem_Click(sender As Object, e As
EventArgs) Handles NewToolStripMenuItem.Click
        MessageBox.Show("New File")
    End Sub
End Class
```

10. **Write a program where a ToolStrip is used to add a Button that shows a message box saying "ToolStrip Button Clicked".**

    Answer:

```
Public Class Form1
    Private Sub ToolStripButton1_Click(sender As Object, e As
EventArgs) Handles ToolStripButton1.Click
        MessageBox.Show("ToolStrip Button Clicked")
    End Sub
End Class
```

2.5 Dialogs and Message Boxes

11. **Create a form with a Button. When the Button is clicked, show an OpenFileDialog to let the user choose a file to open. Display the file path in a Label.**

    Answer:

```
Public Class Form1
    Private Sub Button1_Click(sender As Object, e As EventArgs) Handles
Button1.Click
        OpenFileDialog1.ShowDialog()
        Label1.Text = OpenFileDialog1.FileName
    End Sub
End Class
```

12. **Write a program where a MessageBox is shown with "Yes" and "No" buttons. If the user clicks "Yes", display "You clicked Yes" in a Label.**

    Answer:

```
Public Class Form1
    Private Sub Button1_Click(sender As Object, e As EventArgs) Handles
Button1.Click
        Dim result As DialogResult = MessageBox.Show("Do you want to
continue?", "Confirm", MessageBoxButtons.YesNo)
        If result = DialogResult.Yes Then
            Label1.Text = "You clicked Yes"
        Else
            Label1.Text = "You clicked No"
        End If
    End Sub
End Class
```

2.6 Working with Images and Icons

13. **Create a form that uses an ImageList to store and display icons in a ListView.**

    Answer:

```
Public Class Form1
    Private Sub Form1_Load(sender As Object, e As EventArgs) Handles
MyBase.Load
```

```
        Dim imgList As New ImageList()
        imgList.Images.Add("file", Image.FromFile("file_icon.ico"))
        ListView1.SmallImageList = imgList
        ListView1.Items.Add(New ListViewItem("File", "file"))
    End Sub
End Class
```

14. **Write a program that displays an icon in the taskbar when the application starts.**

Answer:

```
Public Class Form1
    Private Sub Form1_Load(sender As Object, e As EventArgs) Handles
MyBase.Load
        Me.Icon = New Icon("icon.ico")
    End Sub
End Class
```

2.7 Creating Status Bars and Progress Bars

15. **Write a program with a ProgressBar that fills as the user clicks a Button. Each click increases the progress by 10%.**

Answer:

```
Public Class Form1
    Private Sub Button1_Click(sender As Object, e As EventArgs) Handles
Button1.Click
        If ProgressBar1.Value < 100 Then
            ProgressBar1.Value += 10
        End If
    End Sub
End Class
```

CHAPTER 3: MASTERING VB.NET LANGUAGE FEATURES

3.1 Data Types and Variables in VB.NET

In VB.NET, **data types** define the kind of value that a variable can hold. A **variable** is a container that stores data, and each variable must be declared with a specific data type that determines the kind of data it can store. The process of declaring a variable involves specifying its data type and its name. The data type of a variable ensures that it can only store data of the appropriate type (e.g., integers, strings, booleans, etc.).

Common Data Types in VB.NET:

1. **Integer** (`Dim x As Integer`)
   - **Definition**: An integer is a data type used to store whole numbers without decimals.
   - **Range**: Typically stores values between -2,147,483,648 and 2,147,483,647.
   - **Example**:

     ```
     Dim x As Integer = 10
     ```

2. **Double** (`Dim y As Double`)
   - **Definition**: A double is a data type used to store floating-point numbers (decimals). It can store more precise values than `Single` and is often used for calculations involving real numbers.
   - **Range**: It can store very large or very small values, including numbers with many decimal places.
   - **Example**:

     ```
     Dim y As Double = 3.14159
     ```

3. **String** (`Dim name As String`)
   - **Definition**: A string is a data type used to store sequences of characters, such as words or text. A string can hold anything from a single character to entire paragraphs.
   - **Example**:

     ```
     Dim name As String = "Alice"
     ```

4. **Boolean** (`Dim isActive As Boolean`)
   - **Definition**: A boolean is a data type used to store a logical value, which can either be `True` or `False`. It is commonly used for decision-making and condition evaluation.
   - **Example**:

     ```
     Dim isActive As Boolean = True
     ```

5. **Char** (`Dim letter As Char`)
   - **Definition**: A char is a data type used to store a single character, such as a letter, number, or symbol. A char holds one character from the Unicode character set.
   - **Example**:

```
Dim letter As Char = "A"c  ' Note: the 'c' suffix indicates it's
a Char literal.
```

6. **Date** (`Dim currentDate As Date`)
   - **Definition**: A date is a data type used to store date and time information. It can store values such as year, month, day, hours, minutes, seconds, and even fractions of a second.
   - **Example**:

```
Dim currentDate As Date = #12/25/2025 12:00:00 AM#
```

7. **Object** (`Dim obj As Object`)
   - **Definition**: An object is the most general data type in VB.NET. It can hold any data type, including more complex types such as arrays, classes, or user-defined types. It is used when you are uncertain about the data type or when you need to store a variety of different data types.
   - **Example**:

```
Dim obj As Object = 1234  ' You can store an integer, string,
etc., in an Object.
obj = "Hello, World!"  ' Now obj holds a string.
```

Declaring and Assigning Variables:

In VB.NET, variables are declared using the `Dim` keyword followed by the variable name and the data type. Optionally, you can also initialize the variable with a value.

Example of Variable Declaration:

```
Dim x As Integer = 5  ' Declare an Integer and assign a value
Dim name As String = "Alice"  ' Declare a String and assign a value
Dim isActive As Boolean = True  ' Declare a Boolean and assign a value
```

You can also **declare a variable without assigning a value** at the time of declaration:

```
Dim x As Integer  ' Declare an Integer (default value is 0)
Dim name As String  ' Declare a String (default value is Nothing or an empty
string)
Dim isActive As Boolean  ' Declare a Boolean (default value is False)
```

Implicit Data Type Declaration:

VB.NET is a **strongly typed language**, but it also supports **implicit type inference**. When you omit the type explicitly, VB.NET will infer the type based on the assigned value.

```
Dim x = 5  ' Implicitly, VB.NET infers that x is of type Integer
Dim name = "Alice"  ' VB.NET infers that name is of type String
Dim isActive = True  ' VB.NET infers that isActive is of type Boolean
```

Variable Scope and Lifetime:

- **Local variables** are declared within procedures or blocks and exist only during the execution of that block. They are destroyed once the block execution ends.
- **Global or Module-level variables** are declared at the top of a module or class and exist for the lifetime of the application or module.

Casting and Conversions:

You may need to **cast** or **convert** between data types in certain cases. You can use explicit conversion functions to ensure that one type of data is converted into another.

Example of Explicit Conversion:

```
Dim x As Integer = 10
Dim y As Double = 5.5
Dim result As Double = x + y  ' Implicit conversion from Integer to Double

Dim str As String = "123"
Dim num As Integer = Convert.ToInt32(str)  ' Explicit conversion from String
to Integer
```

Example of CType for Casting:

```
Dim number As Object = 1234
Dim intNumber As Integer = CType(number, Integer)  ' Casting an Object to
Integer
```

Type Handling:

- **TypeOf Operator**: Can be used to check the type of an object at runtime.

```
If TypeOf obj Is Integer Then
    Console.WriteLine("The object is an Integer.")
End If
```

3.2 Operators: Arithmetic, Relational, and Logical

In VB.NET, **operators** are special symbols used to perform operations on variables and values. Operators can be categorized into different types based on the kind of operation they perform. In this section, we will cover **arithmetic operators**, **relational operators**, and **logical operators**.

1. Arithmetic Operators:

Arithmetic operators are used to perform basic mathematical operations such as addition, subtraction, multiplication, division, and finding remainders.

Common Arithmetic Operators:

1. **Addition (+)**:
    - Used to add two values.

- **Example**:

```
Dim sum As Integer = 5 + 3   ' sum = 8
```

2. **Subtraction (-)**:
    - Used to subtract one value from another.
    - **Example**:

```
Dim difference As Integer = 5 - 3   ' difference = 2
```

3. **Integer Division ()**:
    - Divides one number by another, but returns only the integer quotient (ignores the remainder).
    - **Example**:

```
Dim quotient As Integer = 5 \ 2   ' quotient = 2 (ignores decimal
part)
```

4. **Division (/)**:
    - Divides two numbers and returns a floating-point result (including decimal part).
    - **Example**:

```
Dim quotient As Double = 5 / 2   ' quotient = 2.5
```

5. **Modulus (Mod)**:
    - Returns the remainder of a division operation.
    - **Example**:

```
Dim remainder As Integer = 5 Mod 2   ' remainder = 1
```

Example of Arithmetic Operations:

```
Dim sum As Integer = 10 + 2    ' sum = 12
Dim difference As Integer = 10 - 3    ' difference = 7
Dim quotient As Double = 10 / 4    ' quotient = 2.5
Dim integerDivision As Integer = 10 \ 4    ' integerDivision = 2
Dim remainder As Integer = 10 Mod 4    ' remainder = 2
```

---

2. Relational Operators:

Relational operators are used to compare two values and determine the relationship between them. They return a **Boolean** value (`True` or `False`).

Common Relational Operators:

1. **Equal to (=)**:
    - Compares if two values are equal.
    - **Example**:

```
Dim isEqual As Boolean = (5 = 3)   ' isEqual = False
```

2. **Not equal to (<>)**:
   - Compares if two values are not equal.
   - **Example**:

```
Dim isNotEqual As Boolean = (5 <> 3)   ' isNotEqual = True
```

3. **Less than (<)**:
   - Compares if the first value is less than the second value.
   - **Example**:

```
Dim isLessThan As Boolean = (5 < 3)   ' isLessThan = False
```

4. **Greater than (>)**:
   - Compares if the first value is greater than the second value.
   - **Example**:

```
Dim isGreaterThan As Boolean = (5 > 3)   ' isGreaterThan = True
```

5. **Less than or equal to (<=)**:
   - Compares if the first value is less than or equal to the second value.
   - **Example**:

```
Dim isLessThanOrEqual As Boolean = (5 <= 3)   ' isLessThanOrEqual
= False
```

6. **Greater than or equal to (>=)**:
   - Compares if the first value is greater than or equal to the second value.
   - **Example**:

```
Dim isGreaterThanOrEqual As Boolean = (5 >= 3)   '
isGreaterThanOrEqual = True
```

Example of Relational Operations:

```
Dim isEqual As Boolean = (5 = 3)   ' isEqual = False
Dim isNotEqual As Boolean = (5 <> 3)   ' isNotEqual = True
Dim isGreaterThan As Boolean = (5 > 3)   ' isGreaterThan = True
Dim isLessThan As Boolean = (5 < 3)   ' isLessThan = False
Dim isGreaterThanOrEqual As Boolean = (5 >= 3)   ' isGreaterThanOrEqual = True
Dim isLessThanOrEqual As Boolean = (5 <= 3)   ' isLessThanOrEqual = False
```

---

3. Logical Operators:

Logical operators are used to combine conditional expressions or to perform logical operations. They return a Boolean value (`True` or `False`) based on the conditions provided.

Common Logical Operators:

1. **And**:
   - Returns `True` if both conditions are `True`, otherwise returns `False`.
   - **Example**:

     ```
     Dim condition1 As Boolean = True
     Dim condition2 As Boolean = False
     Dim result As Boolean = (condition1 And condition2)   ' result =
     False
     ```

2. **Or**:
   - Returns `True` if at least one of the conditions is `True`, otherwise returns `False`.
   - **Example**:

     ```
     Dim condition1 As Boolean = True
     Dim condition2 As Boolean = False
     Dim result As Boolean = (condition1 Or condition2)   ' result =
     True
     ```

3. **Not**:
   - Reverses the truth value of the condition (inverts it).
   - **Example**:

     ```
     Dim condition As Boolean = True
     Dim result As Boolean = Not condition   ' result = False
     ```

Example of Logical Operations:

```
Dim condition1 As Boolean = True
Dim condition2 As Boolean = False
Dim resultAnd As Boolean = (condition1 And condition2)   ' resultAnd = False
Dim resultOr As Boolean = (condition1 Or condition2)   ' resultOr = True
Dim resultNot As Boolean = Not condition1   ' resultNot = False
```

Summary of Operators:

Operator Type	Operator	Description	Example
Arithmetic	`+`	Addition	`5 + 3`
	`-`	Subtraction	`5 - 3`
	`\`	Integer Division	`5 \ 2`
	`/`	Division (floating-point)	`5 / 2`
	`Mod`	Modulus (remainder)	`5 Mod 2`

Operator Type	Operator	Description	Example
Relational	`=`	Equal to	`5 = 3`
	`<>`	Not equal to	`5 <> 3`
	`<`	Less than	`5 < 3`
	`>`	Greater than	`5 > 3`
	`<=`	Less than or equal to	`5 <= 3`
	`>=`	Greater than or equal to	`5 >= 3`
Logical	`And`	Returns `True` if both conditions are true	`(condition1 And condition2)`
	`Or`	Returns `True` if at least one condition is true	`(condition1 Or condition2)`
	`Not`	Reverses the truth value of a condition	`Not condition1`

By understanding how to use these operators, you can effectively manipulate and compare data in VB.NET to create logical flow and solve real-world problems in your applications.

3.3 Conditional Statements: If...Else, Select Case

Conditional statements in programming allow the program to decide which block of code to execute based on certain conditions. In VB.NET, there are two common ways to handle conditions: **If...Else** and **Select Case**.

1. If...Else Statement:

The **If...Else** statement is used to execute a block of code only if a specific condition is **True**, and optionally execute another block of code if the condition is **False**. It is the most common conditional structure in VB.NET.

Syntax of If...Else:

```
If condition Then
    ' Code to execute if the condition is True
Else
    ' Code to execute if the condition is False
End If
```

Explanation:

- The **`If`** keyword checks the condition.
- If the condition evaluates to **True**, the code within the **`Then`** block is executed.
- If the condition evaluates to **False**, the code within the **`Else`** block (if provided) is executed.

Example:

```
Dim age As Integer = 18

If age >= 18 Then
    Console.WriteLine("You are an adult.")
Else
    Console.WriteLine("You are a minor.")
End If
```

- In this example, the program checks if the value of the variable `age` is greater than or equal to 18.
- If the condition **`age >= 18`** is **True**, it will print "You are an adult."
- If the condition is **False**, it will print "You are a minor."

Using ElseIf:

You can also use **`ElseIf`** to check multiple conditions sequentially. The first **`True`** condition will execute its corresponding block of code.

```
Dim grade As Integer = 85

If grade >= 90 Then
    Console.WriteLine("Grade A")
ElseIf grade >= 80 Then
    Console.WriteLine("Grade B")
ElseIf grade >= 70 Then
    Console.WriteLine("Grade C")
Else
    Console.WriteLine("Grade D or below")
End If
```

- Here, multiple conditions are checked in order. The program will print "Grade B" because `grade` is between 80 and 89.

---

2. Select Case Statement:

The **Select Case** statement is used when there are multiple possible conditions based on a single variable. It is often used as a more efficient alternative to multiple **`If...ElseIf`** statements, especially when checking a variable for several possible values.

Syntax of Select Case:

```
Select Case variable
```

```
    Case value1
        ' Code to execute if variable = value1
    Case value2
        ' Code to execute if variable = value2
    Case Else
        ' Code to execute if variable does not match any case
End Select
```

Explanation:

- The **`Select Case`** keyword evaluates the value of a single variable.
- Each **`Case`** statement checks for a specific value.
- If a match is found, the corresponding block of code is executed.
- **`Case Else`** is used as a fallback when none of the previous cases match the value of the variable.

Example:

```
Dim day As Integer = 3

Select Case day
    Case 1
        Console.WriteLine("Monday")
    Case 2
        Console.WriteLine("Tuesday")
    Case 3
        Console.WriteLine("Wednesday")
    Case Else
        Console.WriteLine("Weekend")
End Select
```

- In this example, the variable `day` is checked.
- Since the value of `day` is `3`, the program will output "Wednesday".
- If the value of `day` was not 1, 2, or 3, the program would output "Weekend" because of the **`Case Else`**.

Using Ranges in Select Case:

You can also use **ranges** in a **`Select Case`** to evaluate a variable against a range of values.

```
Dim age As Integer = 25

Select Case age
    Case 0 To 12
        Console.WriteLine("Child")
    Case 13 To 19
        Console.WriteLine("Teenager")
    Case 20 To 64
        Console.WriteLine("Adult")
    Case Else
        Console.WriteLine("Senior")
End Select
```

- Here, the `age` is checked against specific ranges, making it more efficient than using multiple **`If...ElseIf`** statements.
- Since `age` is 25, the output will be "Adult".

Using Multiple Values in a Single Case:

You can also check for multiple values in a single **`Case`** by separating them with commas.

```
Dim grade As Integer = 75

Select Case grade
    Case 90 To 100
        Console.WriteLine("Grade A")
    Case 80 To 89
        Console.WriteLine("Grade B")
    Case 70 To 79
        Console.WriteLine("Grade C")
    Case 60 To 69
        Console.WriteLine("Grade D")
    Case Else
        Console.WriteLine("Grade F")
End Select
```

- Here, `grade` is checked for different ranges. Since `grade` is 75, the program will output "Grade C".

Summary of Differences:

Feature	If...Else	Select Case
Use Case	Best for a small number of conditions	Best for multiple conditions based on one variable
Efficiency	Less efficient with many conditions	More efficient with many conditions
Readability	Easier for fewer conditions	Easier for a large number of conditions
Multiple Conditions	Use `ElseIf` for multiple conditions	Use multiple `Case` statements

---

3.4 Loops in VB.NET: For...Next, Do...Loop, While...End While

In VB.NET, loops are used to repeat a block of code multiple times based on a specific condition. The primary types of loops are **For...Next**, **Do...Loop**, and **While...End While**. Each type of loop serves a particular purpose depending on the needs of your program.

1. For...Next Loop

The **For...Next** loop is used when you want to repeat a block of code a specific number of times. It's ideal when the number of iterations is known before entering the loop.

Syntax of For...Next:

```
For counter As Integer = startValue To endValue [Step stepValue]
    ' Code to be executed in each iteration
Next
```

- **`startValue`**: The initial value of the counter.
- **`endValue`**: The final value that the counter should reach.
- **`Step` (optional)**: Specifies the increment (or decrement) for the counter. If not specified, it defaults to 1.

Example:

```
For i As Integer = 1 To 5
    Console.WriteLine(i)
Next
```

- This loop will print the numbers 1 through 5 because the **`startValue`** is 1, the **`endValue`** is 5, and the default **`Step`** value is 1.

Example with Step:

```
For i As Integer = 1 To 10 Step 2
    Console.WriteLine(i)
Next
```

- This loop will print the numbers 1, 3, 5, 7, and 9 because the **`Step`** value is set to 2, which increments the counter by 2 on each iteration.

---

2. Do...Loop

The **Do...Loop** is more flexible than the **For...Next** loop because you can specify a condition that must be met either **before** the loop starts or **after** it completes. You can use the **Do While** or **Do Until** variation, depending on whether you want the loop to continue while the condition is true or until the condition becomes true.

Syntax of Do...Loop (While):

```
Do While condition
    ' Code to be executed as long as the condition is True
Loop
```

- The loop continues to execute as long as the condition remains **True**.

Syntax of Do...Loop (Until):

```
Do Until condition
```

```
    ' Code to be executed until the condition becomes True
Loop
```

- The loop continues to execute until the condition becomes **True**.

Example of Do While:

```
Dim counter As Integer = 0
Do While counter < 5
    Console.WriteLine(counter)
    counter += 1
Loop
```

- This loop will print the numbers 0 through 4 because the **condition** is **True** while `counter` is less than 5, and **counter** is incremented in each iteration.

Example of Do Until:

```
Dim counter As Integer = 0
Do Until counter >= 5
    Console.WriteLine(counter)
    counter += 1
Loop
```

- This loop will also print the numbers 0 through 4, but it stops when the **counter** is no longer **less than 5**.

---

3. While...End While Loop

The **While...End While** loop is similar to the **Do While** loop, but it checks the condition **before** entering the loop. If the condition is **False** at the start, the loop is never executed.

Syntax of While...End While:

```
While condition
    ' Code to be executed as long as the condition is True
End While
```

- The loop will continue to execute as long as the **condition** is **True**.
- The condition is evaluated **before** the loop starts, meaning if it's **False** initially, the code inside the loop will not run at all.

Example:

```
Dim counter As Integer = 0
While counter < 5
    Console.WriteLine(counter)
    counter += 1
End While
```

- This loop will print the numbers 0 through 4, and just like the **Do While** loop, it checks if the condition (**counter < 5**) is **True** before entering the loop and continues as long as the condition remains **True**.

Key Differences Between the Loops:

Feature	For...Next	Do...Loop	While...End While
Use Case	When the number of iterations is known	When the condition needs to be checked before or after the loop	When the condition is checked before entering the loop
Condition Checking	Checked at the start of each iteration	Can be checked either at the start or at the end	Checked before the first iteration starts
Flexibility	Less flexible, fixed number of iterations	More flexible, can be controlled with While or Until	More rigid as the condition is checked before entering
Default Action	Performs action a fixed number of times	Performs action while/ until condition is met	Executes as long as the condition is True
When to Use	When you know how many iterations you need	When you want to perform actions while or until a condition is met	When the condition needs to be evaluated before starting the loop

---

3.5 Procedures: Subroutines and Functions

Subroutines (Sub):

In VB.NET, **procedures** are blocks of code that perform a specific task. The two primary types of procedures are **Subroutines (Subs)** and **Functions**. Both serve similar purposes but differ in how they interact with the program and whether or not they return values.

---

1. Subroutines (Sub)

A **Subroutine** (or **Sub**) is a procedure that performs a set of operations but **does not return a value**. Subroutines are often used to group a series of statements that perform a specific task, and they help make code more modular and easier to maintain.

Syntax of a Subroutine:

```
Sub ProcedureName(Optional Parameter As DataType)
    ' Code to be executed
End Sub
```

- **ProcedureName**: The name of the subroutine. It is called when you want to execute the subroutine's code.

- **Optional Parameter**: You can pass arguments (parameters) into the subroutine. These parameters are used by the code inside the subroutine. The **Optional** keyword allows you to provide default values for parameters.

Example:
```
Sub GreetUser(name As String)
    Console.WriteLine("Hello, " & name)
End Sub
```

- This subroutine takes a string parameter **`name`** and prints a greeting to the console. When you call the subroutine, you pass a value for **`name`**:

```
GreetUser("Alice")   ' Output: Hello, Alice
```

In this case, "Alice" is passed as the argument to the **`name`** parameter, and the subroutine displays the message "Hello, Alice".

Calling a Subroutine:

To call a subroutine, you simply use its name followed by any necessary arguments (if any):

```
GreetUser("Bob")   ' Calls the GreetUser subroutine and passes "Bob" as an
argument.
```

Subroutines can be used for tasks like displaying messages, updating UI elements, or performing calculations.

---

2. Functions

A **Function** is similar to a **Subroutine**, but the key difference is that **Functions return a value**. Functions are useful when you need to perform a calculation or operation that results in a value you want to use in other parts of your program.

Syntax of a Function:
```
Function FunctionName(Optional Parameter As DataType) As ReturnType
    ' Code to be executed
    Return value
End Function
```

- **FunctionName**: The name of the function.
- **Parameter**: A value or reference passed into the function.
- **ReturnType**: Specifies the type of value that the function will return (e.g., Integer, String, Boolean).
- **Return value**: The value that is returned from the function.

Example:
```
Function AddNumbers(a As Integer, b As Integer) As Integer
```

```
    Return a + b
End Function
```

- This function takes two integer parameters **a** and **b**, and it returns their sum as an integer.

To call a function, you pass the necessary arguments and can store the returned value in a variable or use it directly:

```
Dim result As Integer = AddNumbers(5, 3)
Console.WriteLine(result)   ' Output: 8
```

In this example, the function **AddNumbers** adds **5** and **3** and returns **8**, which is stored in the variable **result** and printed to the console.

---

3. Passing Parameters: By Value and By Reference

In VB.NET, parameters can be passed to procedures in two ways: **By Value** (default) and **By Reference**.

By Value (default)

When you pass a parameter **by value**, the **actual value** is passed to the procedure. Any changes made to the parameter inside the procedure do not affect the original variable.

Example: Passing By Value

```
Sub ChangeValueByValue(num As Integer)
    num += 10
End Sub

Dim x As Integer = 5
ChangeValueByValue(x)
Console.WriteLine(x)   ' Output: 5 (original value of x is unchanged)
```

In this case, the value of **x** remains unchanged because **num** was passed by value, so **num** is a separate copy of **x**.

By Reference (ByRef)

When you pass a parameter **by reference** (using the **ByRef** keyword), the **reference** to the variable is passed, not the actual value. This means that any changes made to the parameter inside the procedure will affect the original variable.

Example: Passing By Reference

```
Sub IncrementValue(ByRef num As Integer)
    num += 1
End Sub
```

```
Dim x As Integer = 5
IncrementValue(x)   ' x is now 6
Console.WriteLine(x)   ' Output: 6 (original value of x is changed)
```

In this case, since **num** was passed by reference, any changes made to **num** (such as incrementing it) affect **x**, so **x** becomes **6**.

Summary of Passing Parameters:

- **By Value (default)**: The function or subroutine gets a copy of the variable. Changes do not affect the original variable.
- **By Reference (ByRef)**: The function or subroutine gets a reference to the original variable. Changes will affect the original variable.

Key Differences Between Subroutines and Functions:

Aspect	Subroutine (Sub)	Function
Purpose	Performs a task but does not return a value.	Performs a task and returns a value.
Return Type	Does not return any value.	Must return a value of a specific type.
Call	Called by its name, typically used to perform actions.	Called to compute a value, which can be used in expressions.
Example Use	Displaying a message, performing operations.	Performing a calculation, returning a result.
Syntax	`Sub ProcedureName(...)`	`Function FunctionName(...) As ReturnType`

3.6 Error Handling in VB.NET: Using Try...Catch...Finally

Error handling is an essential part of programming, enabling your application to handle unexpected situations (exceptions) in a controlled way, preventing it from crashing and offering a way to respond appropriately. In VB.NET, error handling is typically done using the **Try...Catch...Finally** block.

---

1. Try...Catch...Finally

The **Try...Catch...Finally** construct in VB.NET allows you to handle exceptions in a structured way. It consists of three main parts:

- **Try**: Contains the code that might cause an exception.
- **Catch**: Catches and handles the exception if one occurs.
- **Finally**: Contains code that runs regardless of whether an exception occurs or not. This is typically used for cleanup operations.

Syntax:

```
Try
    ' Code that may throw an exception
Catch ex As ExceptionType
    ' Code to handle the exception
Finally
    ' Code that always runs, whether or not an exception occurred
End Try
```

- **Try**: This is where you write the code that may result in an exception (e.g., division by zero, file access).
- **Catch**: When an exception occurs inside the `Try` block, the control is passed to the corresponding `Catch` block. You can specify the type of exception you want to handle (e.g., `DivideByZeroException`).
- **Finally**: This block of code will always execute, whether an exception was thrown or not. It is typically used for cleanup tasks such as closing files, releasing resources, or logging.

Example of Try...Catch...Finally:

```
Try
    Dim result As Integer = 10 / 0   ' This will cause a division by zero
exception
Catch ex As DivideByZeroException
    Console.WriteLine("Error: Division by zero.")   ' Handling the exception
Finally
    Console.WriteLine("Cleanup code.")   ' This code will always run
End Try
```

- **Try Block**: Contains the division operation, which would throw a `DivideByZeroException`.
- **Catch Block**: Catches the exception and displays a message.
- **Finally Block**: Regardless of whether an exception occurs, this code will run and output "Cleanup code."

Output:

```
Error: Division by zero.
Cleanup code.
```

How It Works:

1. The `Try` block executes the division operation.
2. Since dividing by zero causes an exception, the program jumps to the `Catch` block and executes it.
3. Finally, the `Finally` block runs, ensuring that cleanup code (or other final operations) occurs.

2. Throwing Custom Exceptions

You can also create and **throw your own exceptions** in VB.NET using the **Throw** keyword. This is useful when you want to enforce certain conditions in your program and inform the user or the system about specific error situations.

Syntax for Throwing an Exception:

```
Throw New Exception("Error message here")
```

When an exception is thrown, it will be propagated up the call stack until it is caught by an appropriate `Catch` block or until the program terminates.

Example of Throwing a Custom Exception:

```
Sub CheckAge(age As Integer)
    If age < 18 Then
        Throw New Exception("Age must be 18 or older.")
    End If
End Sub

Sub Main()
    Try
        CheckAge(16)   ' This will throw the exception
    Catch ex As Exception
        Console.WriteLine("Error: " & ex.Message)
    End Try
End Sub
```

In this example:

- The `CheckAge` subroutine throws an exception if the age is less than 18.
- The `Main` subroutine calls `CheckAge(16)`, which triggers the exception because 16 is less than 18.
- The `Catch` block catches the exception and displays the message.

Output:

```
Error: Age must be 18 or older.
```

---

3. Types of Exceptions

VB.NET provides various built-in exceptions that you can catch and handle. Some common exception types include:

- **DivideByZeroException**: Raised when an attempt to divide by zero occurs.
- **FileNotFoundException**: Raised when a file is not found.
- **ArgumentNullException**: Raised when a method receives a `null` argument.
- **InvalidOperationException**: Raised when a method call is invalid for the object's current state.

Example of Handling Multiple Exception Types:

You can handle multiple exception types by using multiple `Catch` blocks. This allows you to take different actions based on the type of exception.

```
Try
    ' Code that may throw an exception
    Dim num As Integer = Integer.Parse("abc")   ' This will cause a
FormatException
Catch ex As FormatException
    Console.WriteLine("Error: Invalid number format.")
Catch ex As InvalidCastException
    Console.WriteLine("Error: Invalid type cast.")
Finally
    Console.WriteLine("Cleanup code.")
End Try
```

In this example:

- If the `Integer.Parse` method fails to parse a non-numeric string, it throws a `FormatException`.
- The corresponding `Catch` block will handle it and display the error message.

Output:

```
Error: Invalid number format.
Cleanup code.
```

---

4. The `Finally` Block

The `Finally` block is optional but highly recommended when you need to ensure that some actions occur after the `Try...Catch` block, regardless of whether an exception is thrown or not. It's commonly used for resource cleanup, closing files, or logging.

Example of Finally Block:

```
Try
    ' Some code that may throw an exception
    Dim fileReader As New System.IO.StreamReader("example.txt")
    Console.WriteLine(fileReader.ReadToEnd())
Catch ex As Exception
    Console.WriteLine("An error occurred: " & ex.Message)
Finally
    Console.WriteLine("This will always execute, even if an exception
occurs.")
End Try
```

In this example, even if an exception occurs (e.g., file not found), the `Finally` block ensures that the message "This will always execute..." is printed.

3.7 Introduction to Classes and Objects

In VB.NET, **classes** and **objects** are fundamental building blocks of object-oriented programming (OOP). Classes define the structure of objects, including their properties, methods, and behaviors. Objects, on the other hand, are instances of a class, which means that they are actual representations of the template (class) that you define.

---

1. Creating Classes

A **class** is a blueprint for creating objects. It can contain:

- **Properties**: Variables that represent the state or attributes of the object.
- **Methods**: Functions or subroutines that define the behavior or actions that the object can perform.

A class is defined using the **`Class`** keyword and is given a name. Inside the class, you can define properties and methods. The **`Public`** keyword makes the class, its properties, and methods accessible from outside the class.

Example of a Simple Class:

```
Public Class Car
    Public Make As String
    Public Model As String
    Public Year As Integer

    Public Sub DisplayCarInfo()
        Console.WriteLine("Car: " & Make & " " & Model & " (" & Year & ")")
    End Sub
End Class
```

In this example:

- **`Make`, `Model`, and `Year`** are properties of the `Car` class, representing the car's make, model, and year.
- **`DisplayCarInfo`** is a method that displays the car's information on the console.

The **`Public`** keyword allows access to these properties and methods outside the class.

---

2. Instantiating Objects

An **object** is an instance of a class. You create an object by using the `New` keyword followed by the class name. Once an object is instantiated, you can access and modify its properties and invoke its methods.

Example of Instantiating an Object:

```
Dim myCar As New Car()   ' Create an object of type Car
myCar.Make = "Toyota"     ' Set the Make property
myCar.Model = "Corolla"   ' Set the Model property
myCar.Year = 2020         ' Set the Year property
myCar.DisplayCarInfo()    ' Call the method to display car information
```

In this example:

- `myCar` is an object of type `Car`.
- The properties (`Make`, `Model`, `Year`) are set to specific values for `myCar`.
- The `DisplayCarInfo()` method is called to print the car's information.

Output:

```
Car: Toyota Corolla (2020)
```

This demonstrates how to instantiate an object from a class, set its properties, and invoke its methods.

---

3. Using Properties and Methods

A class can define **properties** (also known as fields or attributes) that store data, and **methods** that define the operations that can be performed on the object.

Example of Using Properties:

Properties allow access to class data in a controlled manner, using **get** and **set** accessors. The **`Get`** accessor returns the value of a property, while the **`Set`** accessor allows you to assign a value to the property.

```
Public Class Person
    Private _name As String   ' Private backing field

    ' Public property to access the _name field
    Public Property Name As String
        Get
            Return _name
        End Get
        Set(value As String)
            _name = value
        End Set
    End Property
End Class
```

In this example:

- The `Name` property uses a backing field (`_name`), which is declared as **Private**. This means the field can only be accessed through the public property `Name`.
- The **`Get`** accessor retrieves the value of `_name`, and the **`Set`** accessor assigns a value to it.

Example of Using Methods:

Methods define actions that an object can perform. They can be used to manipulate data or perform operations related to the class.

```
Dim person As New Person()
person.Name = "John"      ' Using the Name property to set the value
Console.WriteLine(person.Name)   ' Output: John
```

In this example:

- A `Person` object is created (`person`).
- The `Name` property is used to set the person's name to `"John"`.
- The `Console.WriteLine(person.Name)` outputs `"John"`.

The method in this case is the automatic behavior of the property getter, which retrieves the value.

---

4. Access Modifiers (Public, Private, Protected)

Access modifiers control the visibility and accessibility of members (properties, methods) within a class.

- **Public**: Members declared as `Public` can be accessed from anywhere, including outside the class.
- **Private**: Members declared as `Private` can only be accessed from within the class itself.
- **Protected**: Members declared as `Protected` can be accessed within the class and by derived classes.

Example of Access Modifiers:

```
Public Class Person
    Private _name As String  ' Private field, not accessible outside the
class

    Public Property Name As String
        Get
            Return _name
        End Get
        Set(value As String)
            _name = value
        End Set
    End Property

    Public Sub DisplayPersonInfo()
        Console.WriteLine("Name: " & _name)
    End Sub
End Class
```

In this example:

- The `_name` field is `Private`, so it cannot be accessed directly outside the `Person` class.
- The `Name` property is `Public`, so it can be accessed and modified from outside the class.
- The method `DisplayPersonInfo` is `Public`, so it can be called from outside the class.

---

5. Constructors (Optional)

In VB.NET, classes can have **constructors**, which are special methods used to initialize objects when they are created. Constructors allow you to set initial values for properties when the object is instantiated.

Example of a Constructor:

```
Public Class Car
    Public Make As String
    Public Model As String
    Public Year As Integer

    ' Constructor to initialize the Car object
    Public Sub New(make As String, model As String, year As Integer)
        Me.Make = make
        Me.Model = model
        Me.Year = year
    End Sub

    Public Sub DisplayCarInfo()
        Console.WriteLine("Car: " & Make & " " & Model & " (" & Year & ")")
    End Sub
End Class
```

In this example:

- The `Car` class has a constructor `Sub New`, which takes three parameters: `make`, `model`, and `year`.
- The constructor sets the values of the properties when a new `Car` object is created.

Using the Constructor:

```
Dim myCar As New Car("Toyota", "Corolla", 2020)
myCar.DisplayCarInfo()
```

Output:

```
Car: Toyota Corolla (2020)
```

30 multiple-choice questions (MCQs):

3.1 Data Types and Variables in VB.NET

1. **Which of the following data types is used to store a sequence of characters in VB.NET?**
   - A) Integer
   - B) Double
   - C) String
   - D) Boolean

   Answer: C) String
2. **Which keyword is used to declare a variable in VB.NET?**
   - A) Var
   - B) Dim
   - C) Let
   - D) Const

   Answer: B) Dim
3. **Which of the following data types can store true/false values in VB.NET?**
   - A) Integer
   - B) String
   - C) Boolean
   - D) Date

   Answer: C) Boolean
4. **Which data type is used to store a decimal number in VB.NET?**
   - A) Integer
   - B) Double
   - C) Boolean
   - D) Char

   Answer: B) Double
5. **Which statement is correct for declaring a variable `age` with an initial value of 25 in VB.NET?**
   - A) `Dim age As Integer = 25`
   - B) `Dim age Integer = 25`
   - C) `Dim age = Integer 25`
   - D) `Dim age : Integer = 25`

   Answer: A) `Dim age As Integer = 25`
6. **What does the `Date` data type in VB.NET store?**
   - A) Text
   - B) Decimal numbers
   - C) Boolean values
   - D) Date and time values

   Answer: D) Date and time values

3.2 Operators: Arithmetic, Relational, and Logical

7. **Which of the following is the correct operator for modulus in VB.NET?**
   - A) `/`
   - B) `Mod`

- C) `*`
- D) `Div`

  Answer: B) Mod

8. **Which operator is used to check if two values are not equal in VB.NET?**
   - A) `=`
   - B) `<>`
   - C) `<=`
   - D) `!=`

   Answer: B) `<>`

9. **Which of the following operators will return True only if both conditions are true?**
   - A) `And`
   - B) `Or`
   - C) `Not`
   - D) `Xor`

   Answer: A) `And`

10. **What will be the result of the expression `5 > 3` in VB.NET?**
    - A) True
    - B) False
    - C) Error
    - D) Null

    Answer: A) True

11. **Which of the following will result in a division by zero exception in VB.NET?**
    - A) `10 / 2`
    - B) `10 Mod 2`
    - C) `10 / 0`
    - D) `10 Mod 0`

    Answer: C) `10 / 0`

12. **Which logical operator in VB.NET is used to reverse the truth value?**
    - A) `Not`
    - B) `And`
    - C) `Or`
    - D) `Xor`

    Answer: A) `Not`

3.3 Conditional Statements: If...Else, Select Case

13. **Which of the following statements is used to check multiple conditions in VB.NET?**
    - A) If...ElseIf...Else
    - B) Select Case
    - C) Both A and B
    - D) None of the above

    Answer: C) Both A and B

14. **Which VB.NET keyword is used to start a conditional block?**
    - A) Then

- B) If
- C) Case
- D) Select

Answer: B) If

15. **In which scenario is a `Select Case` structure more efficient than an `If...ElseIf` chain?**
   - A) When comparing multiple values of the same variable
   - B) When checking a single condition
   - C) When handling complex logical operations
   - D) Select Case is never more efficient

   Answer: A) When comparing multiple values of the same variable
16. **What is the correct syntax to handle multiple conditions in an If statement?**
   - A) `If condition1 Then condition2 ElseIf condition3`
   - B) `If condition1 Else condition2`
   - C) `If condition1 Or condition2`
   - D) `If condition1 Then condition2 End If`

   Answer: A) `If condition1 Then condition2 ElseIf condition3`

3.4 Loops in VB.NET: For...Next, Do...Loop, While...End While

17. **What does a `For...Next` loop in VB.NET do?**
   - A) Repeats a block of code a specified number of times
   - B) Repeats a block of code while a condition is true
   - C) Repeats a block of code until a condition becomes true
   - D) Both A and B

   Answer: A) Repeats a block of code a specified number of times
18. **Which of the following loops checks the condition before executing the loop's body?**
   - A) `Do...Loop`
   - B) `While...End While`
   - C) `For...Next`
   - D) All of the above

   Answer: B) `While...End While`
19. **What is the purpose of the `Continue For` statement in a `For...Next` loop?**
   - A) Skip the current iteration and move to the next iteration
   - B) Break out of the loop entirely
   - C) Restart the loop from the beginning
   - D) None of the above

   Answer: A) Skip the current iteration and move to the next iteration
20. **What will happen if the condition in a `Do While` loop is never met in VB.NET?**
   - A) The loop will execute indefinitely
   - B) The loop will execute once and then exit
   - C) The loop will exit immediately without executing
   - D) The loop will throw an error

   Answer: A) The loop will execute indefinitely

21. **Which loop is best suited for iterating over a collection or range of numbers?**
    - A) `Do...Loop`
    - B) `For...Next`
    - C) `While...End While`
    - D) None of the above

    Answer: B) `For...Next`

3.5 Procedures: Subroutines and Functions

22. **Which of the following is true about a Function in VB.NET?**
    - A) A Function cannot return a value
    - B) A Function must return a value
    - C) A Function can only accept one parameter
    - D) A Function is similar to a Subroutine but returns a value

    Answer: D) A Function is similar to a Subroutine but returns a value
23. **Which keyword is used to define a Subroutine in VB.NET?**
    - A) Function
    - B) Sub
    - C) Method
    - D) Procedure

    Answer: B) Sub
24. **Which of the following is the correct syntax for passing parameters by reference in a Subroutine?**
    - A) `Sub Increment(ByRef num As Integer)`
    - B) `Sub Increment(ByVal num As Integer)`
    - C) `Sub Increment(num As Integer)`
    - D) `Sub Increment(ByDef num As Integer)`

    Answer: A) `Sub Increment(ByRef num As Integer)`
25. **In which scenario would you use `ByVal` when passing parameters to a function?**
    - A) When you want the function to modify the original variable
    - B) When you do not want the function to modify the original variable
    - C) When you want to pass a reference to a large object
    - D) None of the above

    Answer: B) When you do not want the function to modify the original variable

---

3.6 Error Handling in VB.NET: Using Try...Catch...Finally

26. **Which part of a Try...Catch block in VB.NET is used for cleanup tasks, regardless of whether an error occurs or not?**
    - A) Try
    - B) Catch
    - C) Finally

- D) None of the above
  Answer: C) Finally

27. **What is the correct syntax for throwing a custom exception in VB.NET?**
    - A) `Throw New CustomException()`
    - B) `Raise New CustomException()`
    - C) `Throw CustomException()`
    - D) `Throw CustomException`

    Answer: A) `Throw New CustomException()`
28. **Which keyword is used to handle exceptions in VB.NET?**
    - A) Catch
    - B) Handle
    - C) Throw
    - D) Try

    Answer: A) Catch
29. **Which of the following is a valid exception handling method in VB.NET?**
    - A) `Try...Catch...End`
    - B) `Try...Catch...Finally`
    - C) `Try...Exception`
    - D) `Try...Raise`

    Answer: B) `Try...Catch...Finally`

3.7 Introduction to Classes and Objects

30. **In VB.NET, what is the purpose of a class?**
    - A) To create and store objects
    - B) To store methods only
    - C) To define templates for creating objects
    - D) To store variables only

    Answer: C) To define templates for creating objects

3.1 Data Types and Variables in VB.NET

1. **Question:** Write a VB.NET program to declare variables of type Integer, String, and Boolean, and assign appropriate values to them. Then print the values.

   Answer:

```
Dim age As Integer = 25
Dim name As String = "Alice"
Dim isStudent As Boolean = True

Console.WriteLine("Age: " & age)
Console.WriteLine("Name: " & name)
Console.WriteLine("Is Student: " & isStudent)
```

3.2 Operators: Arithmetic, Relational, and Logical

2. **Question:** Write a VB.NET program that calculates the sum, difference, product, and modulus of two numbers.

   Answer:

```
Dim num1 As Integer = 10
Dim num2 As Integer = 3
Console.WriteLine("Sum: " & (num1 + num2))
Console.WriteLine("Difference: " & (num1 - num2))
Console.WriteLine("Product: " & (num1 * num2))
Console.WriteLine("Modulus: " & (num1 Mod num2))
```

3. **Question:** Write a VB.NET program to check if a number is greater than 10 using a relational operator.

   Answer:

```
Dim num As Integer = 15
If num > 10 Then
    Console.WriteLine("The number is greater than 10.")
Else
    Console.WriteLine("The number is not greater than 10.")
End If
```

4. **Question:** Write a VB.NET program that uses a logical operator to check if two conditions are true (both numbers are greater than 10).

   Answer:

```
Dim num1 As Integer = 15
Dim num2 As Integer = 20
If num1 > 10 And num2 > 10 Then
    Console.WriteLine("Both numbers are greater than 10.")
Else
    Console.WriteLine("At least one number is not greater than 10.")
End If
```

3.3 Conditional Statements: If...Else, Select Case

5. **Question:** Write a VB.NET program using an If...Else statement to check whether a given number is even or odd.

   Answer:

```
Dim num As Integer = 7
If num Mod 2 = 0 Then
    Console.WriteLine("The number is even.")
```

```
Else
    Console.WriteLine("The number is odd.")
End If
```

6. **Question:** Write a VB.NET program using Select Case to display the day of the week based on an integer input (1-7).

   Answer:

```
Dim day As Integer = 3
Select Case day
    Case 1
        Console.WriteLine("Monday")
    Case 2
        Console.WriteLine("Tuesday")
    Case 3
        Console.WriteLine("Wednesday")
    Case 4
        Console.WriteLine("Thursday")
    Case 5
        Console.WriteLine("Friday")
    Case 6
        Console.WriteLine("Saturday")
    Case 7
        Console.WriteLine("Sunday")
    Case Else
        Console.WriteLine("Invalid day")
End Select
```

3.4 Loops in VB.NET: For...Next, Do...Loop, While...End While

7. **Question:** Write a VB.NET program using a For...Next loop to print the numbers from 1 to 5.

   Answer:

```
For i As Integer = 1 To 5
    Console.WriteLine(i)
Next
```

8. **Question:** Write a VB.NET program that uses a Do...Loop to count from 1 to 5.

   Answer:

```
Dim counter As Integer = 1
Do While counter <= 5
    Console.WriteLine(counter)
    counter += 1
Loop
```

9. **Question:** Write a VB.NET program that uses a While...End While loop to print the first 5 natural numbers.

   Answer:

```
Dim counter As Integer = 1
While counter <= 5
    Console.WriteLine(counter)
    counter += 1
End While
```

3.5 Procedures: Subroutines and Functions

10. **Question:** Write a VB.NET Subroutine to print "Hello, World!" when called.

    Answer:

```
Sub Greet()
    Console.WriteLine("Hello, World!")
End Sub

' Calling the subroutine
Greet()
```

11. **Question:** Write a VB.NET function that takes two integers as parameters and returns their sum.

    Answer:

```
Function AddNumbers(num1 As Integer, num2 As Integer) As Integer
    Return num1 + num2
End Function

' Calling the function
Dim result As Integer = AddNumbers(10, 5)
Console.WriteLine("The sum is: " & result)
```

12. **Question:** Write a VB.NET program to demonstrate passing parameters by reference in a subroutine.

    Answer:

```
Sub IncrementValue(ByRef num As Integer)
    num += 1
End Sub

Dim value As Integer = 10
IncrementValue(value)  ' value becomes 11
Console.WriteLine("Value after increment: " & value)
```

3.6 Error Handling in VB.NET: Using Try...Catch...Finally

13. **Question:** Write a VB.NET program that handles a division by zero exception using Try...Catch...Finally.

    Answer:

    ```
    Try
        Dim result As Integer = 10 / 0
    Catch ex As DivideByZeroException
        Console.WriteLine("Error: Division by zero!")
    Finally
        Console.WriteLine("This is the Finally block.")
    End Try
    ```

14. **Question:** Write a VB.NET program that throws a custom exception when the age entered is less than 18.

    Answer:

    ```
    Sub CheckAge(age As Integer)
        If age < 18 Then
            Throw New Exception("Age must be 18 or older.")
        Else
            Console.WriteLine("Age is valid.")
        End If
    End Sub

    ' Test with age 16
    Try
        CheckAge(16)
    Catch ex As Exception
        Console.WriteLine(ex.Message)
    End Try
    ```

3.7 Introduction to Classes and Objects

15. **Question:** Write a VB.NET program to define a class `Person` with a property `Name`, a method `Greet`, and create an object to call the `Greet` method.

    Answer:

    ```
    Public Class Person
        Public Property Name As String

        Public Sub Greet()
            Console.WriteLine("Hello, " & Name)
        End Sub
    End Class
    ```

```
' Creating an object and calling the method
Dim person1 As New Person()
person1.Name = "John"
person1.Greet()  ' Output: Hello, John
```

CHAPTER 4: OBJECT-ORIENTED PROGRAMMING IN VB.NET

4.1 Fundamentals of OOP (Object-Oriented Programming)

Object-Oriented Programming (OOP) is a programming paradigm that focuses on organizing software design around **objects**, rather than functions or logic. An object is an instance of a **class**, and it can hold both **data** (fields/properties) and **behavior** (methods/functions). This paradigm allows for code to be modular, reusable, and scalable, making it easier to maintain and extend.

There are **four fundamental principles** of OOP: **Encapsulation**, **Inheritance**, **Polymorphism**, and **Abstraction**. Let's dive deeper into each principle:

---

1. Encapsulation

Encapsulation is the concept of **bundling data** (properties) and the methods that operate on that data into a **single unit or class**. This means that the internal workings of an object are hidden from the outside world, and access to the object's data is restricted to only what is necessary. The goal of encapsulation is to protect the integrity of the data and provide a controlled interface for interacting with it.

In VB.NET, encapsulation is implemented using **access modifiers** such as `Public`, `Private`, `Protected`, and `Friend`. These modifiers determine the visibility of the data and methods.

- **Public**: Members are accessible from any class or code.
- **Private**: Members are only accessible within the class in which they are declared.
- **Protected**: Members are accessible within the class and its derived classes.
- **Friend**: Members are accessible within the same assembly (project).

Example:

```
Public Class Car
    ' Private field, not accessible directly from outside
    Private _make As String

    ' Public property to encapsulate access to the private field
    Public Property Make As String
        Get
            Return _make
        End Get
        Set(value As String)
            _make = value
        End Set
    End Property
End Class
```

In the example above, the `Make` property allows controlled access to the private `_make` field. This ensures that the internal state of the object can be modified or retrieved only through the `Property`, thus maintaining data integrity.

---

2. Inheritance

Inheritance is a mechanism in OOP that allows one class (the **child** or **derived class**) to inherit the properties and methods from another class (the **parent** or **base class**). Inheritance promotes **code reuse** and helps create a **hierarchical relationship** between classes.

In VB.NET, a class can inherit another class using the `Inherits` keyword. The derived class can extend or modify the behavior of the base class by adding new members or overriding existing methods.

Example:

```
' Base class
Public Class Animal
    Public Sub Speak()
        Console.WriteLine("The animal makes a sound.")
    End Sub
End Class

' Derived class
Public Class Dog
    Inherits Animal

    ' Overriding the Speak method
    Public Sub Speak()
        Console.WriteLine("The dog barks.")
    End Sub
End Class
```

In the example above:

- `Dog` **inherits** from `Animal`, meaning `Dog` has access to the `Speak` method from `Animal`.
- `Dog` **overrides** the `Speak` method to provide its own implementation, specific to dogs.

Benefits of Inheritance:

- **Code Reusability**: Child classes inherit common behavior from the parent class.
- **Extensibility**: Child classes can add or modify behavior without changing the parent class.

---

3. Polymorphism

Polymorphism allows objects of different types to be treated as instances of a **common parent class**, and it enables the same method to behave differently depending on the object that calls it. Polymorphism provides flexibility in your code and allows for the creation of generic methods or functions that can work with any subclass.

There are two types of polymorphism:

- **Method Overriding**: A method in a base class is overridden by a method in a derived class to provide a specific implementation.
- **Method Overloading**: Multiple methods with the same name, but with different parameters, are defined in a class.

Example of Method Overriding:

```
Public Class Animal
    Public Overridable Sub Speak()
        Console.WriteLine("Animal makes a sound.")
    End Sub
End Class

Public Class Cat
    Inherits Animal

    ' Override the Speak method
    Public Overrides Sub Speak()
        Console.WriteLine("The cat meows.")
    End Sub
End Class

Dim animal As Animal = New Cat()
animal.Speak()   ' Output: The cat meows
```

In this example, `Speak` is overridden in the `Cat` class. Even though the variable `animal` is of type `Animal`, it calls the overridden method in the `Cat` class, demonstrating **runtime polymorphism**.

Example of Method Overloading:

```
Public Class Calculator
    ' Overloaded Add method
    Public Function Add(a As Integer, b As Integer) As Integer
        Return a + b
    End Function

    Public Function Add(a As Double, b As Double) As Double
        Return a + b
    End Function
End Class
```

In the `Calculator` class, the `Add` method is overloaded, allowing it to accept both integers and doubles.

4. Abstraction

Abstraction is the concept of **hiding complex implementation details** and exposing only the necessary functionality to the user. It simplifies interaction with objects by providing clear and concise interfaces. Abstraction helps reduce complexity and allows users to focus on high-level functionality rather than the intricate details of the implementation.

In VB.NET, abstraction is often achieved through the use of **abstract classes** or **interfaces**.

- **Abstract Classes**: An abstract class cannot be instantiated on its own but can provide a base for derived classes. It may have abstract methods that must be implemented by any derived class.
- **Interfaces**: An interface defines a contract that must be implemented by a class, without providing implementation details.

Example of Abstraction with Abstract Class:

```
' Abstract class
Public MustInherit Class Shape
    Public MustOverride Sub Draw()   ' Abstract method
End Class

' Derived class
Public Class Circle
    Inherits Shape

    Public Overrides Sub Draw()
        Console.WriteLine("Drawing a circle.")
    End Sub
End Class
```

In this example, the `Shape` class is abstract, and it defines a `Draw` method that must be implemented in the derived class `Circle`.

Example of Abstraction with Interface:

```
' Interface
Public Interface IDrawable
    Sub Draw()
End Interface

' Implementing the interface
Public Class Circle
    Implements IDrawable

    Public Sub Draw() Implements IDrawable.Draw
        Console.WriteLine("Drawing a circle.")
    End Sub
End Class
```

Here, the `Circle` class implements the `IDrawable` interface and provides its own implementation of the `Draw` method.

4.2 Creating Classes and Objects

In Object-Oriented Programming (OOP), a **class** is a blueprint for creating **objects**. An object is an instance of a class and can have **properties**, **methods**, and **events**. Let's break down these components in detail, as well as constructors and destructors.

---

1. Defining Properties, Methods, and Events

Properties

- **Properties** are variables that belong to a class and represent the attributes or state of an object. They define the data that an object will store.
- Properties can be read from and written to, and in VB.NET, they are defined using **Get** and **Set** blocks.

Example of Property:

```
Public Class Car
    ' Property
    Public Property Make As String
    Public Property Model As String
End Class
```

Here, the `Make` and `Model` properties represent the **attributes** of a `Car` object. These properties hold the car's make and model information.

Methods

- **Methods** are functions or subroutines that define the behavior of an object. They can perform operations using the data stored in the properties or other parameters passed to the method.
- Methods typically define what an object can **do**.

Example of Method:

```
Public Sub DisplayCarInfo()
    Console.WriteLine("Car: " & Make & " " & Model)
End Sub
```

In this example, the `DisplayCarInfo` method outputs the car's make and model to the console.

Events

- **Events** allow objects to communicate with each other by notifying other objects when something has happened. This mechanism is particularly useful when you want to inform other parts of your program that a specific action has occurred (e.g., a button was clicked, a car was started).
- Events are often used in scenarios where an object is interacting with the user interface or other objects.

Example of Event:

```
Public Event CarStarted As EventHandler
```

This event, `CarStarted`, will be triggered when the `StartCar` method is called. The `EventHandler` is a predefined delegate that specifies the method signature that handles the event.

Raising the Event:

```
Public Sub StartCar()
    RaiseEvent CarStarted(Me, EventArgs.Empty)
End Sub
```

The `StartCar` method triggers the `CarStarted` event when called, notifying any objects listening for this event that the car has started.

---

2. Constructors and Destructors

Constructors

- **Constructors** are special methods that are automatically called when an object is instantiated (created). They are used to initialize the object, typically by setting its initial state.
- In VB.NET, a constructor has the same name as the class and does not have a return type.

Example of Constructor:

```
Public Class Car
    ' Properties
    Public Property Make As String
    Public Property Model As String

    ' Constructor
    Public Sub New(make As String, model As String)
        Me.Make = make
        Me.Model = model
    End Sub
End Class
```

In this example, the `Car` class has a constructor (`New` method) that takes two parameters: `make` and `model`. When a new `Car` object is created, the constructor initializes the `Make` and `Model` properties with the passed values.

Creating an Object Using the Constructor:

```
Dim myCar As New Car("Toyota", "Corolla")
```

This line creates a new instance of the `Car` class, and the constructor initializes the `Make` and `Model` properties.

Destructors (Finalizers)

- **Destructors** (in VB.NET, known as `Finalize`) are used for cleanup operations before the object is garbage collected. In VB.NET, the `Finalize` method is automatically called by the garbage collector to clean up any unmanaged resources (e.g., database connections, file handles).
- You typically override `Finalize` when you need to release resources or perform any final cleanup before the object is destroyed.

Example of Destructor (Finalize):

```
Protected Overrides Sub Finalize()
    ' Cleanup code
    Console.WriteLine("Car object is being destroyed.")
    MyBase.Finalize()
End Sub
```

In this example, the `Finalize` method prints a message when the `Car` object is being destroyed (garbage collected). It also calls `MyBase.Finalize()` to ensure that the base class's cleanup code is executed.

Important Note: Destructors are **not explicitly called** by the programmer. They are managed by the .NET runtime's garbage collector. Instead of relying heavily on destructors, it's often better to implement the **`IDisposable` interface** when managing resources that need explicit cleanup.

---

3. Full Example of Class with Properties, Methods, Events, Constructor, and Destructor

```
Public Class Car
    ' Properties
    Public Property Make As String
    Public Property Model As String

    ' Event
    Public Event CarStarted As EventHandler

    ' Constructor
```

```
    Public Sub New(make As String, model As String)
        Me.Make = make
        Me.Model = model
    End Sub

    ' Method
    Public Sub DisplayCarInfo()
        Console.WriteLine("Car: " & Make & " " & Model)
    End Sub

    ' Method to start the car and raise the event
    Public Sub StartCar()
        RaiseEvent CarStarted(Me, EventArgs.Empty)
        Console.WriteLine("The car is now started.")
    End Sub

    ' Destructor (cleanup code)
    Protected Overrides Sub Finalize()
        Console.WriteLine("Car object is being destroyed.")
        MyBase.Finalize()
    End Sub
End Class
```

How It Works:

- **Properties**: `Make` and `Model` hold the car's attributes.
- **Methods**:
  - `DisplayCarInfo` displays information about the car.
  - `StartCar` starts the car and raises the `CarStarted` event.
- **Event**: The `CarStarted` event notifies other objects when the car has started.
- **Constructor**: Initializes a new `Car` object with a `Make` and `Model`.
- **Destructor**: Cleans up resources and displays a message when the object is destroyed.

4.3 Understanding Method Overloading

Method Overloading is a feature in Object-Oriented Programming (OOP) that allows you to define multiple methods within the same class with the **same name** but with **different parameter lists**. This can be especially useful when you want to perform similar tasks but with different types or numbers of parameters.

Method overloading provides the benefit of reusing the same method name for different scenarios, enhancing code readability and making the code easier to maintain.

---

1. Syntax of Method Overloading

In VB.NET, method overloading is accomplished by defining multiple methods with the same name but different parameter types, numbers of parameters, or both. The return type does not contribute to overloading. The method signature is determined by the method name and the types and number of its parameters.

Example of Method Overloading:

```
Public Class Calculator
    ' Overloaded method that accepts two integers
    Public Function Add(x As Integer, y As Integer) As Integer
        Return x + y
    End Function

    ' Overloaded method that accepts two doubles
    Public Function Add(x As Double, y As Double) As Double
        Return x + y
    End Function

    ' Overloaded method that accepts three integers
    Public Function Add(x As Integer, y As Integer, z As Integer) As Integer
        Return x + y + z
    End Function
End Class
```

In the above example:

- The `Add` method is overloaded three times:
    - **First method**: Adds two integers.
    - **Second method**: Adds two doubles.
    - **Third method**: Adds three integers.

Each method performs the same operation (addition), but the number and types of parameters differ. This allows the `Add` method to be used in different situations without the need to create entirely different method names.

---

2. How Method Overloading Works

When you call a method, the **compiler determines which version of the overloaded method to execute** based on the **number and types of arguments** you provide. The method name remains the same, but the appropriate method is chosen based on the provided parameters.

Example Usage:

```
Dim calc As New Calculator()

' Calling the method with two integer parameters
Dim result1 As Integer = calc.Add(3, 5)
Console.WriteLine(result1)   ' Output: 8

' Calling the method with two double parameters
```

```
Dim result2 As Double = calc.Add(3.5, 5.2)
Console.WriteLine(result2)  ' Output: 8.7

' Calling the method with three integer parameters
Dim result3 As Integer = calc.Add(1, 2, 3)
Console.WriteLine(result3)  ' Output: 6
```

Here:

- The first `Add` method accepts two integers (`3` and `5`).
- The second `Add` method accepts two doubles (`3.5` and `5.2`).
- The third `Add` method accepts three integers (`1`, `2`, and `3`).

Based on the number and types of arguments passed, the appropriate overloaded method is invoked.

---

3. When to Use Method Overloading

You should use method overloading in the following situations:

a. Performing the Same Operation with Different Types of Data

If you want to perform the same operation (e.g., addition, subtraction, etc.) with different types of data (e.g., integers, doubles, strings), method overloading allows you to keep the method name the same for each type, making the code more concise and readable.

Example: If you want to provide a method for adding both integers and floating-point numbers, method overloading helps achieve this without creating separate method names like `AddIntegers` and `AddDoubles`.

b. Enhancing Readability

When you use the same method name for similar operations, the code becomes more readable and easier to maintain. You don't have to introduce a new method name for each different scenario.

Example: If you have multiple ways of adding numbers (like adding integers, floating-point numbers, or a list of numbers), method overloading provides a clean and consistent API for the `Add` operation.

c. Providing Flexibility and Ease of Use

Method overloading provides the flexibility to pass a different number or type of parameters without having to remember different method names. It helps streamline the developer experience by allowing them to reuse the method name in different situations.

Example: A developer can easily call `Add(2, 3)` for adding integers or `Add(2.5, 3.7)` for adding floats, without worrying about which method to call based on the parameter types.

---

4. Limitations of Method Overloading

While method overloading offers flexibility, there are some things to keep in mind:

1. **Return type does not affect overloading**: Overloading is determined only by the method signature (name + parameters). You cannot overload methods just by changing the return type.

   Incorrect Overloading Example:

   ```
   Public Function Add(x As Integer, y As Integer) As Integer
   Public Function Add(x As Integer, y As Integer) As Double  ' This will
   result in an error
   ```

2. **Overloaded methods must have different parameters**: The parameters must differ in the number or types of parameters. You cannot overload methods based on parameter names alone.

   Incorrect Overloading Example:

   ```
   Public Function Add(x As Integer, y As Integer) As Integer
   Public Function Add(a As Integer, b As Integer) As Integer  ' This will
   result in an error
   ```

---

5. Advantages of Method Overloading

- **Code Simplicity**: By using the same method name for different input types or quantities, your code becomes simpler and easier to manage.
- **Better User Experience**: Users of your class don't need to learn multiple method names for similar tasks; they can use one method name with different inputs.
- **Increased Flexibility**: You can handle various input types and parameters without cluttering your code with multiple method names.

4.4 Inheritance in VB.NET

Inheritance is one of the core principles of Object-Oriented Programming (OOP). It allows a class (known as the **child** or **derived** class) to inherit properties, methods, and events from another class (known as the **parent** or **base** class). This facilitates code reusability, and you can build on the functionality of existing classes while adding more specific features to the derived class.

---

1. Creating Derived Classes

In VB.NET, inheritance is implemented using the `Inherits` keyword. The child class inherits the attributes and behavior (properties and methods) of the parent class, but it can also have additional attributes or override inherited methods to provide specialized behavior.

Example of Creating a Derived Class:

```
' Parent class
Public Class Vehicle
    Public Property Make As String
    Public Property Model As String

    Public Sub DisplayInfo()
        Console.WriteLine("Make: " & Make & ", Model: " & Model)
    End Sub
End Class

' Derived class
Public Class Car
    Inherits Vehicle
    Public Property Year As Integer
End Class
```

Explanation:

- The `Vehicle` class is the **parent** class, which has two properties (`Make` and `Model`) and a method (`DisplayInfo`).
- The `Car` class is the **child** class that **inherits** from the `Vehicle` class using the `Inherits` keyword.
- The `Car` class can access the `Make` and `Model` properties, as well as the `DisplayInfo` method, from the `Vehicle` class. Additionally, it introduces a new property called `Year`.

Usage Example:

```
Dim myCar As New Car()
myCar.Make = "Toyota"
myCar.Model = "Corolla"
myCar.Year = 2022
myCar.DisplayInfo()  ' Output: Make: Toyota, Model: Corolla
```

In this example, the `myCar` object, which is an instance of the `Car` class, inherits all the functionality from the `Vehicle` class and can also use the `Year` property defined in the `Car` class.

---

2. Overriding Methods

In some cases, you might want to change or **extend** the behavior of an inherited method in the derived class. You can do this by **overriding** a method in the child class. To override a method, the method in the parent class must be marked with the `Overridable` keyword, and the method in the child class must use the `Overrides` keyword.

Example of Method Overriding:

```
' Parent class
Public Class Animal
    ' This method can be overridden in derived classes
    Public Overridable Sub Speak()
        Console.WriteLine("Animal speaks")
    End Sub
End Class

' Derived class
Public Class Dog
    Inherits Animal

    ' Overriding the Speak method to provide a specific implementation
    Public Overrides Sub Speak()
        Console.WriteLine("Dog barks")
    End Sub
End Class
```

Explanation:

- The `Speak` method in the `Animal` class is marked with the `Overridable` keyword, which means it can be overridden in any derived class.
- The `Dog` class inherits from the `Animal` class and **overrides** the `Speak` method using the `Overrides` keyword, providing a specialized implementation (printing `"Dog barks"` instead of `"Animal speaks"`).

Usage Example:

```
Dim animal As New Animal()
animal.Speak()  ' Output: Animal speaks

Dim dog As New Dog()
dog.Speak()  ' Output: Dog barks
```

- When calling the `Speak` method on the `animal` object, the method in the `Animal` class is executed.
- When calling the `Speak` method on the `dog` object (which is of type `Dog`), the overridden method in the `Dog` class is executed.

This is an example of **polymorphism**, as the method `Speak` behaves differently depending on the type of the object (`Animal` or `Dog`).

---

3. Why Use Inheritance?

Inheritance helps you avoid redundant code by allowing you to create base classes with general functionality and then extend or specialize that functionality in derived classes.

Benefits of Inheritance:

1. **Code Reusability**: Common functionality is defined in the parent class, and child classes can inherit it. This avoids duplication of code.
2. **Extensibility**: You can easily add or modify features in derived classes without altering the parent class.
3. **Organizational Structure**: It allows you to create a hierarchical structure, making your code easier to understand and maintain.

Real-World Analogy:

Think of inheritance in the context of vehicles:

- A **Vehicle** class might define general properties like `Make`, `Model`, and methods like `DisplayInfo`.
- A **Car** class can inherit from `Vehicle` and add specific properties like `Year`, without having to redefine the `Make`, `Model`, and `DisplayInfo` properties.
- This allows you to create multiple types of vehicles (cars, trucks, etc.) that share common functionality while having their own unique characteristics.

---

4. Key Concepts of Inheritance:

1. **Base Class**: The class that provides properties and methods to derived classes (e.g., `Vehicle` in the example).
2. **Derived Class**: The class that inherits from another class and can add its own functionality (e.g., `Car` or `Dog`).
3. **Overriding**: A mechanism to change or extend the functionality of a method defined in the base class.
4. **Access to Base Class Members**: The derived class has access to the public and protected members of the base class, but cannot access private members unless specifically exposed.

---

5. Access Modifiers and Inheritance:

In VB.NET, the accessibility of members in a base class can be controlled using access modifiers:

- **Public**: Members are accessible from anywhere.
- **Protected**: Members are accessible within the class and its derived classes.
- **Private**: Members are only accessible within the class itself.

Example of Access Modifiers in Inheritance:

```
Public Class Vehicle
    Public Property Make As String
    Private Property Model As String
    Protected Property Year As Integer

    Public Sub DisplayInfo()
        Console.WriteLine("Make: " & Make)
    End Sub
End Class

Public Class Car
    Inherits Vehicle

    Public Sub DisplayDetails()
        ' Accessing public property from base class
        Console.WriteLine("Make: " & Make)
        ' Console.WriteLine("Model: " & Model) ' Error: Model is Private
        ' Accessing protected property from base class
        Console.WriteLine("Year: " & Year)
    End Sub
End Class
```

In this example:

- The `Car` class can access the `Make` property from `Vehicle` because it is public.
- The `Car` class **cannot** access the `Model` property because it is private to the `Vehicle` class.
- The `Car` class **can** access the `Year` property because it is protected.

4.5 Access Modifiers in VB.NET

Access modifiers in VB.NET control the visibility and accessibility of members (fields, properties, methods) of a class. These modifiers allow you to enforce **encapsulation**, which is one of the core principles of Object-Oriented Programming (OOP). Encapsulation ensures that sensitive data is protected from unauthorized access and modification, promoting data integrity and security.

Here's a detailed explanation of the four main **access modifiers** in VB.NET:

---

1. Public:

- **Visibility**: The `Public` modifier allows members to be accessed from anywhere — both inside and outside the class or assembly.
- **Use Case**: Use `Public` when you want to make a member accessible from anywhere in the application or when the class is part of an API that needs to be accessible globally.

Example:

```
Public Class Person
    Public Property Name As String   ' Accessible anywhere
    Public Property Age As Integer   ' Accessible anywhere
End Class

Dim person As New Person()
person.Name = "Alice"   ' No restriction on accessing Name
person.Age = 30         ' No restriction on accessing Age
```

Explanation:

- Both `Name` and `Age` are `Public` properties. This means they can be accessed and modified from anywhere, even outside the `Person` class.

---

2. Private:

- **Visibility**: The `Private` modifier restricts access to members to only within the **same class**. No other class or object can directly access these members.
- **Use Case**: Use `Private` to encapsulate internal details that should not be exposed to the outside world. This is useful for protecting the state of an object and preventing direct modification.

Example:

```
Public Class Person
    Private _name As String   ' Private field

    Public Property Name As String   ' Public property for controlled access
        Get
            Return _name
        End Get
        Set(value As String)
            _name = value
        End Set
    End Property
End Class

Dim person As New Person()
' person._name = "Alice"   ' Error: _name is Private and cannot be accessed
directly
person.Name = "Alice"      ' Valid: Name property is Public and can be used
```

Explanation:

- The `_name` field is marked as `Private`, so it cannot be accessed directly from outside the `Person` class.
- The `Name` property provides controlled access to the `_name` field through its `Get` and `Set` methods.

---

3. Protected:

- **Visibility**: The `Protected` modifier allows access to members within the **class itself** and any **derived (child) class**, but not from other classes outside the inheritance hierarchy.
- **Use Case**: Use `Protected` when you want to expose functionality or data to derived classes but not to external classes.

Example:

```
Public Class Animal
    Protected Property Name As String   ' Accessible within Animal and derived
classes

    Public Sub SetName(newName As String)
        Name = newName   ' Protected member can be accessed within the class
    End Sub
End Class

Public Class Dog
    Inherits Animal   ' Dog inherits from Animal

    Public Sub DisplayInfo()
        Console.WriteLine("Dog's name is: " & Name)   ' Can access Name
because it's Protected
    End Sub
End Class

Dim dog As New Dog()
dog.SetName("Buddy")   ' Set the Name using the public method
dog.DisplayInfo()      ' Output: Dog's name is: Buddy
```

Explanation:

- The `Name` property is `Protected`, so it can be accessed in the `Dog` class (which inherits from `Animal`) but not from outside the class hierarchy.

---

4. Friend:

- **Visibility**: The `Friend` modifier allows access to members within the **same assembly** (the compiled executable or library). It's similar to `Internal` in other languages like C#.
- **Use Case**: Use `Friend` when you want members to be accessible to other classes within the same project (assembly) but not from external projects.

Example:

```
Friend Class LibraryBook
    Friend Property Title As String   ' Accessible within the same assembly

    Public Sub DisplayInfo()
```

```
        Console.WriteLine("Book Title: " & Title)
    End Sub
End Class

' In another class within the same assembly
Dim book As New LibraryBook()
book.Title = "VB.NET Programming"  ' Valid: Accessible within the same
assembly
book.DisplayInfo()  ' Output: Book Title: VB.NET Programming
```

Explanation:

- The `LibraryBook` class and its `Title` property are marked as `Friend`, so they can be accessed from any other class within the same assembly but not from outside the assembly.

Encapsulation and Data Protection:

- **Encapsulation**: This is the principle of hiding the internal details of an object and only exposing what is necessary for the outside world. Using access modifiers helps to enforce encapsulation.
- **Data Protection**: By using the `Private`, `Protected`, and `Friend` modifiers, you can ensure that critical data is hidden from direct manipulation by external code. The public members can serve as access points to allow safe access and modification of data.

Example: Encapsulation with Private Fields

```
Public Class Person
    Private _name As String  ' Private field to hold the name

    ' Public property for controlled access to the private field
    Public Property Name As String
        Get
            Return _name
        End Get
        Set(value As String)
            If value.Length > 0 Then
                _name = value
            Else
                Console.WriteLine("Name cannot be empty.")
            End If
        End Set
    End Property
End Class

Dim person As New Person()
person.Name = "Alice"  ' Valid: The setter allows controlled access to _name
person.Name = ""       ' Invalid: Name cannot be empty, so it won't be set
```

Explanation:

- The `_name` field is private, so it cannot be modified directly.

- The `Name` property ensures that any changes to `_name` are validated (i.e., the name cannot be set to an empty string).

Summary of Access Modifiers:

Modifier	Description	Access Level
Public	Accessible from anywhere (inside and outside the class or assembly).	Global access
Private	Accessible only within the same class.	Class-level access only
Protected	Accessible within the class and its derived classes.	Class and derived classes only
Friend	Accessible within the same assembly (project).	Assembly-level access only

By using access modifiers appropriately, you can manage the accessibility of your class members, which helps in maintaining a clean, secure, and maintainable codebase. Proper encapsulation ensures that data is protected from unintended modifications, improving the overall reliability of your application.

4.6 Interfaces in VB.NET

An **interface** in VB.NET is a contract or blueprint that defines a set of **methods**, **properties**, **events**, or **indexers** that a class must implement. The interface itself only provides the signatures of these members without defining any behavior or implementation. It's up to the class implementing the interface to provide the actual code for the methods or properties.

Creating and Implementing Interfaces

An interface is defined using the `Interface` keyword. It can contain declarations for **methods** and **properties**, but not any implementation details. A class that implements the interface is required to provide implementations for all the methods and properties defined in the interface.

Syntax to Create an Interface:

```
Public Interface IDriveable
    ' Method to drive the vehicle
    Sub Drive()
```

```
    ' Method to get the fuel level
    Function GetFuelLevel() As Integer
End Interface
```

In this example, `IDriveable` is an interface that defines two members:

- `Drive()`: A `Sub` method that does not return a value.
- `GetFuelLevel()`: A `Function` method that returns an `Integer` value.

Implementing the Interface in a Class:

Once the interface is defined, a class can **implement** it by using the `Implements` keyword. The class must then provide its own implementation for all methods and properties declared in the interface.

```
Public Class Car
    Implements IDriveable  ' Car class implements the IDriveable interface

    ' Implementing the Drive method from IDriveable interface
    Public Sub Drive() Implements IDriveable.Drive
        Console.WriteLine("Car is driving.")
    End Sub

    ' Implementing the GetFuelLevel method from IDriveable interface
    Public Function GetFuelLevel() As Integer Implements
IDriveable.GetFuelLevel
        Return 50  ' Just an example, returns a fixed fuel level of 50
    End Function
End Class
```

Explanation:

- The `Car` class implements the `IDriveable` interface, which means it must provide the implementations for both `Drive()` and `GetFuelLevel()`.
- In the `Drive()` method, the implementation simply outputs a message saying "Car is driving."
- In the `GetFuelLevel()` method, the implementation returns a fixed fuel level of 50.

Using the Interface:

Now that the class `Car` implements the `IDriveable` interface, you can create objects of the `Car` class and invoke the methods defined by the interface.

```
Dim myCar As New Car()
myCar.Drive()  ' Output: Car is driving.
Console.WriteLine("Fuel level: " & myCar.GetFuelLevel())  ' Output: Fuel
level: 50
```

In the above code, we create an instance of the `Car` class, call the `Drive()` method, and retrieve the fuel level using the `GetFuelLevel()` method.

Interface vs. Abstract Classes

While both **interfaces** and **abstract classes** serve as blueprints for derived classes, there are important differences between them:

1. Interfaces:

- An **interface** only provides **method and property declarations** without any implementation.
- A class can implement **multiple interfaces**. This provides flexibility, allowing a class to conform to multiple contracts.
- An interface cannot have fields, constructors, or any implementation code.

Example:

```
Public Interface IDriveable
    Sub Drive()
End Interface

Public Interface INavigable
    Sub Navigate()
End Interface

Public Class Car
    Implements IDriveable, INavigable

    Public Sub Drive() Implements IDriveable.Drive
        Console.WriteLine("Driving the car.")
    End Sub

    Public Sub Navigate() Implements INavigable.Navigate
        Console.WriteLine("Navigating the car.")
    End Sub
End Class
```

In the above example, the `Car` class implements **two interfaces** (`IDriveable` and `INavigable`), meaning it must provide implementations for both sets of methods defined in the interfaces.

2. Abstract Classes:

- An **abstract class** can contain **both method declarations and method implementations**.
- A class can **inherit only one abstract class** due to the single inheritance restriction in VB.NET.
- Abstract classes can contain fields, constructors, and some method implementations.

Example of an abstract class:

```
Public MustInherit Class Vehicle
```

```
    Public Property Make As String
    Public Property Model As String

    ' Abstract method (no implementation)
    Public MustOverride Sub Start()

    ' Regular method with implementation
    Public Sub Stop()
        Console.WriteLine("Vehicle stopped.")
    End Sub
End Class

Public Class Car
    Inherits Vehicle

    ' Implementing the abstract method
    Public Overrides Sub Start()
        Console.WriteLine("Car started.")
    End Sub
End Class
```

In this example:

- `Vehicle` is an **abstract class** with an abstract method `Start()` and a regular method `Stop()`.
- `Car` inherits from `Vehicle` and provides the actual implementation of the `Start()` method.

Key Differences Between Interfaces and Abstract Classes:

Feature	Interface	Abstract Class
Multiple Inheritance	A class can implement **multiple interfaces**.	A class can inherit **only one abstract class**.
Implementation	No implementation, only method signatures.	Can provide both method signatures and implementations.
Fields	Cannot have fields.	Can have fields.
Constructors	Cannot have constructors.	Can have constructors.
Methods	Can only have method declarations (no code).	Can have both declared and implemented methods.
Access Modifiers	Only `Public` access modifiers are allowed.	Can have various access modifiers (e.g., `Private`, `Protected`).

When to Use Interfaces:

- Use interfaces when you want to define a **contract** that multiple classes can adhere to, regardless of where those classes fit into an inheritance hierarchy.
- Use interfaces to achieve **multiple inheritance** in VB.NET, as a class can implement multiple interfaces.

When to Use Abstract Classes:

- Use abstract classes when you want to define **common functionality** for multiple derived classes, but also want to allow for **custom behavior** to be implemented in the derived classes.
- Use abstract classes when you need to define **fields, constructors, and non-abstract methods** that can be shared among derived classes.

4.7 Polymorphism: Achieving Flexibility in Code

Polymorphism is one of the core principles of Object-Oriented Programming (OOP), and it enables you to use a single interface to represent different underlying forms (types). The term polymorphism literally means "many forms," and it allows objects of different classes to be treated as objects of a common base class. This ability enhances the flexibility and scalability of your code by allowing you to write more generalized and reusable code that can work with objects of various types without knowing their specific class at compile time.

In VB.NET, polymorphism is achieved primarily through **method overriding** and **interface implementation**. Here, we'll focus on **method overriding** as the mechanism for achieving polymorphism.

---

1. Method Overriding

Method overriding allows a derived (child) class to provide its own implementation of a method that is already defined in the base (parent) class. This means that the derived class can modify or replace the behavior of the inherited method to suit its own requirements.

Syntax for Method Overriding:

- The base class method should be marked as `Overridable`, meaning it can be overridden in derived classes.
- The derived class method should be marked as `Overrides`, indicating that it is providing its own implementation.

Example of Method Overriding in VB.NET:

```
Public Class Animal
    ' Base class method: This can be overridden by derived classes
    Public Overridable Sub Speak()
        Console.WriteLine("Animal speaks")
    End Sub
End Class

' Derived class: Dog overrides Speak method
Public Class Dog
    Inherits Animal
    Public Overrides Sub Speak()
        Console.WriteLine("Dog barks")
    End Sub
End Class

' Derived class: Cat overrides Speak method
Public Class Cat
    Inherits Animal
    Public Overrides Sub Speak()
        Console.WriteLine("Cat meows")
    End Sub
End Class
```

In the above example:

- The `Animal` class has a method called `Speak`, which is marked with the `Overridable` keyword. This means other classes can override this method.
- The `Dog` and `Cat` classes both inherit from `Animal` and provide their own implementations of the `Speak` method using the `Overrides` keyword.

---

2. Polymorphism in Action

Polymorphism allows for **runtime method binding**, meaning that the method to be called is determined at runtime based on the type of the object that invokes the method. This allows a reference of the base class to point to objects of derived classes, and when a method is called on that reference, the derived class's overridden method will be invoked.

Example of Polymorphism:

```
Public Class Animal
    Public Overridable Sub Speak()
        Console.WriteLine("Animal speaks")
    End Sub
End Class

Public Class Dog
    Inherits Animal
    Public Overrides Sub Speak()
        Console.WriteLine("Dog barks")
    End Sub
```

```
End Class

Public Class Cat
    Inherits Animal
    Public Overrides Sub Speak()
        Console.WriteLine("Cat meows")
    End Sub
End Class

' Usage of Polymorphism
Dim animal As Animal

' Animal reference points to a Dog object
animal = New Dog()
animal.Speak()   ' Output: Dog barks

' Animal reference now points to a Cat object
animal = New Cat()
animal.Speak()   ' Output: Cat meows
```

Explanation of Polymorphism in the Example:

- The variable `animal` is declared as a reference of type `Animal`, but at runtime, it can point to any object that is a subclass of `Animal` (like `Dog` or `Cat`).
- When we assign a `Dog` object to `animal` and call `animal.Speak()`, it calls the `Speak` method in the `Dog` class (because the object at runtime is of type `Dog`).
- When we assign a `Cat` object to `animal` and call `animal.Speak()`, it calls the `Speak` method in the `Cat` class (because the object at runtime is of type `Cat`).

This is an example of **runtime polymorphism**, where the method call is resolved dynamically based on the actual object type (`Dog` or `Cat`) at runtime, even though the reference type (`Animal`) is the same.

Key Concepts in Polymorphism

- **Runtime Polymorphism**: As demonstrated in the above example, polymorphism in VB.NET is typically associated with runtime behavior. The specific method that is invoked is determined during program execution, not at compile-time.
- **Base Class Reference and Derived Class Objects**: The power of polymorphism lies in treating derived class objects as instances of their base class. This allows for generalized code that can work with different objects in a uniform way.
- **Overriding vs Overloading**:
    - **Method Overriding** (used in polymorphism) happens when a base class method is redefined in a derived class, and the runtime determines which method to call based on the actual object type.
    - **Method Overloading** allows multiple methods with the same name but different parameters to coexist. It happens at compile-time, not runtime, and is not related to polymorphism.

When to Use Polymorphism

1. **Generalizing Code**: Polymorphism allows you to write more general and flexible code that can work with objects of different types. You can design code that can operate on any subclass of a base class without knowing the specific subclass at compile-time.
2. **Extending Functionality**: Polymorphism allows you to extend the functionality of existing classes without changing their implementation. By overriding methods in derived classes, you can change how the inherited functionality works.
3. **Reducing Conditional Logic**: Polymorphism helps you avoid writing conditional statements (e.g., `If...Else`) to decide which behavior to invoke. Instead, polymorphism lets the system decide which method to call based on the actual object type at runtime.
4. **Simplifying Code**: Polymorphism helps reduce code duplication and increases maintainability. You can handle different object types using the same code that works with the base class, allowing for easier updates and modifications.

Real-World Example of Polymorphism

Imagine a system for an online store where various types of products (e.g., books, electronics, and clothes) are handled. Each product may have different behaviors for calculating the price (e.g., discounts, shipping costs). Instead of writing separate code for each product type, polymorphism allows you to write a generalized function that can calculate the price for any product type by overriding a base `Product` class method.

```
Public Class Product
    Public Overridable Function CalculatePrice() As Decimal
        ' Base price calculation for generic product
        Return 100
    End Function
End Class

Public Class Book
    Inherits Product
    Public Overrides Function CalculatePrice() As Decimal
        ' Price calculation for book (e.g., applying a book discount)
        Return 80
    End Function
End Class

Public Class Electronics
    Inherits Product
    Public Overrides Function CalculatePrice() As Decimal
        ' Price calculation for electronics (e.g., adding a warranty cost)
        Return 150
    End Function
End Class

' Usage
Dim product As Product
product = New Book()
```

```
Console.WriteLine("Book Price: " & product.CalculatePrice())   ' Output: Book
Price: 80

product = New Electronics()
Console.WriteLine("Electronics Price: " & product.CalculatePrice())   '
Output: Electronics Price: 150
```

In this example, the `Product` class provides a general price calculation, while the `Book` and `Electronics` classes override this method to provide their specific price calculation. You can now use polymorphism to calculate prices for different product types without needing to know the specific type of product.

30 multiple-choice questions (MCQs):

4.1 Fundamentals of OOP

1. **Which of the following is NOT one of the four fundamental principles of Object-Oriented Programming (OOP)?**
   - a) Encapsulation
   - b) Inheritance
   - c) Modularity
   - d) Polymorphism

     Answer: c) Modularity
2. **Which OOP principle allows objects of different classes to be treated as objects of a common base class?**
   - a) Encapsulation
   - b) Inheritance
   - c) Polymorphism
   - d) Abstraction

     Answer: c) Polymorphism
3. **What does the principle of encapsulation ensure in OOP?**
   - a) Objects can communicate with each other
   - b) Code is reusable through inheritance
   - c) Data is protected and hidden within the object
   - d) Objects can take many forms

     Answer: c) Data is protected and hidden within the object
4. **Which of the following is an example of method overriding in OOP?**
   - a) A method in a base class is redefined in a derived class.
   - b) A method with the same name but different parameters is created in a class.
   - c) A class can be used to create multiple objects.
   - d) A class inherits properties from another class.

     Answer: a) A method in a base class is redefined in a derived class.
5. **What is the primary goal of abstraction in OOP?**
   - a) To allow objects to take on different forms
   - b) To expose only necessary details and hide the complex implementation

- c) To ensure code is reusable
- d) To provide multiple methods for similar tasks

  Answer: b) To expose only necessary details and hide the complex implementation

---

4.2 Creating Classes and Objects

6. **In VB.NET, what is the purpose of a constructor?**
   - a) To destroy an object
   - b) To initialize an object when it is created
   - c) To define the properties of a class
   - d) To change the behavior of a method

   Answer: b) To initialize an object when it is created
7. **Which method is automatically called when an object is instantiated in VB.NET?**
   - a) Destructor
   - b) Finalize
   - c) Constructor
   - d) Overridable method

   Answer: c) Constructor
8. **Which of the following defines a property of a class in VB.NET?**
   - a) A variable that represents the state of the object
   - b) A function that changes the state of the object
   - c) A method that interacts with other objects
   - d) A special function that is automatically called

   Answer: a) A variable that represents the state of the object
9. **What is the purpose of the `Finalize` method in VB.NET?**
   - a) To initialize an object
   - b) To provide cleanup operations before the object is destroyed
   - c) To create new methods for the object
   - d) To raise events

   Answer: b) To provide cleanup operations before the object is destroyed
10. **Which keyword is used to define an event in a class in VB.NET?**
    - a) Event
    - b) Sub
    - c) Function
    - d) Raise

    Answer: a) Event

4.3 Understanding Method Overloading

11. **What is method overloading in VB.NET?**
    - a) Changing the method signature to provide different implementations

- b) Providing multiple methods with the same name but different parameters
- c) Overriding methods in the derived class
- d) Declaring methods that don't return any value

  Answer: b) Providing multiple methods with the same name but different parameters

12. **Which of the following is a valid method overloading scenario in VB.NET?**
    - a) Two methods with the same name but different return types
    - b) Two methods with the same name but different parameter types
    - c) Two methods with the same name and the same parameter list
    - d) Two methods with different names

    Answer: b) Two methods with the same name but different parameter types
13. **When should you use method overloading?**
    - a) When you need to provide different implementations for different parameters
    - b) To provide the same method signature in different classes
    - c) To reuse code in a class
    - d) When the method requires dynamic polymorphism

    Answer: a) When you need to provide different implementations for different parameters
14. **What happens if you define two overloaded methods with the same number of parameters and identical types in VB.NET?**
    - a) The code will result in a compilation error
    - b) The method that is defined later will be executed
    - c) Both methods will be ignored
    - d) The method that is defined first will be executed

    Answer: a) The code will result in a compilation error
15. **Which of the following is NOT a benefit of method overloading?**
    - a) Provides flexibility to handle different data types
    - b) Allows the same functionality with different parameters
    - c) Increases code redundancy
    - d) Improves code readability

    Answer: c) Increases code redundancy

4.4 Inheritance in VB.NET

16. **Which keyword is used to indicate that a class inherits from another class in VB.NET?**
    - a) Implements
    - b) Inherits
    - c) Subclass
    - d) Extends

    Answer: b) Inherits
17. **Which of the following is a valid reason for using inheritance in VB.NET?**
    - a) To restrict access to data
    - b) To reuse code from a base class in derived classes

- c) To declare events in a class
- d) To override method implementations

  Answer: b) To reuse code from a base class in derived classes

18. **What does the `Overrides` keyword do in VB.NET?**
    - a) It defines a new method with the same name in a derived class.
    - b) It modifies an inherited method to add functionality in the base class.
    - c) It indicates that a derived class is overriding a base class method.
    - d) It ensures that the method is available to all objects.

    Answer: c) It indicates that a derived class is overriding a base class method.
19. **Which of the following is an example of inheritance in VB.NET?**
    - a) A base class method is overridden in a derived class.
    - b) A method is defined with the same name but different parameters.
    - c) A class contains multiple methods of different names.
    - d) A class includes a private property.

    Answer: a) A base class method is overridden in a derived class.
20. **Which of the following methods is called when an object is being destroyed in VB.NET?**
    - a) Destructor
    - b) Finalize
    - c) Initialize
    - d) Create

    Answer: b) Finalize

4.5 Access Modifiers in VB.NET

21. **Which access modifier allows access to class members from anywhere within the same assembly?**
    - a) Private
    - b) Friend
    - c) Protected
    - d) Public

    Answer: b) Friend
22. **Which of the following access modifiers restricts access to class members within the same class only?**
    - a) Private
    - b) Public
    - c) Protected
    - d) Friend

    Answer: a) Private
23. **Which access modifier allows class members to be accessed by derived classes but not from outside the class hierarchy?**
    - a) Private
    - b) Protected
    - c) Friend

- d) Public

  Answer: b) Protected

24. **What is the purpose of encapsulation in OOP?**
    - a) To hide the implementation details of a class
    - b) To create multiple classes
    - c) To allow method overloading
    - d) To inherit methods from the base class

    Answer: a) To hide the implementation details of a class
25. **What does the `Public` access modifier do in VB.NET?**
    - a) Allows access only within the same class
    - b) Allows access within the same assembly
    - c) Allows access from anywhere, inside or outside the class
    - d) Allows access only from derived classes

    Answer: c) Allows access from anywhere, inside or outside the class

---

4.6 Interfaces in VB.NET

26. **Which keyword is used to define an interface in VB.NET?**
    - a) Interface
    - b) Implements
    - c) Class
    - d) Abstract

    Answer: a) Interface
27. **What is the key difference between an interface and an abstract class?**
    - a) An interface can provide method implementations, while an abstract class cannot.
    - b) An abstract class provides method signatures, while an interface provides both signatures and implementations.
    - c) An interface can be implemented by multiple classes, while an abstract class can only be inherited by one class.
    - d) An interface is used for inheritance, while an abstract class is used for abstraction.

    Answer: c) An interface can be implemented by multiple classes, while an abstract class can only be inherited by one class.
28. **What happens when a class implements an interface in VB.NET?**
    - a) The class inherits the implementation of all methods in the interface.
    - b) The class must implement all methods defined in the interface.
    - c) The class is not allowed to implement any methods.
    - d) The class can only use methods defined in other interfaces.

    Answer: b) The class must implement all methods defined in the interface.

4.7 Polymorphism: Achieving Flexibility in Code

29. **What is the main benefit of polymorphism in OOP?**
    - a) It allows objects to change their type at runtime.
    - b) It ensures methods are always overridden in derived classes.
    - c) It allows multiple classes to share common behavior without inheriting from a common base class.
    - d) It lets methods in the base class be executed in the derived class.
    Answer: a) It allows objects to change their type at runtime.
30. **Which of the following is an example of polymorphism in VB.NET?**
    - a) A method with multiple parameter signatures
    - b) A base class method being overridden in a derived class
    - c) A class containing multiple properties
    - d) An interface being implemented by multiple classes
    Answer: b) A base class method being overridden in a derived class

15 programming questions with answers based on the topics you've mentioned:

4.1 Fundamentals of OOP

1. **What is the primary purpose of inheritance in OOP? Write a simple example demonstrating inheritance in VB.NET.**

   Answer: The primary purpose of inheritance is to allow a new class (child or derived class) to inherit properties and methods from an existing class (parent or base class), promoting code reuse.

   Example:

```
Public Class Animal
    Public Property Name As String

    Public Sub Speak()
        Console.WriteLine("Animal makes a sound.")
    End Sub
End Class

Public Class Dog
    Inherits Animal

    Public Sub Bark()
        Console.WriteLine("Dog barks.")
    End Sub
End Class
```

4.2 Creating Classes and Objects

2. **Define a class `Person` with a property `Name` and a method `Greet` that prints a greeting message using the `Name` property.**

   Answer:

```
Public Class Person
    Public Property Name As String

    Public Sub Greet()
        Console.WriteLine("Hello, " & Name)
    End Sub
End Class
```

---

3. **Write a `Car` class with a constructor that accepts `Make` and `Model` as parameters and assigns them to properties.**

   Answer:

```
Public Class Car
    Public Property Make As String
    Public Property Model As String

    Public Sub New(make As String, model As String)
        Me.Make = make
        Me.Model = model
    End Sub
End Class
```

---

4. **How would you create an event `OnSpeedChange` in a `Car` class that notifies when the car's speed changes?**

   Answer:

```
Public Class Car
    Public Event OnSpeedChange As EventHandler

    Private _speed As Integer

    Public Property Speed As Integer
        Get
            Return _speed
        End Get
        Set(value As Integer)
            _speed = value
            RaiseEvent OnSpeedChange(Me, EventArgs.Empty)
        End Set
    End Property
End Class
```

4.3 Understanding Method Overloading

5. **Write an overloaded method `Add` in a `Calculator` class that can add two integers or two doubles.**

   Answer:

```
Public Class Calculator
    Public Function Add(x As Integer, y As Integer) As Integer
        Return x + y
    End Function

    Public Function Add(x As Double, y As Double) As Double
        Return x + y
    End Function
End Class
```

---

6. **What would happen if you attempt to overload two methods with the same name and identical parameters in VB.NET?**

   Answer: This would result in a compile-time error because method overloading requires at least one different parameter (type, number, or order) for each method with the same name.

---

7. **When would you use method overloading in a program? Provide an example.**

   Answer: You would use method overloading when you need to perform the same operation with different types of data or different numbers of parameters.

   Example:

```
Public Function Multiply(x As Integer, y As Integer) As Integer
    Return x * y
End Function

Public Function Multiply(x As Double, y As Double) As Double
    Return x * y
End Function
```

4.4 Inheritance in VB.NET

8. **Write a derived class `Car` that inherits from a base class `Vehicle`. The `Vehicle` class should have properties `Make` and `Model`. The `Car` class should have an additional property `Year`.**

Answer:

```
Public Class Vehicle
    Public Property Make As String
    Public Property Model As String
End Class

Public Class Car
    Inherits Vehicle
    Public Property Year As Integer
End Class
```

---

9. **In VB.NET, how would you override a method from a base class in a derived class? Provide an example where the base class method `Speak` is overridden in the `Dog` class.**

   Answer:

```
Public Class Animal
    Public Overridable Sub Speak()
        Console.WriteLine("Animal speaks")
    End Sub
End Class

Public Class Dog
    Inherits Animal

    Public Overrides Sub Speak()
        Console.WriteLine("Dog barks")
    End Sub
End Class
```

---

10. **What is the difference between the `Overridable` and `Overrides` keywords in VB.NET?**

    Answer:

    - `Overridable` is used in the base class to indicate that a method can be overridden in a derived class.
    - `Overrides` is used in the derived class to indicate that a method is overriding a base class method.

4.5 Access Modifiers in VB.NET

11. **What access modifier should you use to ensure that a class member is only accessible within the same class?**

Answer: The `Private` access modifier should be used to restrict access to class members within the same class.

---

12. **What is the difference between `Friend` and `Protected` access modifiers in VB.NET?**

    Answer:

    - `Friend` makes the class members accessible within the same assembly (project).
    - `Protected` makes the class members accessible within the class itself and any derived classes, but not from outside the class hierarchy.

---

13. **Write a `Person` class with a `Private` field `_name` and a `Public` property `Name` to access and modify the `_name` field.**

    Answer:

```
Public Class Person
    Private _name As String

    Public Property Name As String
        Get
            Return _name
        End Get
        Set(value As String)
            _name = value
        End Set
    End Property
End Class
```

4.6 Interfaces in VB.NET

14. **Create an interface `IDriveable` with a method `Drive` and a function `GetFuelLevel`. Then implement it in a `Car` class.**

    Answer:

```
Public Interface IDriveable
    Sub Drive()
    Function GetFuelLevel() As Integer
End Interface

Public Class Car
    Implements IDriveable

    Public Sub Drive() Implements IDriveable.Drive
```

```
        Console.WriteLine("Car is driving.")
    End Sub

    Public Function GetFuelLevel() As Integer Implements
IDriveable.GetFuelLevel
        Return 75
    End Function
End Class
```

4.7 Polymorphism: Achieving Flexibility in Code

15. **Write an example demonstrating polymorphism where the `Speak` method is overridden in derived classes (`Dog` and `Cat`) of a base class `Animal`.**

Answer:

```
Public Class Animal
    Public Overridable Sub Speak()
        Console.WriteLine("Animal speaks")
    End Sub
End Class

Public Class Dog
    Inherits Animal

    Public Overrides Sub Speak()
        Console.WriteLine("Dog barks")
    End Sub
End Class

Public Class Cat
    Inherits Animal

    Public Overrides Sub Speak()
        Console.WriteLine("Cat meows")
    End Sub
End Class

' Usage
Dim myAnimal As Animal

myAnimal = New Dog()
myAnimal.Speak()   ' Output: Dog barks

myAnimal = New Cat()
myAnimal.Speak()   ' Output: Cat meows
```

CHAPTER 5: EXCEPTION HANDLING IN VB.NET

5.1 Understanding Exceptions

What is an Exception?

An **exception** is an event that disrupts the normal flow of execution in a program. It occurs when the program encounters an unexpected or erroneous situation, typically at **runtime**. When an exception is thrown, the program stops executing the current code and looks for an exception handler (usually a `Try...Catch` block) to resolve or handle the issue. If the exception is not handled properly, the program may terminate unexpectedly.

For example:

- **Divide by zero**: If a program tries to divide a number by zero, an exception is raised.
- **Null reference**: If a program tries to access an object that has not been initialized (i.e., a `null` reference), it will raise an exception.
- **File access issues**: If the program tries to access a file that doesn't exist, an exception will be triggered.

Handling exceptions is crucial because it prevents the program from crashing and allows you to manage errors in a graceful manner.

Types of Exceptions in VB.NET

In VB.NET, exceptions can be broadly categorized into **System Exceptions** and **Application Exceptions**. These two categories help to differentiate between errors that are due to system-level issues and those that are a result of the application's logic.

---

1. System Exceptions

System Exceptions are errors that are generated by the .NET runtime or system environment. These exceptions typically occur due to issues like invalid operations, accessing resources incorrectly, or incorrect use of system components. They are predefined by .NET and represent conditions that the runtime cannot handle automatically.

Common **System Exceptions** include:

1. **`DivideByZeroException`**:
   - This exception occurs when an attempt is made to divide a number by zero, which is mathematically undefined.
   - Example:

```
Dim result As Integer = 10 / 0 ' This will throw a
DivideByZeroException
```

2. **`NullReferenceException`**:
   - This exception occurs when the program attempts to access an object or call a method on a null object reference.
   - Example:

```
Dim obj As String = Nothing
Console.WriteLine(obj.Length) ' This will throw a
NullReferenceException
```

3. **`FileNotFoundException`**:
   - This exception occurs when the program tries to access a file that does not exist in the specified location.
   - Example:

```
Dim sr As New System.IO.StreamReader("nonexistentfile.txt") '
This will throw a FileNotFoundException
```

4. **`IndexOutOfRangeException`**:
   - This exception occurs when an index is used that is outside the bounds of an array or collection.
   - Example:

```
Dim arr As Integer() = {1, 2, 3}
Console.WriteLine(arr(5)) ' This will throw an
IndexOutOfRangeException
```

Other **System Exceptions** include:

- **`InvalidCastException`**: Raised when an invalid cast is performed (e.g., trying to cast an object to an incompatible type).
- **`OutOfMemoryException`**: Raised when there is insufficient memory to continue the program's execution.

---

2. Application Exceptions

Application Exceptions are exceptions that are raised by the application itself. These are typically thrown when the program encounters an invalid state or when specific logic conditions are violated. Developers create custom exceptions or use standard exceptions to handle specific business logic errors.

Common **Application Exceptions** include:

1. **`ArgumentException`**:

- This exception occurs when a method receives invalid or inappropriate arguments.
- Example:

```
Sub SetAge(age As Integer)
    If age < 0 Then
        Throw New ArgumentException("Age cannot be negative.")
    End If
End Sub
SetAge(-5) ' This will throw an ArgumentException
```

2. **`InvalidOperationException`**:
   - This exception occurs when a method is called in an invalid state for the current object. For example, calling a method when an object is not initialized or when the method's operation cannot be completed due to the object's current state.
   - Example:

```
Public Class BankAccount
    Private balance As Integer

    Public Sub Withdraw(amount As Integer)
        If balance <= 0 Then
            Throw New InvalidOperationException("Insufficient
funds.")
        End If
        balance -= amount
    End Sub
End Class
```

3. **`FormatException`**:
   - Raised when the format of a data value is invalid (e.g., invalid date or number format).
   - Example:

```
Dim result As Integer = Integer.Parse("abc") ' This will throw a
FormatException
```

4. **`TimeoutException`**:
   - Raised when a time operation exceeds the specified time limit.
   - Example:

```
' If a database operation or network call takes too long, a
TimeoutException might occur.
```

5. **`Custom Application Exceptions`**:
   - Developers can define their own exceptions to handle specific application logic. For example, a `ProductNotFoundException` could be defined to handle errors when a product is not found in a database.

Custom Exception Example:

```
Public Class ProductNotFoundException
    Inherits Exception
```

```
    Public Sub New(message As String)
        MyBase.New(message)
    End Sub
End Class

' Usage
Try
    Throw New ProductNotFoundException("Product not found in the database.")
Catch ex As ProductNotFoundException
    Console.WriteLine(ex.Message) ' Output: Product not found in the
database.
End Try
```

5.2 Structured Exception Handling

In VB.NET, **Structured Exception Handling (SEH)** is a programming paradigm that enables you to handle errors or exceptions in a controlled and structured manner, preventing the program from crashing and providing an opportunity to respond to errors appropriately. It is achieved using the `Try...Catch...Finally` block structure, which allows the programmer to catch exceptions, handle them, and ensure that certain code is always executed (such as cleanup code).

The Structure of Try...Catch...Finally

1. **Try Block**:
   - The `Try` block contains the code that may throw an exception. If an error occurs during the execution of the code in the `Try` block, the program immediately jumps to the corresponding `Catch` block.
   - The `Try` block is where you place the code that you suspect might cause errors (e.g., accessing an array element, performing file operations, dividing numbers, etc.).
2. **Catch Block**:
   - The `Catch` block is used to catch and handle exceptions that occur in the `Try` block.
   - You can have one or more `Catch` blocks, each designed to handle a specific type of exception. If an exception matches the type specified in a `Catch` block, that block will be executed.
   - The `Catch` block provides an opportunity to log the error, show an error message, or take corrective action.
3. **Finally Block**:
   - The `Finally` block contains code that will be executed **regardless** of whether an exception occurs or not.
   - It is typically used for cleanup activities, such as closing database connections, closing files, or releasing resources.
   - Even if no exception occurs in the `Try` block, the code in the `Finally` block will still run, ensuring that resources are freed or necessary actions are taken after the execution of the `Try` block.

- If an exception occurs and is caught, the `Finally` block will execute after the `Catch` block.

Basic Syntax

Here's the basic syntax of the `Try...Catch...Finally` structure:

```
Try
    ' Code that may throw an exception
    Dim result As Integer = 10 / 0  ' Division by zero
Catch ex As DivideByZeroException
    ' Handle the exception
    Console.WriteLine("Error: Division by zero.")
Finally
    ' Code that will run regardless of exception
    Console.WriteLine("Cleanup code.")
End Try
```

Explanation of Each Part

1. **Try Block**:
    - Here, the division by zero operation `10 / 0` is attempted. Since dividing by zero is an illegal operation, it will throw a `DivideByZeroException`.
2. **Catch Block**:
    - This block catches the specific exception (`DivideByZeroException`) that was raised in the `Try` block. Once the exception is caught, the code inside the `Catch` block is executed.
    - The `Catch ex As DivideByZeroException` part declares the exception type (i.e., `DivideByZeroException`) and the variable `ex` to reference the exception object, allowing you to access details about the error (like the message or stack trace).

    Example output:

    ```
    Error: Division by zero.
    ```

3. **Finally Block**:
    - Regardless of whether an exception occurred or not, the code inside the `Finally` block will be executed. In this case, the message `"Cleanup code."` is printed to the console.

    Example output:

    ```
    Cleanup code.
    ```

Handling Multiple Exception Types

You can also handle multiple types of exceptions in a single `Try...Catch` block by specifying multiple `Catch` blocks. Each `Catch` block handles a different exception type.

Example:

```
Try
    ' Code that may throw different types of exceptions
    Dim number As Integer = Integer.Parse("abc")   ' This will throw a
FormatException
Catch ex As FormatException
    ' Handle FormatException
    Console.WriteLine("Error: Invalid format.")
Catch ex As DivideByZeroException
    ' Handle DivideByZeroException
    Console.WriteLine("Error: Cannot divide by zero.")
Finally
    ' Code that will run regardless of exception
    Console.WriteLine("Cleanup code.")
End Try
```

Best Practices for Using Try...Catch...Finally

- **Catch Specific Exceptions**: It is better to catch specific exceptions (like `FormatException`, `DivideByZeroException`, etc.) rather than using a general `Exception`. This way, you can handle different exceptions in the most appropriate manner.
- **Avoid Empty Catch Blocks**: Catch blocks should not be left empty. If you catch an exception and do nothing with it, it can make debugging difficult and hide potential issues in the code.
- **Log Exceptions**: It's a good practice to log the exception details (such as the message, stack trace, etc.) to a file or logging system to help diagnose issues and ensure the application behaves as expected in the future.
- **Use Finally for Cleanup**: Always use the `Finally` block for cleanup actions such as closing files, releasing resources, or cleaning up data connections, regardless of whether an exception occurred.

Example: Using Try...Catch...Finally in a File Operation

Here's an example of using `Try...Catch...Finally` to handle file operations:

```
Sub ReadFile(filePath As String)
    Try
        ' Attempt to open and read the file
        Dim reader As New System.IO.StreamReader(filePath)
        Dim content As String = reader.ReadToEnd()
        Console.WriteLine(content)
    Catch ex As System.IO.FileNotFoundException
        ' Handle file not found exception
        Console.WriteLine("Error: File not found.")
    Catch ex As UnauthorizedAccessException
```

```
            ' Handle unauthorized access exception
            Console.WriteLine("Error: Unauthorized access to the file.")
        Finally
            ' Always close the file if it was opened
            Console.WriteLine("Cleanup: Closing file if open.")
        End Try
    End Sub
```

In this example:

- The `Try` block attempts to read the file.
- The `Catch` blocks handle different exceptions that might arise, such as the file not being found or unauthorized access.
- The `Finally` block ensures that cleanup code (e.g., closing the file) is always executed, regardless of whether an exception occurred.

5.3 Handling Different Types of Exceptions

In VB.NET, exceptions are categorized into two broad types: **SystemExceptions** and **ApplicationExceptions**. These categories help distinguish between errors that occur due to system-level issues and errors that arise due to application-specific logic problems. Understanding these two types of exceptions is crucial for handling them effectively in your code.

---

1. SystemExceptions:

SystemExceptions are exceptions provided by the .NET runtime (the system), typically signaling errors related to the environment or the system itself. These exceptions are usually unexpected and difficult for the application to recover from without significant changes to the system or environment. When such exceptions occur, they typically indicate problems that need to be fixed either in the application logic or the system configuration.

Common SystemExceptions:

- **NullReferenceException**: Occurs when you try to use an object reference that has not been initialized or is set to `Nothing`. For example, attempting to call a method or access a property of an object that is `Nothing`.

  ```
  Dim obj As MyClass = Nothing
  obj.SomeMethod()   ' Throws NullReferenceException
  ```

- **IndexOutOfRangeException**: Raised when you try to access an array or collection element using an invalid index (an index that is outside its bounds).

```
Dim arr(5) As Integer
Console.WriteLine(arr(10))   ' Throws IndexOutOfRangeException
```

- **FileNotFoundException**: Occurs when attempting to access a file that does not exist in the specified path.

```
Dim reader As New System.IO.StreamReader("nonexistentFile.txt")
' Throws FileNotFoundException if the file doesn't exist
```

Handling SystemExceptions:

SystemExceptions are often handled using specific `Catch` blocks for each type of exception, allowing the program to react appropriately to common system-level issues. These exceptions are usually not recoverable, so the application might need to log the error, alert the user, or terminate the application gracefully.

Example:

```
Try
    Dim num As Integer = 10 / 0   ' Division by zero
Catch ex As DivideByZeroException
    Console.WriteLine("Cannot divide by zero.")
Catch ex As IndexOutOfRangeException
    Console.WriteLine("Array index is out of range.")
Catch ex As FileNotFoundException
    Console.WriteLine("File not found.")
Catch ex As Exception
    Console.WriteLine("An unexpected error occurred: " & ex.Message)
Finally
    Console.WriteLine("End of error handling.")
End Try
```

---

2. ApplicationExceptions:

ApplicationExceptions are exceptions that are specifically designed by developers to handle errors or business logic issues within their application. These exceptions are usually thrown to handle anticipated conditions or situations that are unique to the application's specific needs. These exceptions are **not part of the .NET runtime** and are intended to allow better control over error handling in specific application domains.

Common ApplicationExceptions:

- **InvalidUserInputException**: Thrown when the user enters invalid or unexpected data that the application cannot process.

```
If userInput IsNotValid Then
    Throw New InvalidUserInputException("User input is invalid.")
End If
```

- **DataValidationException**: Raised when the application detects invalid data while performing operations like saving or processing user data.

```
If Not ValidateData(userData) Then
    Throw New DataValidationException("Invalid data.")
End If
```

Handling ApplicationExceptions:

In contrast to system exceptions, which are generally unpredictable and require recovery or logging, **ApplicationExceptions** allow developers to control error handling within the scope of the application's functionality. These can be thrown to indicate application-specific issues, such as invalid input or failed validation, and can be handled by custom `Catch` blocks.

Example of custom exception handling:

```
Try
    ' Code that may throw a custom exception
    If Not ValidateAge(age) Then
        Throw New InvalidUserInputException("Age cannot be less than 18.")
Catch ex As InvalidUserInputException
    Console.WriteLine("User Input Error: " & ex.Message)
Catch ex As Exception
    ' General catch for other unexpected exceptions
    Console.WriteLine("An unexpected error occurred: " & ex.Message)
Finally
    Console.WriteLine("End of error handling.")
End Try
```

Handling Multiple Exception Types

You can handle different types of exceptions using multiple `Catch` blocks. The `Catch` block for a specific exception type will execute if that particular exception is thrown. If none of the specific `Catch` blocks match, the program can use a **general `Catch` block** to handle unexpected exceptions.

Here's how you handle multiple exceptions separately:

```
Try
    ' Code that may throw different exceptions
    Dim number As Integer = Integer.Parse("abc")   ' This throws
FormatException
Catch ex As FormatException
    Console.WriteLine("Error: Invalid format for number.")
Catch ex As DivideByZeroException
    Console.WriteLine("Error: Cannot divide by zero.")
Catch ex As FileNotFoundException
    Console.WriteLine("Error: File not found.")
Catch ex As Exception
    ' General catch block for unexpected exceptions
    Console.WriteLine("An unexpected error occurred: " & ex.Message)
Finally
```

```
    Console.WriteLine("End of error handling.")
End Try
```

Key Points:

1. **SystemExceptions**: These are predefined exceptions that occur due to system-level errors. They are typically fatal or beyond the control of the application. Common system exceptions include `DivideByZeroException`, `NullReferenceException`, and `FileNotFoundException`.
2. **ApplicationExceptions**: These are custom exceptions created by the application itself to handle specific application errors or issues. Examples include `InvalidUserInputException` and `DataValidationException`.
3. **Catch Multiple Exceptions**: You can use multiple `Catch` blocks to handle different exception types separately. Specific exceptions should be handled before a general `Catch ex As Exception` block.
4. **Graceful Error Handling**: Handling both `SystemExceptions` and `ApplicationExceptions` properly allows the program to respond appropriately without crashing, providing feedback to the user, logging errors, or recovering from failures.

By distinguishing between system-level and application-specific errors, you can design a more robust error-handling strategy, improve user experience, and ensure that the program can handle a variety of error conditions in a structured way.

5.4 Creating Custom Exceptions

Creating custom exceptions in VB.NET is a powerful feature that allows developers to define specific error conditions unique to their applications. By extending the built-in `Exception` class, you can create exceptions tailored to your specific needs, providing meaningful error messages and error-handling functionality. Custom exceptions make your application more robust and help maintain clear communication about error conditions, especially when dealing with complex business logic or specific domain issues.

Steps to Create Custom Exceptions:

To create a custom exception in VB.NET, you need to follow these basic steps:

1. Inherit from the `Exception` Class:

- In VB.NET, all exceptions are derived from the `Exception` class. To create a custom exception, simply inherit from the `Exception` class.
- By inheriting from `Exception`, your custom exception will have all the properties and methods of the `Exception` class, such as `Message`, `StackTrace`, `InnerException`, etc.

2. Define a Constructor:

- The custom exception class typically has one or more constructors that accept parameters like error messages or other relevant data. The constructor should call the base `Exception` class constructor to initialize the exception properly.
- If needed, you can also add custom properties to carry additional information about the exception.

Example of Creating a Custom Exception:

Let's walk through an example of creating a custom exception named `InvalidAgeException`, which will be thrown when the age input is invalid (i.e., a negative value).

```
Public Class InvalidAgeException
    Inherits Exception

    ' Constructor that accepts a custom message
    Public Sub New(message As String)
        MyBase.New(message)   ' Calls the base class (Exception) constructor
    End Sub
End Class
```

In the example above:

- **Inherits Exception**: The `InvalidAgeException` class inherits from the `Exception` class.
- **Constructor**: The constructor accepts a `message` string parameter that will be passed to the base class constructor (`MyBase.New(message)`). This initializes the `Message` property of the exception with the provided message.

Using the Custom Exception:

Once the custom exception class is defined, it can be used in the application. Here is an example of how the custom exception can be used in the `Try...Catch` block:

```
Try
    Dim age As Integer = -1

    ' Check for invalid age
    If age < 0 Then
        ' Throw the custom exception with a message
        Throw New InvalidAgeException("Age cannot be negative.")
    End If

Catch ex As InvalidAgeException
    ' Handle the custom exception
    Console.WriteLine("Custom Error: " & ex.Message)
```

```
End Try
```

Explanation:

- **Throwing the Custom Exception**: If the `age` variable is negative, we throw the `InvalidAgeException` with the message "Age cannot be negative."
- **Catching the Custom Exception**: The `Catch` block catches the `InvalidAgeException`, and the error message is printed to the console.

Output:

```
Custom Error: Age cannot be negative.
```

Extending Custom Exceptions with Additional Properties:

You can also extend the functionality of custom exceptions by adding additional properties that provide more context or information about the error. This is particularly useful when your application needs to carry additional error data (e.g., a specific error code or timestamp).

For example, let's add an `ErrorCode` property to our custom exception:

```
Public Class InvalidAgeException
    Inherits Exception

    ' Additional property for an error code
    Public Property ErrorCode As Integer

    ' Constructor with custom message and error code
    Public Sub New(message As String, errorCode As Integer)
        MyBase.New(message)  ' Calls the base class constructor with the
message
        Me.ErrorCode = errorCode  ' Assigns the custom error code
    End Sub
End Class
```

Now, you can throw the exception with both a custom message and an error code:

```
Try
    Dim age As Integer = -5

    ' Check for invalid age
    If age < 0 Then
        ' Throw the custom exception with a message and error code
        Throw New InvalidAgeException("Age cannot be negative.", 1001)
    End If

Catch ex As InvalidAgeException
    ' Handle the custom exception
    Console.WriteLine("Custom Error: " & ex.Message)
    Console.WriteLine("Error Code: " & ex.ErrorCode)
```

```
End Try
```

Output:

```
Custom Error: Age cannot be negative.
Error Code: 1001
```

Best Practices for Creating Custom Exceptions:

1. **Use Custom Exceptions for Application-Specific Logic**:
   - Custom exceptions are ideal for handling specific application conditions or business logic errors. They provide more clarity than generic exceptions, making the error easier to understand and resolve.
2. **Derive from `Exception`**:
   - Always inherit from the `Exception` class, as this ensures compatibility with the .NET exception handling system.
3. **Provide Meaningful Error Messages**:
   - Always provide a clear and descriptive error message when throwing a custom exception. This makes it easier for developers or users to understand the nature of the problem.
4. **Add Custom Properties if Needed**:
   - Add properties (e.g., error codes, timestamps, or other relevant data) to help troubleshoot issues more efficiently.
5. **Avoid Overuse of Custom Exceptions**:
   - While custom exceptions are useful, avoid creating too many custom exceptions for minor conditions. Overuse can make your exception hierarchy unnecessarily complex.

5.5 Debugging with Exception Handling

Debugging is an essential part of the software development process, especially when working with exception handling. Effective debugging can help developers quickly identify and resolve issues that may otherwise disrupt the execution of the application. With the right tools and techniques, you can troubleshoot problems more efficiently. Below, we'll cover some of the primary tools and methods for debugging code that involves exception handling.

---

1. Visual Studio Debugger

Visual Studio provides an excellent debugging environment to identify and fix exceptions. Here are some key features to help you with debugging exceptions:

Breakpoints:

- **What They Are**: A breakpoint is a marker that you place in your code to pause the execution of the program at a specific line. This allows you to inspect the state of variables, properties, and other aspects of the program's state.
- **How It Helps with Exception Handling**: By setting breakpoints before or after code that may throw an exception, you can examine variables and evaluate whether the exception is being triggered by invalid data, improper logic, or other causes.

Example:

- Set a breakpoint before a block of code that might raise an exception (e.g., a database query, a division operation).
- When the breakpoint is hit, you can step through the code and monitor the variable values that might lead to the exception.

Exception Settings:

- Visual Studio allows you to configure exception handling settings to break when a specific exception type is thrown.
- This is useful when you're trying to catch a specific exception (e.g., `NullReferenceException`) without manually placing try-catch blocks around the code.

How to Use:

- Go to **Debug > Windows > Exception Settings**.
- You can search for the exception you want to break on (e.g., `System.NullReferenceException`) and check the box next to it. The debugger will break the execution when that exception occurs, even if it's not handled.

Immediate Window:

- The Immediate Window in Visual Studio allows you to evaluate expressions and inspect or modify variables during debugging. It's a useful tool for testing expressions and querying the current state of the application at runtime.

Example:

- While debugging, you can use the Immediate Window to test expressions like `? x + y` to check the value of variables `x` and `y` at runtime.
- This helps to quickly determine if the exception is caused by incorrect data or logic.

---

2. Logging

Logging is a powerful technique for tracking and troubleshooting exceptions. By recording detailed information about exceptions (such as the error message, stack trace, and other contextual data), you can analyze and diagnose issues later, even after the program has completed execution.

Logging with `Try...Catch`:

- You can log exceptions to a file, database, or event log using the `Try...Catch` block. This ensures that every exception is captured, providing an audit trail for the errors that occurred.
- In VB.NET, you can use `My.Computer.FileSystem.WriteAllText` or `System.IO.StreamWriter` to log exceptions to a file.

Example of Logging to a File:

```
Try
    ' Code that might throw an exception
    Dim result As Integer = 10 / 0   ' Division by zero
Catch ex As Exception
    ' Log the exception to a file
    My.Computer.FileSystem.WriteAllText("errorlog.txt", ex.ToString(), True)
End Try
```

- In the code above:
    - If an exception occurs (in this case, a division by zero), the `Catch` block logs the entire exception (`ex.ToString()`) to a file named `errorlog.txt`.
    - The third parameter `True` ensures that the log file is appended with each new exception, preserving previous logs.

Benefits of Logging:

- **Persistent Record**: Logging creates a record of the exception that can be reviewed after the application has stopped running.
- **Remote Debugging**: If your application is deployed on a server or client machine, logging can help capture errors that occur on remote systems without requiring direct access to the machine.
- **Troubleshooting Over Time**: A well-maintained log can help identify recurring issues and patterns over time, leading to better code maintenance and quality improvements.

---

3. Using StackTrace

The `StackTrace` class in VB.NET provides detailed information about the sequence of method calls that led to an exception. This includes the method names, the line numbers, and the file names where the exception occurred.

What is a Stack Trace?:

- A **stack trace** shows the call stack at the point where the exception was thrown, indicating which methods were invoked and where the error happened in the program flow.
- This is particularly useful in identifying the specific line of code where an error occurred, helping you understand the context of the exception.

Using `StackTrace` in Exception Handling:

- You can access the `StackTrace` property of an exception to output this information for debugging purposes. The `StackTrace` will help you pinpoint the exact method and line number of where the exception occurred, making it easier to resolve the issue.

Example of Using `StackTrace`:

```
Try
    ' Some code that throws an exception
    Dim result As Integer = 10 / 0   ' Division by zero
Catch ex As Exception
    ' Display the stack trace to the console
    Console.WriteLine("Exception occurred: " & ex.StackTrace)
End Try
```

Output:

```
Exception occurred:    at Program.Main() in
C:\path\to\your\project\Program.vb:line 18
```

- In this example:
  - If an exception occurs, the `Catch` block displays the stack trace of the exception to the console. This tells you exactly where the exception happened (line 18 in `Program.vb`).
  - This information helps you trace the flow of execution leading to the exception, making it easier to isolate the cause of the issue.

Benefits of Stack Trace:

- **Precise Error Location**: Helps you quickly locate the line of code where the exception was triggered.
- **Understanding the Call Stack**: Provides insights into the method call sequence, making it easier to trace back to the root cause of the error.
- **Effective Debugging**: The stack trace can save time by reducing the amount of manual debugging required, as it provides a direct reference to the problem area.

---

4. Other Debugging Techniques

Here are a few additional tips and techniques for troubleshooting exceptions effectively:

Use Visual Debugging Tools:

- Visual Studio offers tools like **Watch**, **Autos**, and **Locals** windows to monitor variables and their values during debugging. These tools help you observe changes in variables and track the flow of your program.

Conditional Breakpoints:

- Sometimes, exceptions only occur under specific conditions (e.g., when a variable reaches a certain value). You can set conditional breakpoints to pause the execution when a certain condition is met, allowing you to catch the exception at the right moment.

Unit Testing:

- Writing unit tests can help identify exceptions before they occur in a live environment. Tests can simulate different scenarios and trigger exceptions under controlled conditions, allowing you to catch errors earlier in the development process.

5.6 Best Practices for Exception Handling

Exception handling is essential for building resilient and robust applications, but it's important to follow best practices to ensure the code is maintainable, efficient, and easy to debug. Below, we will discuss some of the most effective best practices for exception handling in VB.NET.

---

1. Catch Specific Exceptions

Why?

Catching specific exceptions allows you to handle errors more precisely, making your code more robust and easier to debug. It also prevents unintended behavior in your application because you can address different types of errors appropriately.

How?

Instead of using a generic `Catch ex As Exception`, always catch exceptions that are relevant to the code you're working with. For instance, if you're working with file operations, catch a `FileNotFoundException`, or if performing division, catch a `DivideByZeroException`.

Example:

```
Try
    ' Code that may throw an exception
    Dim result As Integer = 10 / 0 ' Division by zero
Catch ex As DivideByZeroException
```

```
    Console.WriteLine("Cannot divide by zero!")
Catch ex As FileNotFoundException
    Console.WriteLine("The specified file was not found!")
Catch ex As Exception
    ' Catching any other unexpected exceptions
    Console.WriteLine("An unexpected error occurred: " & ex.Message)
End Try
```

Benefits:

- **More meaningful error messages**: Helps in debugging because the exception types are more specific.
- **Finer control over handling**: You can deal with different exceptions in different ways (e.g., retrying on `TimeoutException` or logging on `FileNotFoundException`).

---

2. Avoid Empty Catch Blocks

Why?

Leaving a `Catch` block empty is bad practice because it suppresses the exception and makes it difficult to identify the source of the error. An empty `Catch` block leads to silent failures where the application may continue running in an unstable state.

How?

Always ensure that you log or handle the exception meaningfully within the `Catch` block. Logging the exception details helps in troubleshooting later and ensures that nothing is ignored.

Example:

```
Try
    ' Code that may throw an exception
    Dim result As Integer = 10 / 0 ' Division by zero
Catch ex As Exception
    ' Handle the exception properly
    Console.WriteLine("Error: " & ex.Message)
    ' Log the error to a file for later analysis
    My.Computer.FileSystem.WriteAllText("errorlog.txt", ex.ToString(), True)
End Try
```

Benefits:

- **Clear error handling**: It gives you insight into what went wrong, aiding in easier debugging and troubleshooting.
- **Maintain program flow**: Even if an error occurs, you can handle it gracefully and possibly allow the program to continue.

---

3. Use Finally for Cleanup

Why?

The `Finally` block is a great place to put any cleanup code (such as closing files, database connections, or releasing other resources) that must always be executed, regardless of whether an exception was thrown. This ensures that the resources are always cleaned up and that no resources are left open, which could lead to memory leaks or other issues.

How?

Place code for closing connections, files, or other resources that need to be released inside the `Finally` block. This ensures that resources are freed even if an error occurs.

Example:

```
Try
    ' Code that may throw an exception
    Dim file As System.IO.StreamWriter = New
System.IO.StreamWriter("file.txt")
    file.WriteLine("Hello, World!")
Catch ex As Exception
    ' Handle the exception if any occurs
    Console.WriteLine("An error occurred: " & ex.Message)
Finally
    ' Cleanup code that always runs
    file.Close() ' Ensure the file is closed, even if an exception occurred
    Console.WriteLine("Cleanup code executed.")
End Try
```

Benefits:

- **Guaranteed cleanup**: Ensures that critical cleanup tasks are executed, preventing resource leaks.
- **Safer resource handling**: Makes your code more robust, as resources are always freed, preventing issues like file locks or memory leaks.

---

4. Throwing Exceptions

Why?

Sometimes, you need to raise exceptions when certain conditions occur in your code that can't be handled locally. Using `Throw` allows you to pass the responsibility of handling the exception up to the caller, allowing higher-level logic to address the issue.

How?

Use `Throw` to create and propagate exceptions when errors are detected, especially when they cannot be corrected at the current level of the code.

Example:

```
If age < 0 Then
    ' Throw a custom exception if the age is invalid
    Throw New ArgumentException("Age cannot be negative.")
End If
```

Benefits:

- **Control error propagation**: Helps to delegate error handling responsibility to higher-level components.
- **Custom exception messages**: Allows you to provide specific details about the error (e.g., why the error occurred) so that the caller can handle it appropriately.

---

5. Custom Exceptions

Why?

In complex applications, sometimes predefined exceptions are not enough to convey the exact nature of the error. Custom exceptions allow you to define more specific exceptions tailored to your application logic, making it easier to debug and understand the problem.

How?

To create custom exceptions, inherit from the base `Exception` class and define your own constructor and properties if needed.

Example:

```
Public Class InvalidAgeException
    Inherits Exception

    ' Constructor to accept a custom error message
    Public Sub New(message As String)
        MyBase.New(message)
    End Sub
End Class

' Usage of custom exception
Try
    Dim age As Integer = -1
    If age < 0 Then
        Throw New InvalidAgeException("Age cannot be negative.")
    End If
Catch ex As InvalidAgeException
    Console.WriteLine("Custom Error: " & ex.Message)
```

```
End Try
```

Benefits:

- **Better error reporting**: Custom exceptions can provide more context about specific errors within your application's business logic.
- **Tailored to application needs**: Custom exceptions make the error-handling code more readable and specific to your domain.

---

6. Don't Overuse Exception Handling

Why?

Exception handling is a powerful tool, but it should not be used for regular control flow. Using exceptions as a mechanism for controlling normal logic flow can lead to inefficiency and reduced performance. Exceptions are intended for exceptional cases, not for routine operations.

How?

Use conditions (`If` statements) for normal flow control and reserve exceptions for truly exceptional cases where the application cannot continue without addressing the error.

Example:

Bad Practice:

```
Try
    ' Regular code that should not cause an exception
    If someValue = 0 Then
        Throw New InvalidOperationException("Cannot process value 0.")
    End If
Catch ex As InvalidOperationException
    Console.WriteLine("Error occurred.")
End Try
```

Better Practice:

```
If someValue = 0 Then
    Console.WriteLine("Error: Value cannot be zero.")
    Return ' Handle the condition without throwing an exception
End If
```

Benefits:

- **Improved performance**: Exceptions can be expensive to handle in terms of both performance and code readability, so using them for flow control can cause unnecessary overhead.
- **Clearer intent**: Using `If` statements for routine logic improves code clarity and intent, making the program easier to read and understand.

Summary of Best Practices

By following these best practices, your VB.NET applications will handle exceptions in a more structured, efficient, and maintainable manner. Proper exception handling ensures that your program remains stable, improves debugging, and enhances the user experience by dealing with errors gracefully.

- **Catch specific exceptions** to address precise errors.
- **Avoid empty `Catch` blocks** by logging or handling errors.
- **Use the `Finally` block** for cleanup tasks.
- **Throw exceptions** when an error cannot be handled locally.
- **Create custom exceptions** to provide more context in error messages.
- **Avoid overusing exception handling** for regular control flow.

By adhering to these principles, you ensure that your code is resilient, clear, and efficient in the face of errors.

30 multiple-choice questions (MCQs)

5.1 Understanding Exceptions

1. **What is an exception in programming?** a) A syntax error
   b) A runtime error that disrupts the normal flow of execution
   c) A logical error
   d) A memory allocation error

   Answer: b) A runtime error that disrupts the normal flow of execution

2. **Which of the following is a type of exception in VB.NET?** a) SyntaxException
   b) DivideByZeroException
   c) NullReferenceError
   d) FlowControlException

   Answer: b) DivideByZeroException

3. **What type of exception is thrown when an application attempts to divide a number by zero?** a) FileNotFoundException
   b) DivideByZeroException
   c) ArgumentNullException
   d) NullReferenceException

   Answer: b) DivideByZeroException

4. **Which exception type occurs when an attempt is made to access a null object reference?** a) FileNotFoundException
b) NullReferenceException
c) IndexOutOfRangeException
d) ArgumentException

Answer: b) NullReferenceException

5. **What is a SystemException in VB.NET?** a) Exception thrown by user code
b) Exception thrown by the operating system
c) Predefined exception type provided by the .NET framework
d) Exception caused by hardware failure

Answer: c) Predefined exception type provided by the .NET framework

6. **Which of the following is an example of an ApplicationException in VB.NET?** a) IndexOutOfRangeException
b) FileNotFoundException
c) InvalidUserInputException
d) NullReferenceException

Answer: c) InvalidUserInputException

7. **Which exception is thrown when attempting to access an array element out of bounds?** a) IndexOutOfRangeException
b) DivideByZeroException
c) FileNotFoundException
d) ArgumentOutOfRangeException

Answer: a) IndexOutOfRangeException

8. **What is the general purpose of exceptions in programming?** a) To control the flow of a program
b) To interrupt the program's execution in case of errors
c) To manage memory allocations
d) To handle database connections

Answer: b) To interrupt the program's execution in case of errors

5.2 Structured Exception Handling

9. **What is the correct syntax for structured exception handling in VB.NET?** a) Try...Catch...Finally
b) Try...Catch
c) Catch...Finally
d) Try...Error...End Try

Answer: a) Try...Catch...Finally

10. **Which of the following is the purpose of the `Finally` block in a Try-Catch block?** a) To define the code that might throw an exception
b) To execute code that must run regardless of whether an exception occurred
c) To catch and handle exceptions
d) To skip the rest of the code

Answer: b) To execute code that must run regardless of whether an exception occurred

11. **Which block in structured exception handling is used to catch exceptions?** a) Catch block
b) Finally block
c) Try block
d) Catch/Finally block

Answer: a) Catch block

12. **What happens if no exception is thrown inside the Try block?** a) The Catch block is executed
b) The Finally block is executed
c) The program crashes
d) The code inside the Try block is skipped

Answer: b) The Finally block is executed

13. **In which scenario would you use a Try...Catch block?** a) For handling known errors like syntax issues
b) For handling runtime errors like division by zero or file not found
c) For handling logical errors
d) For controlling program flow

Answer: b) For handling runtime errors like division by zero or file not found

14. **What will happen if an exception is thrown inside a Try block and there is no Catch block to handle it?** a) The program will crash immediately
b) The exception will be passed to the operating system
c) The Finally block will still execute
d) The exception will be logged automatically

Answer: c) The Finally block will still execute

5.3 Handling Different Types of Exceptions

15. **What is the difference between a SystemException and an ApplicationException?** a) SystemExceptions are user-defined, and ApplicationExceptions are system-defined

b) SystemExceptions are predefined by the .NET runtime, while ApplicationExceptions are user-defined
c) SystemExceptions are not handled, while ApplicationExceptions must be handled
d) SystemExceptions are thrown in application code, while ApplicationExceptions are thrown by the system

Answer: b) SystemExceptions are predefined by the .NET runtime, while ApplicationExceptions are user-defined

16. **Which of the following is a common example of a system exception?** a) DivideByZeroException
b) InvalidOperationException
c) ArgumentException
d) CustomException

Answer: a) DivideByZeroException

17. **Which exception type should you use to handle an invalid argument passed to a method?** a) DivideByZeroException
b) ArgumentException
c) NullReferenceException
d) FileNotFoundException

Answer: b) ArgumentException

18. **What is the purpose of catching a generic `Exception` type in a Catch block?** a) To catch any type of exception, providing a fallback handler
b) To handle all exceptions precisely
c) To handle only file-related exceptions
d) To create a custom exception

Answer: a) To catch any type of exception, providing a fallback handler

19. **Which of the following should NOT be caught by a generic `Catch` block?** a) NullReferenceException
b) DivideByZeroException
c) SystemExitException
d) Application-specific exceptions

Answer: c) SystemExitException

20. **Which of the following is true about handling exceptions in VB.NET?** a) Always catch only SystemExceptions
b) Catch specific exceptions first, then use a generic exception to handle any others
c) You should always use a generic Catch block for all exceptions
d) Exception handling is unnecessary in VB.NET

Answer: b) Catch specific exceptions first, then use a generic exception to handle any others

5.4 Creating Custom Exceptions

21. **How can you create a custom exception in VB.NET?** a) By creating a new method that returns a string
    b) By inheriting the `Exception` class and adding a constructor
    c) By creating a new class with no base class
    d) By modifying an existing exception type

    Answer: b) By inheriting the `Exception` class and adding a constructor

22. **Which keyword is used to propagate an exception in VB.NET?** a) Throw
    b) Catch
    c) Finally
    d) Raise

    Answer: a) Throw

23. **When creating a custom exception, what constructor should you define?** a) A constructor that accepts only an integer
    b) A constructor that accepts a message string
    c) A constructor that accepts a boolean flag
    d) A default constructor with no arguments

    Answer: b) A constructor that accepts a message string

24. **How do you throw a custom exception in your code?** a) `Throw New CustomException()`
    b) `Throw CustomException("message")`
    c) `Raise Exception("message")`
    d) `Throw Message("Custom error message")`

    Answer: a) `Throw New CustomException()`

25. **What is a common benefit of using custom exceptions?** a) To handle low-level system exceptions
    b) To simplify generic exception handling
    c) To add more context and specific details to errors
    d) To make error messages harder to understand

    Answer: c) To add more context and specific details to errors

5.5 Debugging with Exception Handling

26. **Which Visual Studio tool allows you to pause execution when an exception is thrown?** a) Immediate Window
b) Call Stack
c) Breakpoint
d) Exception Settings

Answer: d) Exception Settings

27. **What is the role of the StackTrace class in exception handling?** a) It provides a detailed error message
b) It helps inspect local variables
c) It shows the sequence of method calls that led to the exception
d) It logs exception details to a file

Answer: c) It shows the sequence of method calls that led to the exception

28. **How can you log exceptions to a file in VB.NET?** a) By using the `Console.WriteLine` method
b) By using `My.Computer.FileSystem.WriteAllText` method
c) By using the `Debug.WriteLine` method
d) By using the `Exception.ToString` method

Answer: b) By using `My.Computer.FileSystem.WriteAllText` method

5.6 Best Practices for Exception Handling

29. **Which of the following is a best practice for exception handling in VB.NET?** a) Always catch the `Exception` type to handle all errors
b) Use exception handling for regular program control flow
c) Log the exception details and avoid empty Catch blocks
d) Rely only on `Finally` blocks for cleanup

Answer: c) Log the exception details and avoid empty Catch blocks

30. **What should you do if you detect an error in a method and cannot handle it locally?**
a) Ignore the error and continue
b) Throw the exception to propagate it to higher levels
c) Use the `Finally` block to handle it
d) Modify the program flow to avoid the error

Answer: b) Throw the exception to propagate it to higher levels

5.1 Understanding Exceptions

1. **Question**: What happens if an exception is not handled in VB.NET?

- **Answer**: If an exception is not handled, the program will terminate abruptly, and an error message will be displayed to the user, potentially causing a crash.

2. **Question**: What type of exception occurs when an application attempts to divide a number by zero in VB.NET?
   - **Answer**: `DivideByZeroException`
3. **Question**: What type of exception is thrown when a method tries to use a null object reference?
   - **Answer**: `NullReferenceException`
4. **Question**: Which exception type is thrown when an application tries to open a file that does not exist?
   - **Answer**: `FileNotFoundException`
5. **Question**: What is the main difference between `SystemException` and `ApplicationException` in VB.NET?
   - **Answer**: `SystemException` is a predefined exception provided by the .NET runtime for system-level errors, while `ApplicationException` is used for exceptions that are defined by the application code for specific business logic errors.

5.2 Structured Exception Handling

6. **Question**: Which block in VB.NET handles exceptions in a Try-Catch structure?
   - **Answer**: The `Catch` block.
7. **Question**: What does the `Finally` block in a Try-Catch-Finally statement do?
   - **Answer**: The `Finally` block contains code that is always executed, regardless of whether an exception occurred or not. It is typically used for cleanup operations like closing files or releasing resources.
8. **Question**: What will happen if you omit the `Catch` block in a Try-Catch-Finally structure in VB.NET?
   - **Answer**: If you omit the `Catch` block, the exception will propagate up the call stack, and the `Finally` block will still be executed.
9. **Question**: What type of exception will be caught by the following code?

```
Try
    Dim result = 10 / 0
Catch ex As DivideByZeroException
    Console.WriteLine("Cannot divide by zero")
End Try
```

   - **Answer**: `DivideByZeroException`
10. **Question**: Can the `Finally` block be omitted in a Try-Catch-Finally structure in VB.NET?
    - **Answer**: Yes, the `Finally` block is optional. If it's omitted, the program will execute without it, but the code inside the `Catch` block will still handle exceptions.

5.3 Handling Different Types of Exceptions

11. **Question**: Which type of exception should be caught first in a multi-Catch structure to ensure that more specific exceptions are handled before more general ones?
    - **Answer**: Specific exceptions (e.g., `FileNotFoundException`, `DivideByZeroException`) should be caught before the more general `Exception` type.
12. **Question**: Write a Try-Catch block that catches a `FileNotFoundException` and prints a message indicating that the file could not be found.
    - **Answer**:

```
Try
    Dim reader As New System.IO.StreamReader("nonexistentfile.txt")
Catch ex As FileNotFoundException
    Console.WriteLine("File not found.")
End Try
```

13. **Question**: How can you handle a custom exception, `InvalidAgeException`, in VB.NET within a Try-Catch block?
    - **Answer**:

```
Try
    Throw New InvalidAgeException("Age cannot be negative.")
Catch ex As InvalidAgeException
    Console.WriteLine(ex.Message)
End Try
```

14. **Question**: How can you differentiate between `SystemException` and `ApplicationException` in VB.NET when handling exceptions?
    - **Answer**: `SystemException` is used for exceptions thrown by the .NET runtime due to system-level issues, while `ApplicationException` is used for exceptions that the application itself explicitly throws to handle specific application logic errors.

5.4 Creating Custom Exceptions

15. **Question**: Write a custom exception class `InvalidAgeException` that inherits from the base `Exception` class and accepts a custom error message.
    - **Answer**:

```
Public Class InvalidAgeException
    Inherits Exception

    Public Sub New(message As String)
        MyBase.New(message)
    End Sub
End Class
```

16. **Question**: How can you throw the custom exception `InvalidAgeException` with a specific message in VB.NET?
    - **Answer**:

```
If age < 0 Then
    Throw New InvalidAgeException("Age cannot be negative.")
End If
```

5.5 Debugging with Exception Handling

17. **Question**: What tool in Visual Studio allows you to break the execution when an exception is thrown?
    - **Answer**: The "Exception Settings" window in Visual Studio allows you to break the execution when specific exceptions are thrown.
18. **Question**: How can you log an exception's details (message, stack trace) to a file in VB.NET?
    - **Answer**:

```
Try
    ' Code that may throw an exception
Catch ex As Exception
    My.Computer.FileSystem.WriteAllText("errorlog.txt", ex.Message &
Environment.NewLine & ex.StackTrace, True)
End Try
```

19. **Question**: How would you use the `StackTrace` class to view where an exception occurred in your application?
    - **Answer**:

```
Try
    ' Code that may throw an exception
Catch ex As Exception
    Console.WriteLine(ex.StackTrace)
End Try
```

20. **Question**: How can you use breakpoints to debug exceptions in Visual Studio?
    - **Answer**: You can set breakpoints in Visual Studio by clicking on the left margin next to the code line. The execution will pause when the breakpoint is hit, allowing you to inspect variables, the call stack, and the exception details.
21. **Question**: What is the benefit of using a `Try...Catch...Finally` block over a basic `If` statement to handle exceptions?
    - **Answer**: A `Try...Catch...Finally` block provides a structured way to handle runtime errors and allows for more robust error handling, including logging, resource cleanup, and reporting, whereas `If` statements are typically used for conditional logic.
22. **Question**: Can you use `Try...Catch` to handle an exception that has already been thrown?
    - **Answer**: No, you can only catch exceptions that are thrown during the execution of the code inside the `Try` block. You cannot catch an exception after it has been thrown outside the `Try` block.
23. **Question**: What is the purpose of the `Catch ex As Exception` block in exception handling?

- **Answer**: The `Catch ex As Exception` block is used to catch any exception of type `Exception` or its derived types. It is used as a general handler for any unexpected exceptions that were not specifically handled earlier in the code.

24. **Question**: What happens if you have multiple `Catch` blocks for different types of exceptions?
    - **Answer**: The first `Catch` block that matches the type of exception thrown will handle the exception. If no match is found, the exception will propagate to the next level or be handled by a generic `Catch` block.
25. **Question**: What should you do in a `Finally` block?
    - **Answer**: You should use the `Finally` block to release resources such as closing files, database connections, or freeing memory, ensuring that these operations are executed regardless of whether an exception occurred or not.

CHAPTER 6: UNDERSTANDING AND USING NAMESPACES IN VB.NET

6.1 Introduction to NameSpaces

A **namespace** in programming is essentially a container that holds a collection of related identifiers such as classes, structures, methods, properties, etc. It allows you to logically group related code elements together, preventing naming conflicts and enhancing code organization. By using namespaces, you can manage the complexity of your code and avoid issues where different parts of the program or different libraries might use the same identifier name.

In VB.NET, namespaces serve as a way to structure code in a manageable way. Without namespaces, all classes and other members would be placed in a single global space, which could lead to naming conflicts if different developers or libraries used the same names for different purposes.

Key Points About Namespaces:

1. **Avoiding Naming Conflicts**:
    - In larger programs, especially when combining multiple libraries, two different libraries might have classes with the same name. For example, both `Library1` and `Library2` could have a class called `Logger`. If namespaces are not used, the program would not know which `Logger` class to use, leading to a conflict.
    - Namespaces allow you to distinguish between these two classes by placing them in different namespaces, preventing conflicts. Even though they share the same name, they exist in separate namespaces, and thus, can coexist without issues.
2. **Improves Code Organization**:
    - By grouping related classes, structures, and methods together, namespaces help keep the codebase organized and structured. For instance, all utility-related classes might be grouped under a `Utilities` namespace, while classes related to data access can be grouped under a `DataAccess` namespace.
    - This organization makes it easier for developers to locate and maintain specific parts of the code, especially in large projects.

How Namespaces Work in VB.NET

In VB.NET, the `Namespace` keyword is used to define a namespace. Everything within the `Namespace` block is part of that namespace, including classes, methods, variables, etc. To access members from a specific namespace, you use the fully-qualified name (including the namespace) or you can use the `Imports` keyword to simplify references.

Example of Using Namespaces

Consider an example where we have a class `Logger` inside a custom namespace `Utilities`. This is how we define and use the `Logger` class:

1. Defining a Namespace and Class:

```
Namespace Utilities
    ' Defining a class called Logger inside the Utilities namespace
    Public Class Logger
        ' Method to log a message to the console
        Public Sub LogMessage(message As String)
            Console.WriteLine(message)
        End Sub
    End Class
End Namespace
```

In this example, we defined a class called `Logger` inside the `Utilities` namespace. This class has a method called `LogMessage` that simply prints a message to the console.

2. Using the Namespace and Class:

To use the `Logger` class in another part of your program, you would reference it by fully qualifying its name with the namespace or use the `Imports` keyword to make the class available without the need to prefix the namespace.

Using Fully Qualified Name:

```
' Using the fully qualified name to access the Logger class
Dim log As New Utilities.Logger()
log.LogMessage("This is a log message.")
```

Using the `Imports` Keyword:

To avoid having to type the full namespace each time, you can use the `Imports` statement at the top of your file:

```
' Importing the Utilities namespace so you don't have to fully qualify the
class name
Imports Utilities

' Now you can directly use the Logger class
Dim log As New Logger()
log.LogMessage("This is a log message.")
```

Why Use Namespaces?

- **Prevents Naming Conflicts**: As previously mentioned, namespaces allow you to use the same name for different classes or methods if they belong to different namespaces. This is especially helpful when working with external libraries or frameworks.
- **Organizes Code**: Namespaces make it easy to organize your code logically. For instance, all user interface-related classes can be in a `UI` namespace, all database-related classes in a `Data` namespace, and so on.
- **Improves Code Maintenance**: Large projects benefit from namespaces because they make the codebase easier to understand and maintain. Developers can quickly locate the code they need, knowing it's grouped logically.

Common Practices for Naming Namespaces:

- Use a consistent naming scheme across your projects. A common practice is to use the company or project name as the root namespace (e.g., `CompanyName.ProjectName`) followed by sub-namespaces to categorize the functionality (e.g., `CompanyName.ProjectName.UI`, `CompanyName.ProjectName.Data`).
- Keep namespaces short and meaningful. Avoid deeply nested namespaces that could complicate your code structure.

6.2 Commonly Used NameSpaces

In .NET, there are many built-in namespaces that provide access to a wide variety of functionality for different types of applications. These namespaces contain classes, structures, and other members that can help you perform specific tasks efficiently. Below are some of the most commonly used namespaces in VB.NET, along with their key components and examples.

---

1. System Namespace

The `System` namespace is the root namespace for many core .NET types and operations. It includes basic types for data manipulation, mathematical operations, I/O handling, and more. Most of the fundamental classes are defined under this namespace, making it essential for everyday programming in .NET.

Key Classes in `System`:

- **System.String**: Represents a sequence of characters.
- **System.Int32**: Represents a 32-bit signed integer.
- **System.Console**: Provides basic methods for input and output operations.
- **System.Math**: Contains mathematical functions (e.g., `Sqrt`, `Pow`, `Abs`).

Example:

```
Dim myString As String = "Hello, World!"   ' Declaration of a string.
Dim myNumber As Integer = 100   ' Declaration of an integer.
Console.WriteLine(myString)   ' Printing the string.
Console.WriteLine(myNumber)   ' Printing the integer.
```

In the example, `System.String` is used to represent the text "Hello, World!", and `System.Int32` is used to represent the integer `100`.

---

2. System.IO Namespace

The `System.IO` namespace provides classes to work with file input and output operations. It is essential when performing tasks like reading from and writing to files, managing directories, and handling file streams.

Key Classes in `System.IO`:

- **FileStream**: Provides a stream for reading from and writing to a file.
- **StreamReader**: Reads characters from a byte stream in a specific encoding.
- **Directory**: Provides static methods for manipulating directories, such as creating, deleting, and querying directories.
- **File**: Provides methods for working with files, like reading, writing, and copying files.

Example:

```
Imports System.IO

Dim filePath As String = "C:\temp\file.txt"  ' Path to a text file.
Dim fileContent As String = File.ReadAllText(filePath)  ' Reading the entire
file content.
Console.WriteLine(fileContent)  ' Displaying the content on the console.
```

In this example, `System.IO.File.ReadAllText` is used to read all the text from the specified file (`file.txt`) and print its content to the console.

---

3. System.Net Namespace

The `System.Net` namespace provides classes for working with network protocols like HTTP, FTP, and TCP. It is primarily used for networking tasks, such as downloading or uploading files, sending web requests, and managing network connections.

Key Classes in `System.Net`:

- **WebClient**: Allows you to download or upload data to and from a resource over the web.
- **HttpWebRequest**: Sends an HTTP request to a specified URL.
- **IPAddress**: Represents an IP address (IPv4 or IPv6).
- **WebRequest**: Base class for web requests.

Example:

```
Imports System.Net

Dim client As New WebClient()
Dim data As String = client.DownloadString("http://example.com")  '
Downloading a web page content.
Console.WriteLine(data)  ' Displaying the content from the web page.
```

In this example, `System.Net.WebClient.DownloadString` is used to download the content of a web page (`http://example.com`) and print it to the console.

4. System.Windows.Forms Namespace

The `System.Windows.Forms` namespace is used in Windows Forms applications. It provides a set of classes for creating graphical user interfaces (GUIs), such as windows, buttons, textboxes, labels, and more. This namespace is essential for building desktop applications with a GUI.

Key Classes in `System.Windows.Forms`:

- **Form**: Represents a window or dialog box in a Windows Forms application.
- **Button**: Represents a clickable button control.
- **TextBox**: Represents a text box control for user input.
- **MessageBox**: Displays a message box to the user.

Example:

```
Imports System.Windows.Forms

Public Class MyForm
    Inherits Form  ' Inheriting from the Form class to create a form window.

    Private button As Button

    Public Sub New()
        ' Initializing a new Button control.
        button = New Button()
        button.Text = "Click Me"  ' Setting button text.
        button.Location = New Point(100, 100)  ' Setting button position on
the form.

        ' Adding event handler for the button click event.
        AddHandler button.Click, AddressOf Me.ButtonClick
        Controls.Add(button)  ' Adding button to the form's controls.
    End Sub

    ' Event handler for button click.
    Private Sub ButtonClick(sender As Object, e As EventArgs)
        MessageBox.Show("Button clicked!")  ' Displaying a message box when
button is clicked.
    End Sub
End Class
```

In this example, `System.Windows.Forms.Form` is used to create a form window, and `System.Windows.Forms.Button` is used to create a button control that shows a message box when clicked.

6.3 Custom NameSpaces in Your Project

In VB.NET, namespaces provide a powerful mechanism for organizing your code logically, especially when working on large-scale projects. Custom namespaces allow you to group related classes, functions, and other types of data under a single, cohesive name. By using custom namespaces, you can avoid naming conflicts, improve code modularity, and make the codebase more maintainable and easier to navigate.

Benefits of Custom Namespaces:

1. **Organization**: Custom namespaces help keep code organized, especially when a project contains many classes or modules.
2. **Avoid Naming Conflicts**: You can use the same class names in different namespaces without them conflicting.
3. **Scalability**: As projects grow, custom namespaces allow you to easily categorize functionality, making it easier for developers to find and modify code.

Creating and Using Custom NameSpaces

Let's walk through how to create and use custom namespaces in your project.

---

1. Creating a Custom Namespace

To create a custom namespace, use the `Namespace` keyword, followed by the desired name of your namespace. Inside the namespace, you define the classes, structures, enums, and other elements that belong to that namespace. This allows you to logically group related code together.

Example:

Here is an example of creating a custom namespace named `MyCompany.ProjectX` with a class `Calculator` inside it:

```
Namespace MyCompany.ProjectX
    Public Class Calculator
        ' Method to add two integers
        Public Function Add(x As Integer, y As Integer) As Integer
            Return x + y
        End Function

        ' Method to subtract two integers
        Public Function Subtract(x As Integer, y As Integer) As Integer
            Return x - y
        End Function
    End Class
End Namespace
```

In this example:

- The `MyCompany.ProjectX` namespace encapsulates the `Calculator` class.
- The `Calculator` class contains methods for performing basic arithmetic operations such as addition and subtraction.

2. Using a Custom Namespace

Once you have defined a custom namespace and added classes to it, you can use them in other parts of your application. There are two ways to access classes or members within a custom namespace:

- **Fully Qualifying the Class Name**: You can reference the class by specifying the full namespace path each time you use it.
- **Using the `Imports` Statement**: This allows you to import the entire namespace, so you can refer to the classes directly without needing to fully qualify them.

Example 1: Fully Qualifying the Class Name

If you choose not to use the `Imports` statement, you can reference the `Calculator` class by fully qualifying its name, including the namespace:

```
Public Sub Main()
    ' Fully qualify the class name with the namespace
    Dim calc As New MyCompany.ProjectX.Calculator()
    Console.WriteLine(calc.Add(3, 5))  ' Output: 8
    Console.WriteLine(calc.Subtract(10, 4))  ' Output: 6
End Sub
```

In this case, you are directly referencing the class with its full namespace path `MyCompany.ProjectX.Calculator` every time you use it.

Example 2: Using the `Imports` Statement

Alternatively, you can use the `Imports` keyword to import the entire `MyCompany.ProjectX` namespace at the beginning of your code file. Once imported, you no longer need to fully qualify class names, making your code cleaner and more readable.

```
Imports MyCompany.ProjectX  ' Import the custom namespace

Public Sub Main()
    ' Now you can directly use the Calculator class without qualifying the
namespace
    Dim calc As New Calculator()
    Console.WriteLine(calc.Add(3, 5))  ' Output: 8
    Console.WriteLine(calc.Subtract(10, 4))  ' Output: 6
End Sub
```

Here, the `Imports` statement imports the `MyCompany.ProjectX` namespace, so you can directly create instances of the `Calculator` class without using the full namespace path.

Best Practices for Custom Namespaces

1. **Use Descriptive Names**: Name your namespaces according to their functionality to make it clear what type of classes or methods they contain. For example, use `MyCompany.Data` for classes related to data processing or `MyCompany.UI` for user interface components.
2. **Avoid Over-Nesting**: While namespaces allow for nested structures, try to keep them simple and avoid over-complicating the hierarchy. For example, instead of `MyCompany.ProjectX.UI.Forms.Controls`, consider using something more concise like `MyCompany.UI.Controls`.
3. **Use Consistent Naming Conventions**: Stick to a consistent naming pattern for namespaces throughout your project. This makes it easier for other developers to navigate and understand your codebase.
4. **Group Related Code**: Place classes that belong together in the same namespace. For example, classes related to file operations might belong in `MyCompany.FileOperations`, while those related to network communication might be in `MyCompany.Network`.

6.4 Organizing Code with NameSpaces

In large-scale applications, the importance of organizing code into namespaces cannot be overstated. As projects grow, the complexity of the code increases, and proper organization becomes critical for ensuring maintainability, readability, and scalability. Namespaces provide a way to group related classes, structures, functions, interfaces, and other types into logical units. This logical grouping enables developers to manage and work with large codebases more effectively.

How Namespaces Help in Organizing Code

Namespaces allow developers to structure the code logically and modularly. This is particularly important in large projects, where there can be thousands of lines of code. Without proper organization, it can become very difficult to locate and manage individual classes, functions, and methods. By using namespaces effectively, you can ensure that related code is grouped together, making the development process smoother and the application easier to maintain.

Benefits of Using Namespaces in Large Projects

1. **Improving Maintainability**
   - In a large project, code is likely to evolve, and new features will be added over time. Grouping related functionality into namespaces makes it easier to manage and extend the codebase. Instead of searching through the entire codebase for a specific class or function, developers can focus on specific namespaces.
   - Example: In a project that deals with both user interface (UI) and data access, you could create separate namespaces for each. `MyApp.UI` could contain all UI-related classes, and `MyApp.DataAccess` could contain all classes related to database access. This structure improves maintainability as the code grows.
2. **Enhancing Code Readability**

- Namespaces provide clear indications of where a particular class or function fits within the overall application. When developers understand which namespace a class belongs to, they immediately know its purpose or functionality.
- Example: If you see a class like `MyApp.DataAccess.DatabaseConnection`, you can easily infer that this class is related to database connectivity. This eliminates ambiguity and improves readability, especially for new developers joining the project.

3. **Preventing Naming Collisions**
   - One of the biggest advantages of using namespaces is that they help prevent naming collisions. Two classes can have the same name as long as they are in different namespaces. Without namespaces, developers would face problems when integrating multiple libraries or modules with overlapping class names.
   - Example: If you have two different libraries, one for handling user authentication and the other for handling logging, both may have a class named `Logger`. If they are in different namespaces (e.g., `MyApp.Authentication.Logger` and `MyApp.Logging.Logger`), there won't be any conflict, and you can use both classes in the same project.

Key Benefits of Namespaces in Large Projects

1. **Avoiding Name Conflicts**
   - In large projects or when integrating third-party libraries, it's common to encounter class name conflicts. With namespaces, you can create unique names by placing classes in different namespaces.
   - **Example**: Let's say you have two third-party libraries that both contain a `FileProcessor` class. Without namespaces, you'd face a conflict when using both libraries. However, by placing each class in a different namespace (e.g., `LibraryA.FileProcessor` and `LibraryB.FileProcessor`), you can use both classes without issues.
2. **Logical Grouping**
   - Code is grouped logically based on functionality, which makes it easier to locate specific features within the application. For instance, related functionality (e.g., all file-related classes) should be in the same namespace. This not only helps with searching but also clarifies the role of each class within the larger system.
   - **Example**: In a large application, you might have namespaces such as:
     - `MyApp.UserManagement` for classes related to user authentication, registration, and profile management.
     - `MyApp.Reporting` for classes that handle report generation and exporting data to different formats.
     - `MyApp.Utils` for utility functions that are shared across different parts of the application.
3. **Scalability**
   - As your project grows, namespaces allow you to scale your application without overwhelming a single namespace. New features and modules can be added in a way that doesn't clutter the global namespace. This makes it easier to scale the project as the number of classes and modules increases.
   - **Example**: Imagine a project that starts as a small application but eventually grows into a multi-functional system. With namespaces, you can continuously add new namespaces

for each new functionality, like `MyApp.Payments`, `MyApp.Inventory`, or `MyApp.Integrations`. This modular approach helps keep the codebase clean and organized.

Best Practices for Organizing Code with Namespaces

1. **Use Descriptive Names**
   - Ensure that namespaces have meaningful names that describe their contents. For example, `MyApp.DataProcessing` is much clearer than simply `MyApp.Module1`. A well-chosen namespace helps other developers understand the purpose of the code inside it.
2. **Group Related Code Together**
   - Organize your code logically by grouping related classes, functions, or modules under a common namespace. For instance, if you have multiple classes for different types of databases, you could create a namespace like `MyApp.Database.MySQL` and `MyApp.Database.SQLServer`.
3. **Avoid Deep Nesting of Namespaces**
   - While nesting namespaces is possible, excessive nesting can make code harder to read. Try to avoid deeply nested namespaces unless absolutely necessary. For instance, `MyApp.UI.Controls.Button` is fine, but something like `MyApp.UI.Controls.Button.Widgets.StandardButton` may be excessive unless there's a good reason for the deeper hierarchy.
4. **Consistent Naming Conventions**
   - Follow consistent naming conventions for namespaces. For example, you could use your company name or project name as the root namespace (e.g., `MyCompany` or `MyApp`), and then branch out for specific features or modules (e.g., `MyApp.UI`, `MyApp.Database`).
5. **Keep Business Logic Separate from UI**
   - In larger applications, it's a good practice to keep the business logic separate from user interface (UI) elements. This not only helps with organization but also makes the application more maintainable. For example, `MyApp.BusinessLogic` and `MyApp.UI` should be separate namespaces.

Example of Organizing Code with Namespaces

Let's consider an example of organizing a simple application that has user authentication, reporting, and file handling functionality:

```
Namespace MyApp.UserManagement
    Public Class User
        ' User-related logic goes here
    End Class

    Public Class Authentication
        ' Authentication logic goes here
    End Class
End Namespace

Namespace MyApp.Reporting
```

```
    Public Class ReportGenerator
        ' Report generation logic goes here
    End Class
End Namespace

Namespace MyApp.FileHandling
    Public Class FileManager
        ' File handling logic goes here
    End Class
End Namespace
```

Here, we've created three namespaces: `MyApp.UserManagement`, `MyApp.Reporting`, and `MyApp.FileHandling`. Each namespace contains relevant classes that implement specific functionality. As the application grows, new namespaces can be added, and this modular structure will allow for easier maintenance.

6.5 Working with Assemblies and References

In .NET, an assembly is a compiled unit of code that contains one or more namespaces, types, and resources. It is the fundamental building block of .NET applications, and all executable code or libraries are packaged into assemblies. Understanding how to work with assemblies and references is crucial for organizing and utilizing code in .NET projects.

What is an Assembly?

An **assembly** is a compiled version of the code in .NET, and it can be either an **executable file (.exe)** or a **dynamic link library (.dll)**. Assemblies contain the necessary code and metadata to define types, such as classes and interfaces, and they are the smallest unit of deployment in .NET. Assemblies also provide versioning, security, and metadata about the code, helping to ensure compatibility between different components in an application.

Key points about assemblies:

- **Contains Code and Metadata:** Assemblies contain both the compiled code (IL - Intermediate Language) and metadata that describes the types and their relationships within the assembly.
- **Two Types of Assemblies:**
    - **Executable Assembly (.exe):** A standalone application that can be run on its own.
    - **Library Assembly (.dll):** A library of reusable code that can be referenced by other applications.

Example: An assembly might look like this in your project structure:

```
MyApp.exe
MyApp.dll
```

References in .NET

In .NET, when you want to use external code (such as classes or methods defined in another assembly), you need to **add a reference** to that assembly in your project. Adding a reference makes the types and members of the external assembly accessible in your code.

How to Add a Reference to an Assembly:

1. **Add a Reference:**
    - Right-click on the project in **Solution Explorer**.
    - Select **Add** > **Reference**.
    - Choose the assembly you want to reference. For example, if you are working with XML, you might reference `System.Xml.dll`.
2. **Import the Namespace:**
    - Once you've added the reference, you can import the namespaces from the referenced assembly into your code using the `Imports` keyword.
    - **Example:**

```
Imports System.Xml
```

Now, you can use the classes and types from `System.Xml.dll` without needing to fully qualify their names.

Working with Assemblies:

Once an assembly is referenced, you can use its classes and methods directly in your code. The reference allows your application to access the types defined in the assembly.

Example:

```
Imports System.Xml

Public Class XmlProcessor
    Public Sub LoadXmlData(xmlFile As String)
        Dim xmlDoc As New XmlDocument()
        xmlDoc.Load(xmlFile)
        Console.WriteLine("XML Loaded")
    End Sub
End Class
```

In this example, `XmlDocument` is a class from the `System.Xml` namespace, which has been added as a reference in the project.

Tools for Working with Assemblies

- **ILSpy:** ILSpy is an open-source tool that can decompile .NET assemblies into readable C# code. It allows you to inspect the contents of an assembly to see what types, methods, and properties are defined inside.
- **Reflector:** Another tool for inspecting assemblies. Reflector lets you explore compiled assemblies and see the internal workings of classes and methods.

These tools are particularly useful when working with third-party libraries or when you want to inspect the metadata and code of an assembly you're referencing.

Example of Working with a Third-Party Assembly:

Let's say you're working with a third-party assembly called `ThirdPartyLibrary.dll`, and you want to use a class `ThirdPartyClass` that is defined inside this library.

1. **Add Reference:**
   - You would add a reference to `ThirdPartyLibrary.dll` by following the same steps mentioned earlier.
2. **Import the Namespace:**
   - If the class `ThirdPartyClass` is inside the `ThirdPartyLibrary` namespace, you would import it like this:

```
Imports ThirdPartyLibrary
```

3. **Using the Third-Party Class:**
   - After importing the namespace, you can create objects and call methods from the third-party assembly.

```
Public Sub UseLibrary()
    Dim obj As New ThirdPartyClass()
    obj.Method()  ' Call method from the third-party library
End Sub
```

By adding a reference and importing the namespace, you gain access to the functionality provided by the third-party library, just as if it were part of your own codebase.

Versioning in Assemblies

Assemblies in .NET support **versioning**. This means that when a new version of an assembly is created, you can continue to use the older version in your project, as long as it is compatible. This is especially important when working with shared libraries or external dependencies.

.NET uses **strong names** (a combination of the assembly's name, version, culture, and public key) to manage versioning and ensure that the correct version of an assembly is loaded at runtime. If you reference a particular version of an assembly, .NET will load that version, preventing any conflicts with other versions that may be installed.

Example:

```
<configuration>
  <runtime>
    <assemblyBinding xmlns="urn:schemas-microsoft-com:asm.v1">
      <dependentAssembly>
        <assemblyIdentity name="System.Xml" publicKeyToken="b77a5c561934e089"
culture="neutral" />
```

```
        <bindingRedirect oldVersion="0.0.0.0-2.0.0.0" newVersion="2.0.0.0" />
      </dependentAssembly>
    </assemblyBinding>
  </runtime>
</configuration>
```

In this example, the `bindingRedirect` element ensures that any request for an older version of `System.Xml` will be redirected to version `2.0.0.0`.

30 multiple-choice questions (MCQs) :

6.1 Introduction to NameSpaces

1. **What is the primary purpose of a namespace in VB.NET?**
   - A) To store the values of variables
   - B) To define access modifiers for variables
   - C) To organize classes and avoid naming conflicts
   - D) To store methods of a program
   - **Answer: C** (To organize classes and avoid naming conflicts)
2. **Which keyword is used to define a namespace in VB.NET?**
   - A) Module
   - B) Class
   - C) Namespace
   - D) Imports
   - **Answer: C** (Namespace)
3. **Which of the following is true about namespaces in VB.NET?**
   - A) They cannot be nested.
   - B) They are used only to define classes.
   - C) They help avoid name conflicts.
   - D) They cannot contain methods or properties.
   - **Answer: C** (They help avoid name conflicts)
4. **How do you refer to a class in a specific namespace in VB.NET?**
   - A) Use the 'using' keyword
   - B) Use the 'Import' keyword
   - C) Fully qualify the class name with the namespace
   - D) Both B and C
   - **Answer: D** (Both B and C)
5. **Which of the following is an advantage of using namespaces?**
   - A) Simplified exception handling
   - B) Code organization and collision avoidance
   - C) Reduces memory consumption
   - D) Increases application speed
   - **Answer: B** (Code organization and collision avoidance)

6.2 Commonly Used NameSpaces

6. **Which namespace contains basic types like `String`, `Integer`, and `Boolean`?**
   - A) System.IO
   - B) System.Net
   - C) System
   - D) System.Windows.Forms
   - **Answer: C** (System)
7. **Which namespace is used to work with file input and output (I/O) operations?**
   - A) System.Net
   - B) System.IO
   - C) System.Windows.Forms
   - D) System.Threading
   - **Answer: B** (System.IO)
8. **Which class is used in `System.IO` to read text files?**
   - A) FileStream
   - B) StreamReader
   - C) Directory
   - D) FileInfo
   - **Answer: B** (StreamReader)
9. **Which namespace is primarily used to handle network communications in VB.NET?**
   - A) System.IO
   - B) System.Net
   - C) System.Threading
   - D) System.Windows.Forms
   - **Answer: B** (System.Net)
10. **In which namespace can you find classes like `Form`, `Button`, and `Label` for Windows Forms applications?**
    - A) System.Net
    - B) System.Windows.Forms
    - C) System.IO
    - D) System.Data
    - **Answer: B** (System.Windows.Forms)
11. **What class in `System.Net` is used to send HTTP requests to a specified URL?**
    - A) HttpWebRequest
    - B) WebClient
    - C) HttpClient
    - D) NetworkStream
    - **Answer: A** (HttpWebRequest)
12. **Which of the following is a class in `System.Windows.Forms` used to create a form window?**
    - A) Button
    - B) Form
    - C) TextBox
    - D) Label

- **Answer: B** (Form)

6.3 Custom NameSpaces in Your Project

13. **How do you define a custom namespace in VB.NET?**
    - A) By using the `Module` keyword
    - B) By using the `Namespace` keyword
    - C) By using the `Imports` keyword
    - D) By using the `Class` keyword
    - **Answer: B** (By using the `Namespace` keyword)
14. **Which of the following is the correct way to create a custom class within a custom namespace?**
    - A) `Namespace MyNamespace; Class MyClass; End Namespace`
    - B) `Namespace MyNamespace : Class MyClass : End Namespace`
    - C) `Namespace MyNamespace Public Class MyClass End Class End Namespace`
    - D) `MyNamespace = Class MyClass End Namespace`
    - **Answer: C** (Namespace MyNamespace Public Class MyClass End Class End Namespace)
15. **Which keyword is used to make a custom namespace accessible from another file or class?**
    - A) Namespace
    - B) Imports
    - C) Reference
    - D) Include
    - **Answer: B** (Imports)
16. **How do you instantiate an object from a class defined in a custom namespace?**
    - A) `Dim obj As New CustomNamespace.ClassName()`
    - B) `Dim obj As CustomNamespace.ClassName = New ClassName()`
    - C) `Dim obj As ClassName()`
    - D) `Imports CustomNamespace.ClassName`
    - **Answer: A** (Dim obj As New CustomNamespace.ClassName())

6.4 Organizing Code with NameSpaces

17. **What is one key benefit of using namespaces in large projects?**
    - A) They increase the memory usage of the project
    - B) They help prevent name conflicts between different libraries
    - C) They slow down the application execution
    - D) They increase the number of classes
    - **Answer: B** (They help prevent name conflicts between different libraries)
18. **Which of the following is a valid reason to use namespaces in large applications?**

- A) To make code more difficult to understand
- B) To keep related functionality together for better maintainability
- C) To store global variables
- D) To provide access to private methods
- **Answer: B** (To keep related functionality together for better maintainability)

19. **Which of the following is NOT a benefit of namespaces?**
    - A) They help in logical grouping of related code
    - B) They prevent name collisions
    - C) They make code more readable
    - D) They improve program execution time
    - **Answer: D** (They improve program execution time)
20. **What happens if two classes in different namespaces have the same name?**
    - A) The compiler will give an error.
    - B) There will be no conflict, and they can be accessed using their full namespace.
    - C) The last defined class will overwrite the previous one.
    - D) The program will crash.
    - **Answer: B** (There will be no conflict, and they can be accessed using their full namespace)

6.5 Working with Assemblies and References

21. **What is an assembly in .NET?**
    - A) A collection of namespaces and types, compiled into a DLL or EXE
    - B) A tool to manage database connections
    - C) A type of runtime exception
    - D) A reference to a third-party library
    - **Answer: A** (A collection of namespaces and types, compiled into a DLL or EXE)
22. **Which file type is NOT an example of an assembly?**
    - A) .exe
    - B) .dll
    - C) .xml
    - D) .pdb
    - **Answer: C** (.xml)
23. **Which of the following tools can be used to inspect the contents of an assembly?**
    - A) Visual Studio
    - B) ILSpy
    - C) Reflector
    - D) All of the above
    - **Answer: D** (All of the above)
24. **How do you add a reference to an external assembly in a VB.NET project?**
    - A) Use the `Add-Reference` command in the terminal
    - B) Right-click on the project and select Add Reference
    - C) Manually add a reference in the source code
    - D) Use the `Imports` keyword directly

- **Answer: B** (Right-click on the project and select Add Reference)

25. **Which of the following is NOT a common type of assembly?**
    - A) .dll (Dynamic Link Library)
    - B) .exe (Executable File)
    - C) .pdb (Program Database)
    - D) .xml (eXtensible Markup Language)
    - **Answer: D** (.xml)
26. **What is the purpose of the `Imports` keyword in VB.NET?**
    - A) To import a class from a custom namespace into the project
    - B) To manage file imports
    - C) To import external libraries into the project
    - D) To refer to an external database
    - **Answer: C** (To import external libraries into the project)
27. **What does versioning in assemblies ensure?**
    - A) The correct class is used when there are multiple versions of an assembly.
    - B) The application only works with one version of the operating system.
    - C) The assembly code can be executed more efficiently.
    - D) The code within the assembly is only accessible during debugging.
    - **Answer: A** (The correct class is used when there are multiple versions of an assembly)
28. **What tool allows you to decompile an assembly back to readable code?**
    - A) Assembly Binder
    - B) ILSpy
    - C) GAC Viewer
    - D) C# Compiler
    - **Answer: B** (ILSpy)
29. **Which of the following is true about assembly references in .NET?**
    - A) References to external assemblies are automatically added during build.
    - B) You can reference an assembly only if it is present in the Global Assembly Cache (GAC).
    - C) You must manually specify assembly versions if not in GAC.
    - D) Assemblies are referenced only by their filenames.
    - **Answer: C** (You must manually specify assembly versions if not in GAC)
30. **Which of the following can be used to ensure compatibility between different versions of an assembly?**
    - A) Strong names and versioning
    - B) Namespace collisions
    - C) Global variables
    - D) Using a single version of an assembly throughout the application
    - **Answer: A** (Strong names and versioning)

6.1 Introduction to NameSpaces

1. **Question:** Define a namespace in VB.NET and demonstrate how you can create a simple namespace that contains a class named `Calculator`.

Answer:

```
Namespace MyApplication
    Public Class Calculator
        Public Function Add(x As Integer, y As Integer) As Integer
            Return x + y
        End Function
    End Class
End Namespace
```

6.2 Commonly Used NameSpaces

2. **Question:** Using the `System.IO` namespace, write a code snippet that reads the contents of a file named `example.txt` and prints it to the console.

   Answer:

```
Imports System.IO

Sub Main()
    Dim filePath As String = "C:\path\to\example.txt"
    If File.Exists(filePath) Then
        Dim content As String = File.ReadAllText(filePath)
        Console.WriteLine(content)
    Else
        Console.WriteLine("File not found.")
    End If
End Sub
```

3. **Question:** Write a program that uses `System.Net.WebClient` to download the HTML content from the URL `http://example.com` and print it to the console.

   Answer:

```
Imports System.Net

Sub Main()
    Dim client As New WebClient()
    Dim htmlContent As String =
client.DownloadString("http://example.com")
    Console.WriteLine(htmlContent)
End Sub
```

4. **Question:** How would you create a simple form with a `Button` and a `Label` using `System.Windows.Forms` in VB.NET? Write the code to display "Hello World" when the button is clicked.

   Answer:

```
Imports System.Windows.Forms
```

```
Public Class MyForm
    Inherits Form
    Private button As Button
    Private label As Label

    Public Sub New()
        button = New Button()
        label = New Label()
        button.Text = "Click Me"
        button.Location = New Point(100, 100)
        label.Location = New Point(100, 150)
        label.Size = New Size(200, 30)

        AddHandler button.Click, AddressOf Me.ButtonClick
        Controls.Add(button)
        Controls.Add(label)
    End Sub

    Private Sub ButtonClick(sender As Object, e As EventArgs)
        label.Text = "Hello World"
    End Sub
End Class

Public Sub Main()
    Application.Run(New MyForm())
End Sub
```

6.3 Custom NameSpaces in Your Project

5. **Question:** Create a custom namespace named `MyCompany.Utilities` and define a class `Logger` within that namespace. The `Logger` class should have a method `LogMessage` that writes a message to the console.

   Answer:

```
Namespace MyCompany.Utilities
    Public Class Logger
        Public Sub LogMessage(message As String)
            Console.WriteLine(message)
        End Sub
    End Class
End Namespace

Sub Main()
    Dim logger As New MyCompany.Utilities.Logger()
    logger.LogMessage("This is a custom namespace example.")
End Sub
```

6. **Question:** How would you access the `Logger` class from the `MyCompany.Utilities` namespace in another file?

Answer:

```
Imports MyCompany.Utilities

Sub Main()
    Dim logger As New Logger()
    logger.LogMessage("This is accessed from a different file.")
End Sub
```

6.4 Organizing Code with NameSpaces

7. **Question:** Write an example of how you can group classes logically using namespaces in a large application. Consider namespaces for database, UI, and business logic.

   Answer:

```
' Namespace for Database Access
Namespace MyApplication.Database
    Public Class DatabaseConnection
        Public Sub Connect()
            Console.WriteLine("Connecting to database...")
        End Sub
    End Class
End Namespace

' Namespace for Business Logic
Namespace MyApplication.BusinessLogic
    Public Class OrderProcessor
        Public Sub ProcessOrder()
            Console.WriteLine("Processing order...")
        End Sub
    End Class
End Namespace

' Namespace for User Interface
Namespace MyApplication.UI
    Public Class UserInterface
        Public Sub ShowUI()
            Console.WriteLine("Displaying User Interface...")
        End Sub
    End Class
End Namespace

Sub Main()
    ' Accessing classes from different namespaces
    Dim db As New MyApplication.Database.DatabaseConnection()
    db.Connect()

    Dim order As New MyApplication.BusinessLogic.OrderProcessor()
    order.ProcessOrder()

    Dim ui As New MyApplication.UI.UserInterface()
    ui.ShowUI()
```

```
End Sub
```

6.5 Working with Assemblies and References

8. **Question:** How do you add a reference to an external assembly (like `System.Xml.dll`) in a VB.NET project?

   Answer:

   - Right-click the project in **Solution Explorer**.
   - Select **Add Reference**.
   - In the **Assemblies** tab, check `System.Xml` and click **OK**.

---

9. **Question:** Write a VB.NET program that uses the `System.Xml` namespace to read and display the content of an XML file named `data.xml`.

   Answer:

```
Imports System.Xml

Sub Main()
    Dim xmlDoc As New XmlDocument()
    xmlDoc.Load("C:\path\to\data.xml")

    Dim root As XmlElement = xmlDoc.DocumentElement
    For Each node As XmlNode In root.ChildNodes
        Console.WriteLine(node.Name & ": " & node.InnerText)
    Next
End Sub
```

10. **Question:** Write a code snippet to reference an external assembly named `MyLibrary.dll` in your project and use a class `MyClass` from that assembly.

Answer:

```
' First, add the reference to MyLibrary.dll through Add Reference
Imports MyLibrary

Sub Main()
    Dim obj As New MyClass()
    obj.MyMethod()
End Sub
```

11. **Question:** How can you use an external assembly that you added as a reference, say `ThirdPartyLibrary.dll`, in your VB.NET project?

Answer:

```
Imports ThirdPartyLibrary

Sub Main()
    Dim obj As New ThirdPartyClass()
    obj.ExecuteMethod()
End Sub
```

12. **Question:** How do you check the version of an assembly reference in a VB.NET project?

Answer:

- Right-click the reference in **Solution Explorer**.
- Select **Properties**.
- The version number will be displayed in the **Version** field under the **Properties** window.

13. **Question:** Create a program that uses the `System.Net.HttpWebRequest` class to send a GET request to a URL and display the response status.

Answer:

```
Imports System.Net

Sub Main()
    Dim request As HttpWebRequest =
CType(WebRequest.Create("http://example.com"), HttpWebRequest)
    Dim response As HttpWebResponse = CType(request.GetResponse(),
HttpWebResponse)

    Console.WriteLine("Response Status: " & response.StatusCode)
    response.Close()
End Sub
```

14. **Question:** Write a VB.NET program that references the `System.Reflection` namespace to load an assembly dynamically and call a method from it.

Answer:

```
Imports System.Reflection

Sub Main()
    ' Load an assembly dynamically
    Dim assembly As Assembly = Assembly.LoadFrom("C:\path\to\MyLibrary.dll")
    ' Get a type from the assembly
    Dim type As Type = assembly.GetType("MyLibrary.MyClass")
    ' Create an instance of the class
    Dim obj As Object = Activator.CreateInstance(type)
    ' Call a method from the class
    type.GetMethod("MyMethod").Invoke(obj, Nothing)
End Sub
```

15. **Question:** Demonstrate how to use versioning for assemblies in a VB.NET project. How can you reference a specific version of an assembly?

Answer:

- In **Solution Explorer**, right-click on **References** and select **Add Reference**.
- Choose the assembly you want and check its version in the **Properties** window.
- To reference a specific version, set the version number when you add the reference or specify it in the `App.config` file under the **assemblyBinding** section.

CHAPTER 7: WORKING WITH DATABASES IN VB.NET

7.1 Introduction to Databases and VB.NET

In the context of software development, **databases** play a critical role in storing and managing data. They provide a structured way to store, retrieve, update, and delete data, making them essential for most applications, especially when dealing with large amounts of dynamic data, such as user information, transactions, or product inventories.

In VB.NET, you can easily work with various types of databases, including SQL Server, MySQL, Oracle, and more. VB.NET has built-in support for interacting with databases using **ADO.NET (ActiveX Data Objects .NET)**, which is a set of libraries that allow applications to communicate with databases, send SQL commands, and process results.

Understanding Databases

A **database** is a collection of data organized in a way that allows for easy retrieval, manipulation, and management. Databases can be thought of as a container for storing structured information (often in tables), which can be queried or modified using **SQL (Structured Query Language)**.

- **Data Retrieval**: SQL queries (e.g., SELECT statements) are used to retrieve data from tables in a database.
- **Data Insertion**: Data can be added to the database using SQL commands like `INSERT INTO`.
- **Data Update**: You can modify existing data with SQL `UPDATE` commands.
- **Data Deletion**: Records can be deleted using SQL `DELETE` commands.

Databases are typically managed by **Database Management Systems (DBMS)** like **SQL Server**, **MySQL**, **Oracle**, and others, which provide the interface for applications to interact with the database.

Working with Databases in VB.NET

VB.NET provides the tools needed to interact with databases, primarily through **ADO.NET**. ADO.NET is a set of libraries that handle data access by providing a series of objects to work with database connections, execute SQL commands, and process data.

ADO.NET supports a wide range of database providers, enabling your VB.NET application to connect to different types of databases. These database providers include:

1. **SQL Server**: For interacting with Microsoft SQL Server databases.
2. **OLEDB**: A general-purpose provider used for connecting to databases like Microsoft Access, Excel, or other non-SQL databases.
3. **ODBC (Open Database Connectivity)**: A standardized method for accessing various database types.
4. **Oracle**: For connecting to Oracle databases.

Key ADO.NET Components

1. **Connection**: The `Connection` object is used to establish a link to a specific database. For example, the `SqlConnection` class is used to connect to SQL Server databases.
2. **Command**: The `Command` object is used to execute SQL queries or stored procedures. In SQL Server, the `SqlCommand` class allows you to execute queries, updates, and stored procedures.
3. **DataReader**: The `DataReader` is used for reading data from the database in a forward-only, read-only manner. It retrieves data efficiently, making it ideal for large datasets.
4. **DataAdapter**: The `DataAdapter` acts as a bridge between the database and the `DataSet` or `DataTable`. It retrieves data from the database and fills the dataset. It also handles updating the database when changes are made to the dataset.
5. **DataSet and DataTable**: These are in-memory representations of data. A `DataSet` can hold multiple tables of data, while a `DataTable` represents a single table of data. These objects are used to hold and manipulate data locally in memory.

Example of Using ADO.NET for Database Interaction

Here's a basic example to demonstrate how VB.NET can interact with a SQL Server database using ADO.NET:

1. Establishing a Connection

To begin working with a database, you first need to establish a connection. This requires a **connection string** that specifies the location of the database, the database name, and authentication details.

```
Dim connectionString As String = "Data Source=localhost;Initial
Catalog=MyDatabase;Integrated Security=True"
Dim connection As New SqlConnection(connectionString)
```

In the connection string:

- `Data Source` specifies the server name (e.g., `localhost` or a specific server IP).
- `Initial Catalog` is the name of the database.
- `Integrated Security=True` means that Windows Authentication is being used for authentication.

2. Executing a Query

Once the connection is established, you can execute a query. Here, we will use the `SqlCommand` object to execute a `SELECT` query and retrieve data.

```
Dim query As String = "SELECT * FROM Employees"
Dim command As New SqlCommand(query, connection)

' Open the connection
```

```
connection.Open()

' Execute the query and retrieve data using SqlDataReader
Dim reader As SqlDataReader = command.ExecuteReader()

' Iterate through the results
While reader.Read()
    Console.WriteLine("Employee ID: " & reader("EmployeeID") & " - Name: " &
reader("EmployeeName"))
End While

' Close the reader and connection
reader.Close()
connection.Close()
```

- `ExecuteReader` executes the query and retrieves the result set.
- We use `SqlDataReader` to read each row of data from the query result.

3. Inserting Data

You can also insert data into the database using the `INSERT INTO` SQL command. Here's how you would insert a new employee into the `Employees` table:

```
Dim insertQuery As String = "INSERT INTO Employees (EmployeeName, Department)
VALUES (@Name, @Department)"
Dim insertCommand As New SqlCommand(insertQuery, connection)

' Add parameters to avoid SQL injection
insertCommand.Parameters.AddWithValue("@Name", "John Doe")
insertCommand.Parameters.AddWithValue("@Department", "Sales")

' Open the connection and execute the insert command
connection.Open()
insertCommand.ExecuteNonQuery()
connection.Close()
```

- The `ExecuteNonQuery` method is used when executing SQL statements that do not return data (e.g., `INSERT`, `UPDATE`, `DELETE`).
- We use **parameterized queries** (`@Name`, `@Department`) to avoid SQL injection attacks and ensure proper handling of user input.

Summary of ADO.NET and Database Interaction in VB.NET

- **ADO.NET** is the main technology used to interact with databases in VB.NET. It provides classes for connecting to a database, executing SQL commands, and retrieving results.
- **SQL commands** are used to interact with databases. VB.NET allows the execution of SQL commands using objects like `SqlCommand`, `OleDbCommand`, or `OdbcCommand`.
- **SqlConnection** is used to establish a connection to a database.
- The **DataReader** provides a fast, efficient way to read data from the database in a forward-only manner.

- The **DataAdapter** is used for more complex scenarios where you need to fill a `DataSet` with data, which can then be manipulated locally in memory.
- Error handling and validation are essential when working with databases to ensure data integrity and avoid runtime errors.

By using these ADO.NET components, VB.NET allows you to create powerful, data-driven applications that can interact with various types of databases, from SQL Server to MySQL and beyond.

7.2 Database Connectivity in VB.NET

In VB.NET, **database connectivity** is essential for creating data-driven applications. You can connect to databases, execute SQL commands, and retrieve or manipulate data directly from your VB.NET code. The process of establishing a connection to a database involves using a **connection string**, which contains all the necessary information for the application to communicate with the database.

Establishing a Connection to a Database

To interact with a database, you must first establish a connection. This is done by creating an instance of the appropriate connection object and providing a **connection string**. The connection string specifies key details about the database, including:

- **Server Name**: The name of the database server (or IP address).
- **Database Name**: The name of the database to which you want to connect.
- **Authentication Details**: Information about how to authenticate (e.g., Windows Authentication or SQL Server authentication).

Connection String Format

A connection string is a string that contains all the parameters needed to establish a connection. It varies depending on the type of database being used (e.g., SQL Server, MySQL, or Oracle). Different **data providers** are used for different types of databases.

1. SQL Server Connection String

SQL Server is one of the most commonly used databases in VB.NET. To connect to a SQL Server database, you use the `SqlConnection` class. The connection string for SQL Server typically contains the server name, database name, and authentication information.

Here is an example of a **SQL Server connection string**:

```
Dim connectionString As String = "Data Source=localhost;Initial
Catalog=MyDatabase;Integrated Security=True"
Dim connection As New SqlConnection(connectionString)
```

- **Data Source**: Specifies the SQL Server instance (in this case, `localhost` refers to the local machine).
- **Initial Catalog**: The name of the database you want to connect to (`MyDatabase` in this example).
- **Integrated Security=True**: Indicates that Windows Authentication is used for authentication. If you need to use SQL Server authentication (with a username and password), you can specify `User ID` and `Password` instead.

Example using SQL Server authentication:

```
Dim connectionString As String = "Data Source=localhost;Initial
Catalog=MyDatabase;User ID=sa;Password=your_password"
Dim connection As New SqlConnection(connectionString)
```

2. OLEDB Connection String

For other databases, such as Microsoft Access or older databases, the **OLEDB** provider is commonly used. An **OLEDB connection string** would look like this:

```
Dim connectionString As String = "Provider=Microsoft.ACE.OLEDB.12.0;Data
Source=C:\path\to\your\database.accdb;"
Dim connection As New OleDbConnection(connectionString)
```

- **Provider**: Specifies the OLEDB provider (e.g., Microsoft Access Database Engine).
- **Data Source**: The path to the database file.

3. ODBC Connection String

The **ODBC** (Open Database Connectivity) provider is a more generic connection string used for a variety of databases, including SQL Server, MySQL, PostgreSQL, etc. An example of an ODBC connection string for SQL Server would look like this:

```
Dim connectionString As String = "Driver={SQL
Server};Server=localhost;Database=MyDatabase;Trusted_Connection=yes;"
Dim connection As New OdbcConnection(connectionString)
```

- **Driver**: Specifies the database driver (e.g., SQL Server).
- **Server**: The database server address.
- **Database**: The name of the database.
- **Trusted_Connection**: When set to `yes`, Windows Authentication is used.

Providers and Their Use Cases

1. **SQL Server (SqlConnection)**:
   - Used for connecting to Microsoft SQL Server databases.
   - Provides rich support for SQL Server-specific features like stored procedures and advanced data types.
2. **OLEDB (OleDbConnection)**:
   - Used to connect to older or non-SQL databases (e.g., Microsoft Access, Excel, or Oracle).

- Provides a general-purpose connectivity option, especially for older or legacy systems.

3. **ODBC (OdbcConnection)**:
   - A standardized way to connect to various database systems, such as MySQL, Oracle, and PostgreSQL.
   - Useful when working with databases that don't have their own .NET provider.

Example Code to Establish a Connection

Let's walk through an example where we connect to a SQL Server database and retrieve some data:

```
Imports System.Data.SqlClient

Public Class DatabaseExample
    Public Sub ConnectToDatabase()
        ' Define the connection string for the SQL Server database
        Dim connectionString As String = "Data Source=localhost;Initial
Catalog=MyDatabase;Integrated Security=True"

        ' Create a new connection object
        Dim connection As New SqlConnection(connectionString)

        Try
            ' Open the connection to the database
            connection.Open()
            Console.WriteLine("Connected to the database successfully.")

            ' Create a SQL query
            Dim query As String = "SELECT * FROM Employees"
            Dim command As New SqlCommand(query, connection)

            ' Execute the query and retrieve data using DataReader
            Dim reader As SqlDataReader = command.ExecuteReader()

            ' Loop through the data and display the results
            While reader.Read()
                Console.WriteLine("Employee ID: " & reader("EmployeeID") & ",
Name: " & reader("EmployeeName"))
            End While

            ' Close the reader
            reader.Close()

        Catch ex As Exception
            Console.WriteLine("An error occurred: " & ex.Message)
        Finally
            ' Close the connection
            connection.Close()
            Console.WriteLine("Connection closed.")
        End Try
    End Sub
End Class
```

Key Steps in the Example:

1. **Creating the Connection**: We create a `SqlConnection` object and pass the connection string that contains all the necessary information to establish a connection.
2. **Opening the Connection**: We use the `Open` method of the `SqlConnection` object to establish the actual connection with the database.
3. **Executing SQL Commands**: We create a `SqlCommand` object to represent the SQL query (in this case, a simple `SELECT` query) and execute it using `ExecuteReader`.
4. **Handling Exceptions**: The code is wrapped in a `Try...Catch` block to handle any potential errors, such as invalid connection strings, unavailable databases, or permission issues.
5. **Closing the Connection**: The connection is closed in the `Finally` block to ensure that it's always properly closed, regardless of whether an error occurred or not.

7.3 Using Server Explorer for Database Connections

Server Explorer in Visual Studio is a powerful tool that allows developers to interact with and manage databases directly within the Visual Studio IDE. It makes working with databases more streamlined by providing a graphical interface to connect, view, and modify database objects without needing to leave the development environment.

Accessing and Managing Databases in Visual Studio

To start using Server Explorer for managing databases, follow these steps:

1. Opening Server Explorer

- To open the **Server Explorer** in Visual Studio, go to the **View** menu and select **Server Explorer**.
    - Alternatively, you can press **Ctrl + Alt + S**.
- The **Server Explorer** window will appear, typically on the left side of the Visual Studio workspace.

2. Adding a Database Connection

Once the **Server Explorer** is open, you can add a connection to a database. Here's how you can do it:

- **Right-click** on the **Data Connections** node (or the empty space under it) and select **Add Connection**.

  This will open the **Add Connection** dialog box where you will be able to specify the database provider and connection details.

3. Selecting a Database Provider

In the **Add Connection** dialog box, you will need to select the type of database you want to connect to. Some common options include:

- **SQL Server**: For connecting to Microsoft SQL Server databases.

- **Microsoft Access**: For connecting to Microsoft Access databases using OLEDB.
- **ODBC**: For connecting to any database that supports ODBC, such as MySQL or PostgreSQL.

Example: Connecting to a SQL Server Database

1. **Select Data Source**: In the "Data source" field, select **Microsoft SQL Server (SqlClient)**.
2. **Server Name**: Enter the **server name** where the SQL Server instance is hosted (e.g., `localhost`, `myserver`, or `192.168.1.100`).
3. **Authentication**: Choose the type of authentication:
   - **Windows Authentication**: Uses your Windows credentials to authenticate to the database.
   - **SQL Server Authentication**: Requires a **username** and **password** for login.
4. **Database Name**: In the **Select or enter a database name** field, enter the name of the database to which you want to connect.
5. **Test Connection**: You can click the **Test Connection** button to ensure that your connection settings are correct.
6. **Click OK**: After entering all necessary information, click **OK** to establish the connection.

Once connected, the database will appear under the **Data Connections** node in the **Server Explorer**.

4. Viewing and Managing Database Objects

After a successful connection, you can expand the **Data Connections** node in the **Server Explorer** to view various objects within the database, such as:

- **Tables**: Lists all the tables in the connected database.
- **Views**: Displays the views (virtual tables) available in the database.
- **Stored Procedures**: Shows the stored procedures that have been defined in the database.
- **Functions**: Displays any user-defined functions in the database.
- **Indexes and Triggers**: These are also visible if you expand the database objects further.

You can interact with these objects in a number of ways:

- **Viewing Table Data**: Right-click on a table and select **Show Table Data** to view the rows in the table.
- **Viewing Table Schema**: Right-click on a table and select **Design** to view and edit the table's schema.
- **Running SQL Queries**: You can execute SQL queries directly from the **Server Explorer**.

5. Running SQL Queries Using Server Explorer

One of the most useful features of **Server Explorer** is the ability to run SQL queries directly against the database:

1. **Right-click** on the database or connection in **Server Explorer**.
2. Select **New Query** from the context menu.

3. A new query window will open where you can type your SQL commands (such as `SELECT`, `INSERT`, `UPDATE`, or `DELETE`).
4. Once you've written your query, click **Execute** (or press **F5**) to run the query against the connected database.
    - The results of the query (if any) will be shown in the **Results** window below the query editor.
    - You can also see the **Messages** tab, which displays any messages or errors returned from the database.

6. Managing Tables and Other Database Objects

Within **Server Explorer**, you can also manage your database objects. For example:

- **Creating Tables**: Right-click on **Tables** and select **New Table** to create a new table in the database.
- **Editing Tables**: Right-click on a table and select **Design** to modify the schema (add or remove columns).
- **Creating Stored Procedures**: Right-click on **Stored Procedures** and select **Add New Stored Procedure** to create stored procedures directly from the UI.
- **Viewing Table Data**: Right-click on a table and choose **Show Table Data** to view the current rows in the table.

7. Benefits of Using Server Explorer

Using **Server Explorer** to manage database connections has several benefits:

- **Integrated Environment**: You don't need to switch between multiple tools or programs to manage your database. Everything can be done directly in Visual Studio.
- **Query Execution**: Quickly run queries and view results without needing a separate SQL tool like SQL Server Management Studio.
- **Ease of Navigation**: You can easily navigate between databases, tables, views, and other objects using a tree structure.
- **Data Viewing and Editing**: You can view and edit your database tables, run queries, and test changes on the fly, making it very convenient for small projects and rapid development.

7.4 Querying Databases with ADO.NET

ADO.NET (ActiveX Data Objects .NET) is a set of classes in the .NET Framework used to interact with data sources like SQL Server, Oracle, and other databases. It allows you to execute SQL commands, retrieve and manipulate data, and manage database connections. In VB.NET, you use **ADO.NET** to interact with databases by executing SQL commands (such as SELECT, INSERT, UPDATE, DELETE) and fetching data using data readers like `SqlDataReader`.

Executing SQL Commands

To execute SQL commands like **SELECT**, **INSERT**, **UPDATE**, and **DELETE**, you need to create a connection to the database, construct the SQL query, and execute it using the `SqlCommand` class.

Here's an example where we execute a **SELECT** SQL command to retrieve data from a database:

Step-by-Step Example: Executing a SELECT Command

1. **Establish a Database Connection**: First, you need to establish a connection to the database using a connection string.
2. **Define SQL Query**: Next, define the SQL query string that you want to execute. For example, a simple `SELECT` query to fetch all records from an `Employees` table.
3. **Create SqlCommand Object**: The `SqlCommand` object is used to send the SQL query to the database for execution.
4. **Execute the Command**: You execute the query using methods like `ExecuteReader()`, `ExecuteNonQuery()`, or `ExecuteScalar()` depending on the nature of the query.

Example: Querying Data (SELECT)

```
' 1. Define the connection string
Dim connectionString As String = "Data Source=localhost;Initial
Catalog=MyDatabase;Integrated Security=True"

' 2. Create a new SQL connection using the connection string
Dim connection As New SqlConnection(connectionString)

' 3. Define the SQL query
Dim query As String = "SELECT * FROM Employees"

' 4. Create a SqlCommand object
Dim command As New SqlCommand(query, connection)

' 5. Open the connection to the database
connection.Open()

' 6. Execute the command using ExecuteReader and fetch the results
Dim reader As SqlDataReader = command.ExecuteReader()

' 7. Loop through the results and display them
While reader.Read()
    Console.WriteLine(reader("EmployeeName"))
End While

' 8. Close the reader and the connection
reader.Close()
connection.Close()
```

Explanation of Code:

- **SqlConnection**: This class is used to establish a connection to the database using the provided connection string.

- **SqlCommand**: This class represents the SQL query to be executed and the connection to the database.
- **ExecuteReader()**: This method is used to execute a query that returns multiple rows of data. It returns a `SqlDataReader` that allows you to read the data in a forward-only, read-only manner.
- **SqlDataReader**: This class provides a way to read data row by row from the database. It only supports forward reading, which means once you have moved to the next row, you cannot go back.

In this example, we're executing a `SELECT` query to retrieve all rows from the `Employees` table, and then displaying the `EmployeeName` of each row.

Retrieving Data Using SqlDataReader

The `SqlDataReader` class is used to retrieve data from a database in a forward-only, read-only manner. You can use it to iterate through the rows of the result set and access the data using column names or column indexes.

Here is a more detailed example of using `SqlDataReader` to retrieve and display multiple columns from the result set:

Example: Retrieving Multiple Columns

```
' Define the connection string
Dim connectionString As String = "Data Source=localhost;Initial
Catalog=MyDatabase;Integrated Security=True"

' Create a new SQL connection using the connection string
Dim connection As New SqlConnection(connectionString)

' Define the SQL query to select data from Employees table
Dim query As String = "SELECT EmployeeID, EmployeeName FROM Employees"

' Create a SqlCommand object to execute the query
Dim command As New SqlCommand(query, connection)

' Open the connection to the database
connection.Open()

' Execute the command and obtain a SqlDataReader
Dim reader As SqlDataReader = command.ExecuteReader()

' Iterate through the result set
While reader.Read()
    ' Access each column by name or index and display the values
    Console.WriteLine("Employee ID: " & reader("EmployeeID").ToString())
    Console.WriteLine("Employee Name: " & reader("EmployeeName").ToString())
End While

' Close the SqlDataReader and the connection
```

```
reader.Close()
connection.Close()
```

Explanation:

- **Accessing Columns**: In the `While reader.Read()` loop, we access each column using either the **column name** (`reader("EmployeeID")`) or the **column index** (`reader(0)`).
- **ToString()**: Since `SqlDataReader` returns the data as an object, we call `ToString()` to convert it to a string for display.
- **Forward-Only**: `SqlDataReader` allows you to read data in a forward-only direction. Once you move to the next row, you cannot move backward, so data must be processed as you read through it.

Executing Other SQL Commands (INSERT, UPDATE, DELETE)

In addition to SELECT queries, you can execute other SQL commands like **INSERT**, **UPDATE**, and **DELETE** using ADO.NET.

For **INSERT**, **UPDATE**, and **DELETE**, instead of using `ExecuteReader()`, you would use the `ExecuteNonQuery()` method. This method returns the number of rows affected by the command (e.g., how many rows were updated).

Example: INSERT Command

```
' Define the connection string
Dim connectionString As String = "Data Source=localhost;Initial
Catalog=MyDatabase;Integrated Security=True"

' Create a new SQL connection
Dim connection As New SqlConnection(connectionString)

' Define the INSERT query
Dim query As String = "INSERT INTO Employees (EmployeeName, Department)
VALUES ('John Doe', 'HR')"

' Create a SqlCommand object
Dim command As New SqlCommand(query, connection)

' Open the connection
connection.Open()

' Execute the INSERT command
Dim rowsAffected As Integer = command.ExecuteNonQuery()

' Display the number of rows affected
Console.WriteLine("Rows affected: " & rowsAffected)

' Close the connection
connection.Close()
```

In this example, an `INSERT` command is executed to add a new employee to the `Employees` table, and the number of rows affected is displayed.

Summary of Key ADO.NET Methods for Executing SQL Commands

1. **ExecuteReader()**: Used to execute a `SELECT` query that returns a result set (multiple rows of data).
2. **ExecuteNonQuery()**: Used for `INSERT`, `UPDATE`, and `DELETE` queries that do not return data but may affect rows.
3. **ExecuteScalar()**: Used for queries that return a single value (e.g., aggregate functions like `COUNT()`, `MAX()`, etc.).

In conclusion, ADO.NET provides a powerful and flexible way to interact with databases in VB.NET. You can execute SQL commands like **SELECT**, **INSERT**, **UPDATE**, and **DELETE**, retrieve data using a `SqlDataReader`, and manage the connection with the database effectively.

7.5 Working with DataGridView Control

The **DataGridView** control in VB.NET is one of the most powerful tools for displaying and interacting with tabular data. It allows you to display, edit, add, and delete data directly within your application. When working with databases, you can bind data to the DataGridView from a data source like a **DataTable** or **BindingSource**. This makes it easy to present and manage large datasets.

Binding Data to DataGridView

The **DataGridView** can display data from various sources such as a **DataTable**, **BindingSource**, or a **List** of objects. One common way of binding data is by using a **DataTable**, which can be populated with data from a database.

Steps to Bind Data to DataGridView:

1. **Create a DataTable**: The `DataTable` will hold the data retrieved from the database.
2. **Retrieve Data from Database**: Use a `SqlDataAdapter` to execute a SQL query and fill the `DataTable` with the data.
3. **Set DataSource**: Once the data is populated into the `DataTable`, you bind it to the `DataGridView` by setting its `DataSource` property.

Example: Binding Data to DataGridView

```
' Create a new DataTable object
Dim dataTable As New DataTable()

' Define the SQL query to fetch data
```

```
Dim query As String = "SELECT * FROM Employees"

' Create a SqlDataAdapter to fetch data
Dim adapter As New SqlDataAdapter(query, connection)

' Fill the DataTable with data from the database
adapter.Fill(dataTable)

' Bind the DataTable to the DataGridView
DataGridView1.DataSource = dataTable
```

Explanation:

- **DataTable**: A `DataTable` object is used to store data in memory. It's a simple in-memory representation of the database table that allows you to manipulate the data programmatically.
- **SqlDataAdapter**: The `SqlDataAdapter` retrieves data from the database and fills the `DataTable`. It acts as a bridge between the database and the `DataTable`.
- **DataSource Property**: The `DataGridView.DataSource` property is set to the `DataTable`, which binds the data to the grid. The `DataGridView` will automatically display all the columns and rows from the `DataTable`.

Once the data is bound to the DataGridView, the user can interact with it directly.

Adding, Editing, and Deleting Records

The DataGridView provides built-in functionality for adding, editing, and deleting records directly in the UI. When the data is bound to a `DataTable`, these changes are reflected in the `DataTable`. However, to persist the changes in the database, you need to write logic that updates the database (e.g., using SQL `UPDATE`, `INSERT`, and `DELETE` commands).

Adding Records

You can add a new row to the `DataTable` bound to the `DataGridView`. This will automatically update the DataGridView. You can do this programmatically by using the `Rows.Add()` method of the `DataTable` object.

```
' Create a new row and add it to the DataTable
Dim newRow As DataRow = dataTable.NewRow()
newRow("EmployeeName") = "Jane Doe"
newRow("Department") = "Sales"

' Add the new row to the DataTable
dataTable.Rows.Add(newRow)
```

Editing Records

If you want to edit a record directly in the `DataGridView`, you can allow users to edit the cells in the grid. After making changes, you need to update the corresponding row in the database. This can be done using an `UPDATE` SQL query.

For example, to update a specific record:

```
' Example of modifying an existing row in DataGridView
DataGridView1.Rows(0).Cells("EmployeeName").Value = "John Smith"

' After editing, write the changes back to the database (using UPDATE
command)
Dim updateQuery As String = "UPDATE Employees SET EmployeeName = @name WHERE
EmployeeID = @id"
Dim command As New SqlCommand(updateQuery, connection)
command.Parameters.AddWithValue("@name",
DataGridView1.Rows(0).Cells("EmployeeName").Value)
command.Parameters.AddWithValue("@id",
DataGridView1.Rows(0).Cells("EmployeeID").Value)

' Execute the update query
connection.Open()
command.ExecuteNonQuery()
connection.Close()
```

Deleting Records

To delete a record from the `DataGridView`, you can remove the selected row from the `DataGridView`. You can do this by calling `Rows.Remove()` on the `DataGridView`. After removing the row from the UI, you also need to delete the corresponding record from the database using a `DELETE` SQL command.

```
' Delete the selected row from the DataGridView
Dim selectedRow As DataGridViewRow = DataGridView1.SelectedRows(0)
DataGridView1.Rows.Remove(selectedRow)

' After deleting, write the changes back to the database (using DELETE
command)
Dim deleteQuery As String = "DELETE FROM Employees WHERE EmployeeID = @id"
Dim command As New SqlCommand(deleteQuery, connection)
command.Parameters.AddWithValue("@id", selectedRow.Cells("EmployeeID").Value)

' Execute the delete query
connection.Open()
command.ExecuteNonQuery()
connection.Close()
```

Explanation of Code:

- **Rows.Remove()**: This method removes the selected row from the `DataGridView`. It's typically used when the user selects a row to delete.

- **ExecuteNonQuery()**: The `ExecuteNonQuery` method is used to execute SQL commands like `INSERT`, `UPDATE`, or `DELETE`, where no data is returned.
- **SQL Commands**: When you delete or update a record in the grid, you need to make sure that the changes are also reflected in the database. This is done by executing the appropriate SQL command (`UPDATE` or `DELETE`) based on the change in the grid.

Important Notes:

1. **Updating the Database**: Changes made to the `DataGridView` (such as adding, editing, or deleting rows) need to be written back to the database to persist those changes. For this, you should execute the appropriate SQL commands (`INSERT`, `UPDATE`, `DELETE`).
2. **Handling Database Connections**: Always ensure that your database connection is open before executing any SQL commands and closed afterward to avoid potential memory leaks or connection issues.
3. **Data Binding**: Once you bind data to a `DataGridView`, any changes you make to the `DataTable` are automatically reflected in the grid. However, make sure to implement proper logic to persist those changes in the database.

7.6 Multiple Table Connections

When working with databases, it's common to interact with data spread across multiple tables. To make sense of these relationships, SQL allows you to combine data from different tables using **JOIN** operations. In VB.NET, you can connect to multiple tables by crafting SQL queries that include these JOIN operations and then execute them using ADO.NET.

Connecting to Multiple Tables

To connect to multiple tables, you'll often perform a **JOIN** operation. This operation allows you to retrieve data from multiple tables based on a common field or relationship between them.

What is a JOIN?

A **JOIN** in SQL is a way to combine columns from two or more tables based on a related column between them. It essentially allows you to pull in related data from different tables into a single result set.

Common types of JOINs include:

1. **INNER JOIN**
2. **LEFT JOIN**
3. **RIGHT JOIN**

Example of Connecting to Multiple Tables Using JOIN

Let's assume you have two tables:

- **Employees** table with columns like `EmployeeID`, `EmployeeName`, `DepartmentID`.
- **Departments** table with columns like `DepartmentID`, `DepartmentName`.

SQL Query with INNER JOIN

An **INNER JOIN** will return only those rows where there is a match in both tables.

```
SELECT Employees.EmployeeID, Employees.EmployeeName,
Departments.DepartmentName
FROM Employees
INNER JOIN Departments ON Employees.DepartmentID = Departments.DepartmentID
```

Explanation of the SQL Query:

- The query selects `EmployeeID` and `EmployeeName` from the **Employees** table.
- It also selects `DepartmentName` from the **Departments** table.
- The `INNER JOIN` keyword is used to join these two tables on the common column `DepartmentID`, which links the employee to their respective department.
- The result will only include employees that are associated with a department (i.e., the join condition is met).

Types of JOINs

1. **INNER JOIN:**
   - The most common type of join.
   - Returns only the rows that have matching values in both tables.
   - If there is no match, the row is excluded from the result set.

   Example:

   ```
   SELECT Employees.EmployeeID, Employees.EmployeeName,
   Departments.DepartmentName
   FROM Employees
   INNER JOIN Departments ON Employees.DepartmentID =
   Departments.DepartmentID
   ```

   - This will return only employees who belong to a department.
2. **LEFT JOIN (or LEFT OUTER JOIN):**
   - Returns all the rows from the left table (in this case, **Employees**), and the matching rows from the right table (**Departments**).
   - If there is no match, the result will still include rows from the left table, but with `NULL` values for columns from the right table.

   Example:

```
SELECT Employees.EmployeeID, Employees.EmployeeName,
Departments.DepartmentName
FROM Employees
LEFT JOIN Departments ON Employees.DepartmentID =
Departments.DepartmentID
```

- This query will return all employees, including those who are not assigned to any department. For employees without a department, the `DepartmentName` will be `NULL`.

3. **RIGHT JOIN (or RIGHT OUTER JOIN):**
   - Similar to the LEFT JOIN, but it returns all rows from the right table and the matching rows from the left table.
   - If no match is found, the result will include `NULL` values for columns from the left table.

Example:

```
SELECT Employees.EmployeeID, Employees.EmployeeName,
Departments.DepartmentName
FROM Employees
RIGHT JOIN Departments ON Employees.DepartmentID =
Departments.DepartmentID
```

- This query will return all departments, including those that do not have any employees. For departments with no employees, the `EmployeeName` will be `NULL`.

4. **FULL OUTER JOIN:**
   - This is a combination of the LEFT JOIN and RIGHT JOIN. It returns all rows when there is a match in either the left (Employees) or the right (Departments) table.
   - If there is no match, `NULL` values are returned for columns of the table without a match.

Example:

```
SELECT Employees.EmployeeID, Employees.EmployeeName,
Departments.DepartmentName
FROM Employees
FULL OUTER JOIN Departments ON Employees.DepartmentID =
Departments.DepartmentID
```

- This query will return all employees and all departments. If an employee has no department, `DepartmentName` will be `NULL`. If a department has no employee, `EmployeeName` will be `NULL`.

Executing a JOIN Query in ADO.NET

In VB.NET, after constructing the appropriate SQL query with a JOIN, you can execute it using **SqlCommand** and retrieve the results with **SqlDataReader**.

Here's how you can connect to a database and execute a JOIN query:

```
Dim connectionString As String = "Data Source=localhost;Initial
Catalog=MyDatabase;Integrated Security=True"
Dim connection As New SqlConnection(connectionString)

Dim query As String = "SELECT Employees.EmployeeID, Employees.EmployeeName,
Departments.DepartmentName " & _
                      "FROM Employees " & _
                      "INNER JOIN Departments ON Employees.DepartmentID =
Departments.DepartmentID"

Dim command As New SqlCommand(query, connection)

connection.Open()

' Execute the query and read the results
Dim reader As SqlDataReader = command.ExecuteReader()

While reader.Read()
    Console.WriteLine(reader("EmployeeID").ToString() & " - " &
reader("EmployeeName").ToString() & " - " &
reader("DepartmentName").ToString())
End While

reader.Close()
connection.Close()
```

Explanation:

- **SqlConnection**: Establishes a connection to the database.
- **SqlCommand**: Executes the SQL query to join the tables.
- **SqlDataReader**: Reads the results returned by the query. You can iterate over the results using `While reader.Read()` and access each column using the column name (e.g., `reader("EmployeeName")`).
- **Open/Close Connection**: The connection is opened before executing the query and closed after the operation is complete to free resources.

Combining Data from Multiple Tables Using JOINs in Practice

When you need to pull data from multiple related tables (e.g., pulling employee and department details), using the appropriate **JOIN** operation can simplify your query and reduce the complexity of your code.

- **INNER JOIN** is useful when you want only matching records.
- **LEFT JOIN** is good when you want to keep all records from the "left" table (even if no match exists in the right table).
- **RIGHT JOIN** helps when you need all records from the "right" table.
- **FULL OUTER JOIN** can be useful when you want to combine all records from both tables, whether they have a match or not.

By utilizing these JOINs effectively in VB.NET with ADO.NET, you can easily manipulate and retrieve combined data from multiple related tables in your application.

7.7 Data Validation and Error Handling

In any application that interacts with databases, two important aspects you must address are **data validation** and **error handling**. These ensure the integrity and reliability of your application by preventing invalid data from being saved and managing unexpected issues that arise during database operations.

Validating Input Data

Validating user input is essential to ensure that the data provided is correct, complete, and in the proper format before it is saved to the database. This prevents issues such as SQL errors, data corruption, and integrity violations.

Types of Validation:

1. **Format Validation:**
    - Ensures that the data entered follows a certain format (e.g., email, phone number, date).
2. **Range/Value Validation:**
    - Ensures that numeric values fall within a specified range or that strings are not empty.
3. **Required Fields Validation:**
    - Ensures that essential fields (e.g., name, email) are not left empty.
4. **Custom Validation:**
    - Involves checks based on your specific application requirements (e.g., ensuring a user doesn't already exist in the system).

Example: Validating an Email Input

One common validation task is ensuring that user input follows the correct format for specific types, like emails. Here's an example of how you can validate an email input using a regular expression (regex) in VB.NET.

```
Dim email As String = txtEmail.Text
If Not Regex.IsMatch(email, "^[\w-]+(\.[\w-]+)*@([\w-]+\.)+[a-zA-Z]{2,7}$")
Then
    MessageBox.Show("Invalid email format.")
    Return
End If
```

- **Regex.IsMatch(email, pattern)**: This method checks if the input matches a given pattern. In this case, the pattern is designed to match valid email formats.
- **MessageBox.Show**: If the input does not match the pattern, a message box alerts the user that the email format is invalid.

By using validation techniques like this, you ensure that only correctly formatted data is sent to the database, which can prevent issues later in the application.

Handling Database Errors

When dealing with databases, errors can occur due to various reasons, such as connection issues, SQL syntax errors, or data integrity violations. To prevent the application from crashing and provide a better user experience, these errors should be handled gracefully.

Common Database Errors:

1. **SQL Syntax Errors:**
    - Occur when the SQL query is incorrectly written or contains invalid syntax.
2. **Connection Issues:**
    - Occur when the application is unable to connect to the database (e.g., network issues, wrong credentials).
3. **Timeouts:**
    - Occur when the database takes too long to respond to a query.
4. **Data Integrity Violations:**
    - Occur when the data does not meet the constraints defined in the database (e.g., inserting a null value in a column that does not allow nulls).

Example: Using Try...Catch for Database Error Handling

To handle database-related errors, you can use a `Try...Catch` block. This allows you to catch exceptions thrown during the execution of database commands and handle them appropriately.

```
Try
    connection.Open()  ' Open the database connection
    ' Execute SQL commands here
    Dim command As New SqlCommand("INSERT INTO Employees (Name, Department)
VALUES ('John Doe', 'HR')", connection)
    command.ExecuteNonQuery()
Catch ex As SqlException
    ' This block will catch SQL-specific errors (e.g., connection issues,
syntax errors)
    MessageBox.Show("Error occurred while accessing the database: " &
ex.Message)
Catch ex As Exception
    ' General exception handling
    MessageBox.Show("An unexpected error occurred: " & ex.Message)
Finally
    ' Ensure that the connection is closed regardless of whether an exception
occurred or not
    connection.Close()
End Try
```

Explanation of Code:

- **Try Block:**
    - The `Try` block contains the code that might generate an exception. In this case, it opens the database connection and executes a SQL command to insert data into the `Employees` table.
- **Catch Block:**
    - The `Catch` block catches exceptions that occur during execution. In the example, the code handles `SqlException` (specific to SQL-related errors) and other general exceptions using `Exception`.
    - `ex.Message` retrieves the error message, which you can display to the user to inform them of the problem.
- **Finally Block:**
    - The `Finally` block ensures that the database connection is always closed, regardless of whether an error occurred. This is crucial for resource management because not closing connections can lead to memory leaks or database connection limits being reached.

Best Practices for Data Validation and Error Handling:

1. **Always validate user input:**
    - Validate all user inputs, whether they are coming from forms, APIs, or other sources, before performing any database operations.
2. **Provide meaningful error messages:**
    - When an error occurs, provide a clear and helpful message that can guide the user to resolve the issue. Avoid exposing sensitive information (like stack traces) to the user.
3. **Use `Try...Catch` for database operations:**
    - Always wrap your database-related operations in `Try...Catch` blocks to handle potential errors gracefully.
4. **Perform logging:**
    - Log errors (but avoid logging sensitive data). This will help you troubleshoot issues during development and in production.
5. **Ensure that resources are released:**
    - Always close database connections and release resources in a `Finally` block or similar structure to avoid memory leaks and connection issues.

Example of Data Validation and Error Handling Combined:

```
Dim connectionString As String = "Data Source=localhost;Initial
Catalog=MyDatabase;Integrated Security=True"
Dim connection As New SqlConnection(connectionString)

' Validate user input (e.g., email)
Dim email As String = txtEmail.Text
```

```
If Not Regex.IsMatch(email, "^[\w-]+(\.[\w-]+)*@([\w-]+\.)+[a-zA-Z]{2,7}$")
Then
    MessageBox.Show("Invalid email format.")
    Return
End If

Try
    connection.Open()   ' Open the connection
    ' Execute SQL commands
    Dim query As String = "INSERT INTO Users (Email) VALUES ('" & email &
"')"
    Dim command As New SqlCommand(query, connection)
    command.ExecuteNonQuery()
    MessageBox.Show("Data inserted successfully.")
Catch ex As SqlException
    MessageBox.Show("Database error: " & ex.Message)
Catch ex As Exception
    MessageBox.Show("An unexpected error occurred: " & ex.Message)
Finally
    connection.Close()   ' Close the connection
End Try
```

In this example, the email is validated first. If the validation passes, the code proceeds to open the connection and execute an SQL query. If an error occurs at any point, the exception is caught, and the user is informed without causing the application to crash.

30 multiple-choice questions (MCQs):

7.1 Introduction to Databases and VB.NET

1. **What does ADO.NET stand for in VB.NET?**
   - A) Active Data Objects .NET
   - B) ActiveX Data Objects .NET
   - C) Advanced Data Objects .NET
   - D) Active Data Online .NET

   Answer: B) ActiveX Data Objects .NET
2. **Which of the following databases can be integrated with VB.NET through ADO.NET?**
   - A) SQL Server
   - B) MySQL
   - C) Oracle
   - D) All of the above

   Answer: D) All of the above
3. **What is the main purpose of a database in VB.NET?**
   - A) Store data
   - B) Manage data
   - C) Perform queries
   - D) All of the above

   Answer: D) All of the above
4. **What does a connection string contain?**

- A) Database Name
- B) Server Name
- C) Authentication Credentials
- D) All of the above

Answer: D) All of the above

7.2 Database Connectivity in VB.NET

5. **What is the first step when establishing a connection to a database in VB.NET?**
   - A) Write the SQL query
   - B) Create a connection string
   - C) Define a DataAdapter
   - D) Create a DataGridView

   Answer: B) Create a connection string
6. **Which ADO.NET class is used to connect to a SQL Server database?**
   - A) SqlConnection
   - B) OdbcConnection
   - C) OleDbConnection
   - D) SqlCommand

   Answer: A) SqlConnection
7. **Which of the following is a correct example of a connection string for SQL Server?**
   - A) "Server=myServer;Database=myDB;User Id=myUser;Password=myPass;"
   - B) "Data Source=myServer;Initial Catalog=myDB;Integrated Security=True"
   - C) "Server=myServer;Database=myDB;Integrated Security=True"
   - D) "DataSource=myServer;Authentication=myAuth;Database=myDB;"

   Answer: B) "Data Source=myServer;Initial Catalog=myDB;Integrated Security=True"
8. **Which ADO.NET provider is used for connecting to Microsoft Access databases?**
   - A) SqlConnection
   - B) OdbcConnection
   - C) OleDbConnection
   - D) OracleConnection

   Answer: C) OleDbConnection
9. **What is the purpose of a connection string in ADO.NET?**
   - A) To hold SQL commands
   - B) To provide the details required for database connection
   - C) To execute queries
   - D) To format the output

   Answer: B) To provide the details required for database connection

---

7.3 Using Server Explorer for Database Connections

10. **Which window in Visual Studio allows you to manage database connections?**
    - A) Solution Explorer
    - B) Properties Window
    - C) Server Explorer
    - D) Object Explorer

    Answer: C) Server Explorer
11. **How do you add a new database connection in Server Explorer?**
    - A) Right-click the project and choose "Add New Database"
    - B) Right-click on "Data Connections" and select "Add Connection"
    - C) Open the "Add New Item" window and select "Database"
    - D) Use the "Query Designer" window

    Answer: B) Right-click on "Data Connections" and select "Add Connection"
12. **What can you view and manage from the Server Explorer in Visual Studio?**
    - A) Tables
    - B) Views
    - C) Stored Procedures
    - D) All of the above

    Answer: D) All of the above
13. **Which of the following can be done directly from the Server Explorer window?**
    - A) Execute SQL queries
    - B) Edit database tables
    - C) View the results of SQL queries
    - D) All of the above

    Answer: D) All of the above

7.4 Querying Databases with ADO.NET

14. **Which class in ADO.NET is used to execute SQL queries?**
    - A) SqlConnection
    - B) SqlCommand
    - C) SqlDataReader
    - D) SqlDataAdapter

    Answer: B) SqlCommand
15. **Which method in ADO.NET is used to execute a SQL query and retrieve data?**
    - A) ExecuteNonQuery()
    - B) ExecuteReader()
    - C) ExecuteScalar()
    - D) ExecuteQuery()

    Answer: B) ExecuteReader()
16. **What is the purpose of SqlDataReader in ADO.NET?**
    - A) To execute SQL commands
    - B) To fetch data from a database in a forward-only manner
    - C) To create database tables

- D) To close database connections

  Answer: B) To fetch data from a database in a forward-only manner

17. **Which of the following statements is used to retrieve data from a database using ADO.NET?**
    - A) SELECT
    - B) INSERT
    - C) UPDATE
    - D) DELETE

    Answer: A) SELECT
18. **Which method in SqlDataReader is used to read a row of data?**
    - A) ReadRow()
    - B) MoveNext()
    - C) Read()
    - D) Next()

    Answer: C) Read()

7.5 Working with DataGridView Control

19. **Which control in VB.NET is used to display tabular data from a database?**
    - A) TextBox
    - B) DataGridView
    - C) Label
    - D) Button

    Answer: B) DataGridView
20. **Which ADO.NET class is used to fill a DataTable with data?**
    - A) SqlConnection
    - B) SqlCommand
    - C) SqlDataAdapter
    - D) SqlDataReader

    Answer: C) SqlDataAdapter
21. **How can you bind a DataTable to a DataGridView control in VB.NET?**
    - A) Using DataGridView1.DataSource
    - B) Using DataGridView1.Items
    - C) Using DataGridView1.Rows
    - D) Using DataGridView1.DataBindings

    Answer: A) Using DataGridView1.DataSource
22. **Which operation can you perform on a DataGridView control?**
    - A) Add records
    - B) Edit records
    - C) Delete records
    - D) All of the above

    Answer: D) All of the above
23. **To update the database after editing a DataGridView, what should you do?**
    - A) Bind the DataGridView again

- B) Refresh the DataGridView
- C) Use SQL commands like UPDATE or INSERT
- D) No action is required

  Answer: C) Use SQL commands like UPDATE or INSERT

7.6 Multiple Table Connections

24. **Which SQL keyword is used to combine data from multiple tables based on a related column?**
    - A) UNION
    - B) JOIN
    - C) MERGE
    - D) COMBINE

    Answer: B) JOIN
25. **Which type of JOIN returns all rows from the left table and matching rows from the right table?**
    - A) INNER JOIN
    - B) LEFT JOIN
    - C) RIGHT JOIN
    - D) FULL JOIN

    Answer: B) LEFT JOIN
26. **Which SQL clause would you use to combine data from two related tables, Employees and Departments?**
    - A) SELECT * FROM Employees INNER JOIN Departments ON Employees.DepartmentID = Departments.DepartmentID
    - B) SELECT * FROM Employees, Departments WHERE Employees.DepartmentID = Departments.DepartmentID
    - C) SELECT * FROM Employees LEFT JOIN Departments ON Employees.DepartmentID = Departments.DepartmentID
    - D) All of the above

    Answer: D) All of the above

7.7 Data Validation and Error Handling

27. **Which VB.NET class is used to handle database errors gracefully?**
    - A) TryCatch
    - B) SqlException
    - C) Exception
    - D) ErrorHandler

    Answer: C) Exception
28. **Which VB.NET function is commonly used to validate email format?**
    - A) Regex.IsMatch

- B) EmailValidator.IsValid
- C) Email.IsValidFormat
- D) IsEmail

Answer: A) Regex.IsMatch

29. **What happens if data fails validation before being inserted into the database?**
    - A) Data is inserted into the database anyway
    - B) The application throws an error and stops
    - C) The data is rejected and an error message is displayed
    - D) Data is saved in a temporary state

    Answer: C) The data is rejected and an error message is displayed
30. **Which of the following is an example of error handling for database operations?**
    - A) If error then exit
    - B) Try…Catch blocks
    - C) If Not Valid then rollback
    - D) Try…Except

    Answer: B) Try…Catch blocks

1. Establishing a Connection to a SQL Server Database

Question:
Write a VB.NET code snippet to establish a connection to a SQL Server database using the `SqlConnection` class.

Answer:

```
Dim connectionString As String = "Data Source=localhost;Initial
Catalog=MyDatabase;Integrated Security=True"
Dim connection As New SqlConnection(connectionString)

Try
    connection.Open()
    Console.WriteLine("Connection successful.")
Catch ex As Exception
    Console.WriteLine("Error: " & ex.Message)
Finally
    connection.Close()
End Try
```

---

2. Executing SQL Query with ADO.NET

Question:
Write a VB.NET code snippet that executes a SELECT SQL query to retrieve all records from a table named `Employees` using ADO.NET.

Answer:

```
Dim connectionString As String = "Data Source=localhost;Initial
Catalog=MyDatabase;Integrated Security=True"
Dim connection As New SqlConnection(connectionString)
Dim query As String = "SELECT * FROM Employees"
Dim command As New SqlCommand(query, connection)

Try
    connection.Open()
    Dim reader As SqlDataReader = command.ExecuteReader()
    While reader.Read()
        Console.WriteLine(reader("EmployeeName"))
    End While
    reader.Close()
Catch ex As Exception
    Console.WriteLine("Error: " & ex.Message)
Finally
    connection.Close()
End Try
```

---

3. Retrieving Data with SqlDataReader

Question:
Write a VB.NET code to retrieve employee names and their IDs from the `Employees` table using `SqlDataReader`.

Answer:

```
Dim connectionString As String = "Data Source=localhost;Initial
Catalog=MyDatabase;Integrated Security=True"
Dim connection As New SqlConnection(connectionString)
Dim query As String = "SELECT EmployeeID, EmployeeName FROM Employees"
Dim command As New SqlCommand(query, connection)

Try
    connection.Open()
    Dim reader As SqlDataReader = command.ExecuteReader()
    While reader.Read()
        Console.WriteLine("ID: " & reader("EmployeeID") & " Name: " &
reader("EmployeeName"))
    End While
    reader.Close()
Catch ex As Exception
    Console.WriteLine("Error: " & ex.Message)
Finally
    connection.Close()
End Try
```

---

4. Binding Data to DataGridView

Question:
Write a VB.NET code to bind data from the `Employees` table to a `DataGridView` control.

Answer:

```
Dim connectionString As String = "Data Source=localhost;Initial
Catalog=MyDatabase;Integrated Security=True"
Dim connection As New SqlConnection(connectionString)
Dim query As String = "SELECT * FROM Employees"
Dim adapter As New SqlDataAdapter(query, connection)
Dim dataTable As New DataTable()

Try
    adapter.Fill(dataTable)
    DataGridView1.DataSource = dataTable
Catch ex As Exception
    MessageBox.Show("Error: " & ex.Message)
End Try
```

---

5. Adding a Record to a Database

Question:
Write a VB.NET code to insert a new record into the `Employees` table.

Answer:

```
Dim connectionString As String = "Data Source=localhost;Initial
Catalog=MyDatabase;Integrated Security=True"
Dim connection As New SqlConnection(connectionString)
Dim query As String = "INSERT INTO Employees (EmployeeName, Department)
VALUES ('John Doe', 'HR')"
Dim command As New SqlCommand(query, connection)

Try
    connection.Open()
    command.ExecuteNonQuery()
    MessageBox.Show("Record added successfully.")
Catch ex As Exception
    MessageBox.Show("Error: " & ex.Message)
Finally
    connection.Close()
End Try
```

---

6. Updating a Record in the Database

Question:
Write a VB.NET code to update an employee's department in the `Employees` table where `EmployeeID` is 101.

Answer:

```
Dim connectionString As String = "Data Source=localhost;Initial
Catalog=MyDatabase;Integrated Security=True"
Dim connection As New SqlConnection(connectionString)
Dim query As String = "UPDATE Employees SET Department = 'Finance' WHERE
EmployeeID = 101"
Dim command As New SqlCommand(query, connection)

Try
    connection.Open()
    command.ExecuteNonQuery()
    MessageBox.Show("Record updated successfully.")
Catch ex As Exception
    MessageBox.Show("Error: " & ex.Message)
Finally
    connection.Close()
End Try
```

---

7. Deleting a Record from the Database

Question:
Write a VB.NET code to delete a record from the `Employees` table where `EmployeeID` is 101.

Answer:

```
Dim connectionString As String = "Data Source=localhost;Initial
Catalog=MyDatabase;Integrated Security=True"
Dim connection As New SqlConnection(connectionString)
Dim query As String = "DELETE FROM Employees WHERE EmployeeID = 101"
Dim command As New SqlCommand(query, connection)

Try
    connection.Open()
    command.ExecuteNonQuery()
    MessageBox.Show("Record deleted successfully.")
Catch ex As Exception
    MessageBox.Show("Error: " & ex.Message)
Finally
    connection.Close()
End Try
```

---

8. Using INNER JOIN to Combine Data from Two Tables

Question:
Write a SQL query to combine data from two tables `Employees` and `Departments` where `DepartmentID` matches in both tables. Display `EmployeeName` and `DepartmentName`.

Answer:

```
SELECT Employees.EmployeeName, Departments.DepartmentName
FROM Employees
```

```
INNER JOIN Departments ON Employees.DepartmentID = Departments.DepartmentID
```

---

9. Validating Email Input with Regular Expressions

Question:
Write a VB.NET code to validate an email input using regular expressions before saving it to the database.

Answer:

```
Dim email As String = txtEmail.Text
Dim emailPattern As String = "^[\w-]+(\.[\w-]+)*@([\w-]+\.)+[a-zA-Z]{2,7}$"

If Not Regex.IsMatch(email, emailPattern) Then
    MessageBox.Show("Invalid email format.")
    Return
End If

' Proceed to save email to the database
```

---

10. Error Handling for Database Operations

Question:
Write a VB.NET code that handles SQL errors using a Try…Catch block while trying to open a database connection.

Answer:

```
Dim connectionString As String = "Data Source=localhost;Initial
Catalog=MyDatabase;Integrated Security=True"
Dim connection As New SqlConnection(connectionString)

Try
    connection.Open()
    ' Perform database operations here
    MessageBox.Show("Connection successful.")
Catch ex As SqlException
    MessageBox.Show("Error while accessing the database: " & ex.Message)
Finally
    connection.Close()
End Try
```

CHAPTER 8: ADVANCED FEATURES IN VB.NET

8.1 Working with Files and Streams

In VB.NET, handling files and streams is essential for reading from and writing to files. The **System.IO** namespace provides various classes to help developers interact with files. Specifically, classes like `StreamReader`, `StreamWriter`, and `File` are commonly used for reading and writing files in a variety of formats. Here's a detailed explanation of how to work with files and streams in VB.NET:

Reading Files

Reading files can be done in different ways depending on the requirements, such as reading the entire file at once or reading it line-by-line. VB.NET provides the `StreamReader` class for line-by-line reading or the `File.ReadAllText` method for reading an entire file at once.

Using StreamReader to Read Files Line-by-Line:

`StreamReader` is ideal for reading text files in a sequential manner. The `StreamReader` reads characters from a byte stream and can be used for efficient reading, especially when you need to process files line by line.

- **Example: Reading a file line by line**:

```
Dim reader As New StreamReader("C:\path\to\yourfile.txt")
While Not reader.EndOfStream
    ' Read the next line from the file
    Console.WriteLine(reader.ReadLine())
End While
reader.Close()
```

  - **Explanation**:
    - `StreamReader` is initialized with the file path.
    - The `While` loop reads each line of the file until `EndOfStream` is reached.
    - `ReadLine` retrieves each line in the file one by one, which is then printed to the console.
    - `reader.Close()` ensures the file is properly closed once done.

Using File.ReadAllText to Read an Entire File:

`File.ReadAllText` reads the entire contents of a file into a single string. This method is useful when you need to process the entire file content as one block, rather than reading line by line.

- **Example: Reading an entire file into a string**:

```
Dim content As String = File.ReadAllText("C:\path\to\yourfile.txt")
Console.WriteLine(content)
```

- **Explanation**:
  - `File.ReadAllText` reads the entire file and stores its content into the `content` string.
  - The entire content is then printed to the console.

Writing Files

When you need to write data to a file, VB.NET provides the `StreamWriter` class for more complex writing tasks, such as writing line by line or appending to a file. Additionally, the `File.WriteAllText` method is available for writing an entire string to a file at once.

Using StreamWriter to Write Data to a File:

`StreamWriter` is used for writing characters to a file, and it offers methods such as `WriteLine` for writing a line of text and `Write` for writing text without a newline.

- **Example: Writing a line of text to a file**:

```
Dim writer As New StreamWriter("C:\path\to\yourfile.txt")
writer.WriteLine("Hello, World!")
writer.Close()
```

  - **Explanation**:
    - `StreamWriter` is initialized with the file path.
    - `WriteLine` writes a line of text to the file.
    - `writer.Close()` ensures that the writer is closed and the file is saved.

Using File.WriteAllText to Write an Entire String to a File:

`File.WriteAllText` allows you to write a full string to a file in one go. This is useful when you have all the data ready to be written at once.

- **Example: Writing a full string to a file**:

```
Dim content As String = "This is the content to be written to the
file."
File.WriteAllText("C:\path\to\yourfile.txt", content)
```

  - **Explanation**:
    - `File.WriteAllText` writes the string content to the file. If the file already exists, it is overwritten.

File Handling with StreamReader and StreamWriter

Both `StreamReader` and `StreamWriter` are used for more granular control over file reading and writing.

Using StreamReader:

`StreamReader` is used when you need to read text files in a more controlled manner, such as reading line-by-line or reading the whole file.

- **Example of reading a file with `StreamReader`:**

```
Dim reader As New StreamReader("C:\path\to\yourfile.txt")
Dim line As String
While (reader.Peek() >= 0) ' Peek checks if there is data to read
    line = reader.ReadLine()
    Console.WriteLine(line) ' Print each line
End While
reader.Close()
```

  - **Explanation:**
    - `Peek` checks if there is more data available to read. If there is data, `ReadLine` retrieves one line at a time.
    - This approach is efficient when processing large files line-by-line.
    - After reading all lines, the `StreamReader` is closed to release resources.

Using StreamWriter:

`StreamWriter` is used to write text to files. You can control how text is written, such as appending to a file or creating a new file.

- **Example of writing to a file with `StreamWriter`:**

```
Dim writer As New StreamWriter("C:\path\to\yourfile.txt")
writer.WriteLine("This is a new line of text.")
writer.Close()
```

  - **Explanation:**
    - `StreamWriter` is used to write a line of text to the specified file.
    - `Close` is used to close the stream after writing.

Key Points to Remember:

- **StreamReader**:
  - Efficient for reading text files.
  - Allows reading the file line by line.

    - Can also read the entire file using `ReadToEnd()`.
- **StreamWriter**:
    - Used to write text to files.
    - Can create new files or overwrite existing ones.
    - Use `WriteLine` to add a new line of text and `Write` to append text without a newline.
- **File.ReadAllText** and **File.WriteAllText**:
    - These are simpler methods to read or write an entire file in one go.
- Always ensure that after working with files, the file streams are closed properly (e.g., using `Close()` or a `Using` statement) to release system resources.

By understanding these basic file handling techniques, you can efficiently manage file input/output operations in your VB.NET applications.

8.2 Multithreading in VB.NET

Multithreading is a fundamental concept in modern programming, allowing multiple tasks to run concurrently on separate threads. This is especially useful in making applications more efficient by performing several operations at once without blocking the main execution flow.

Introduction to Threads in VB.NET

In VB.NET, a **thread** represents an individual unit of execution. Each thread can run a task or operation, and when multiple threads run concurrently, this is known as **multithreading**. Multithreading enables a program to perform multiple operations simultaneously, making better use of CPU resources and improving performance, especially for time-consuming operations.

Why Use Multithreading?

- **Background Tasks:** You can offload long-running tasks like file reading, database queries, or network communication to a separate thread to avoid blocking the main thread (UI thread), which keeps the application responsive.
- **Parallel Execution:** It allows different tasks, such as calculations, data processing, or downloading files, to run simultaneously on different processors or cores.
- **Asynchronous Operations:** Time-consuming operations can run asynchronously, which means that the main application thread can continue processing user input or perform other tasks without waiting for the background task to finish.

Creating and Managing Threads

In VB.NET, threads are typically managed using the `Thread` class from the **System.Threading** namespace. Threads can be created, started, and managed with various methods provided by the `Thread` class.

Creating a Thread:

To create a new thread in VB.NET, you can use the `Thread` class and pass a method that will be executed when the thread is started.

- **Example of creating and starting a thread:**

```
Imports System.Threading

Sub Main()
    ' Create a new thread that will execute the PrintNumbers method
    Dim t As New Thread(AddressOf PrintNumbers)
    t.Start()   ' Start the thread
End Sub

Sub PrintNumbers()
    For i As Integer = 1 To 10
        Console.WriteLine(i)
        Thread.Sleep(500)   ' Sleep for 500 milliseconds
    Next
End Sub
```

  - **Explanation:**
    - `Thread(AddressOf PrintNumbers)` creates a new thread and specifies the method (`PrintNumbers`) that the thread will execute.
    - `t.Start()` starts the thread, and it begins executing the `PrintNumbers` method.
    - In the `PrintNumbers` method, the thread prints numbers 1 to 10 with a 500-millisecond delay between each print (using `Thread.Sleep(500)`).
    - `Thread.Sleep(500)` simulates a time-consuming operation, like waiting for a network response or processing a large amount of data.

Managing Threads:

Once you create and start a thread, you may need to manage its execution, such as waiting for it to finish or checking its status. Here are some methods to manage threads in VB.NET:

1. Join:

The `Join` method is used to make the calling thread wait until the thread it is called on completes its execution. This is useful when you want to ensure that a thread finishes before proceeding with further operations.

- **Example of using `Join`:**

```
Dim t As New Thread(AddressOf PrintNumbers)
t.Start()
t.Join()   ' Wait for the thread to complete
Console.WriteLine("Thread finished execution.")
```

  - **Explanation:**
    - After starting the thread `t` using `t.Start()`, the `t.Join()` method is called.
    - `t.Join()` causes the main thread to wait until the thread `t` has completed.
    - After the thread completes, the message "Thread finished execution." is printed to the console.

2. Abort (Not Recommended):

The `Abort` method is used to forcefully terminate a thread. However, it is generally **not recommended** to use this method because it can cause unexpected behavior and leave resources uncleaned. If you need to stop a thread gracefully, consider using flags or cancellation tokens instead.

- **Example (Not Recommended):**

```
Dim t As New Thread(AddressOf PrintNumbers)
t.Start()
' t.Abort()   ' Not recommended
```

3. IsAlive:

The `IsAlive` property checks if a thread is still running. It returns `True` if the thread is running and `False` if the thread has finished its execution.

- **Example of using `IsAlive`:**

```
Dim t As New Thread(AddressOf PrintNumbers)
t.Start()

' Check if the thread is still running
If t.IsAlive Then
    Console.WriteLine("Thread is still running.")
Else
    Console.WriteLine("Thread has finished.")
End If
```

  - **Explanation:**
    - `t.IsAlive` checks the status of the thread.
    - If the thread is still running, it prints "Thread is still running." Otherwise, it prints "Thread has finished."

When working with multiple threads, you must ensure that shared data is accessed in a thread-safe manner to avoid issues like race conditions (where multiple threads try to access the same data simultaneously).

- **Locks and Mutexes:**
  - You can use the `SyncLock` statement in VB.NET to ensure that only one thread can access a block of code at a time.
  - Example:

```
Dim lockObject As New Object()
SyncLock lockObject
    ' Critical section: Only one thread can execute this at a
time
    Console.WriteLine("Thread-safe operation")
End SyncLock
```

- **Thread Synchronization:**
  - Another way to synchronize threads is using `Mutex` or `Monitor` objects for more complex scenarios.

Key Takeaways:

1. **Threading Basics**: Threads allow your program to perform multiple tasks concurrently, leading to better CPU utilization and responsiveness.
2. **Creating Threads**: In VB.NET, threads are created using the `Thread` class, and a method is passed to define the task the thread will execute.
3. **Managing Threads**: You can manage threads with methods like `Join` (wait for the thread to finish), `IsAlive` (check if the thread is still running), and `Abort` (forcefully stop the thread, though this is discouraged).
4. **Thread Safety**: When multiple threads interact with shared data, you need to ensure thread safety using synchronization techniques like `SyncLock`, `Mutex`, or other locking mechanisms.

Multithreading can significantly improve the performance and responsiveness of your applications by allowing long-running tasks to run concurrently while keeping the main thread free for other operations.

8.3 Working with Collections

In VB.NET, collections are used to store, manage, and manipulate groups of objects. Collections allow you to work with multiple elements of the same or different types, providing flexible ways to handle data. The most commonly used collection types are **Arrays**, **Lists**, and **Dictionaries**.

Arrays

An **array** in VB.NET is a fixed-size collection that can hold elements of the same type (e.g., all integers, all strings). Once an array is initialized with a certain size, it cannot grow or shrink. Arrays are useful when you know the number of elements in advance.

Key Characteristics:

- **Fixed Size:** You cannot resize an array after it is created.
- **Indexed Access:** Elements are accessed using a zero-based index.
- **Homogeneous Data:** All elements in an array must be of the same type.

Example of an Array:

```
Dim numbers() As Integer = {1, 2, 3, 4, 5}
Console.WriteLine(numbers(2)) ' Output: 3
```

- **Explanation:** The array `numbers` contains integers. The element at index 2 (which is the value `3`) is accessed and printed.

Lists

A **List(Of T)** is a generic collection in VB.NET that can dynamically resize and is more flexible than an array. Lists are useful when the number of elements might change during runtime, as you can add, remove, and modify items in the list.

Key Characteristics:

- **Dynamic Size:** Lists can grow or shrink dynamically as elements are added or removed.
- **Generic Type:** You can define the type of elements the list will contain (e.g., `List(Of Integer)`).
- **Indexed Access:** Elements can be accessed using an index, similar to arrays.

Example of a List:

```
Dim numbers As New List(Of Integer)()
numbers.Add(1)
numbers.Add(2)
numbers.Add(3)
Console.WriteLine(numbers(1)) ' Output: 2
```

- **Explanation:** A `List(Of Integer)` is created and populated with the values `1`, `2`, and `3`. The element at index `1` (which is `2`) is accessed and printed.

Dictionaries

A **Dictionary(Of TKey, TValue)** is a collection that stores key-value pairs, where each key must be unique. It provides fast lookups based on the key. It is ideal for scenarios where you need to retrieve values using a specific key.

Key Characteristics:

- **Key-Value Pairs:** Each element is stored as a pair consisting of a unique key and an associated value.
- **Fast Lookups:** You can access the value of an element by using its key.
- **Key Type and Value Type:** You define the types of both the key and the value when creating the dictionary.

Example of a Dictionary:

```
Dim studentGrades As New Dictionary(Of String, Integer)()
studentGrades.Add("Alice", 90)
studentGrades.Add("Bob", 85)
Console.WriteLine(studentGrades("Alice")) ' Output: 90
```

- **Explanation:** A `Dictionary` is created with `String` as the key type (representing student names) and `Integer` as the value type (representing student grades). The grade for "Alice" is accessed using the key `"Alice"`.

Collection Manipulation and LINQ

LINQ (Language Integrated Query) is a powerful feature in VB.NET that allows you to query collections, arrays, and other data sources in a concise and readable way. LINQ can be used to filter, sort, group, and aggregate data in collections.

Filtering Data with LINQ:

You can use LINQ to filter data based on specific criteria, making it easy to extract only the data you need.

Example: Filtering even numbers from a List

```
Dim numbers As New List(Of Integer)({1, 2, 3, 4, 5, 6})
Dim evenNumbers = From n In numbers Where n Mod 2 = 0 Select n
For Each num In evenNumbers
    Console.WriteLine(num)
Next
```

- **Explanation:** The LINQ query `From n In numbers Where n Mod 2 = 0 Select n` selects only the even numbers from the list `numbers`. The `For Each` loop prints each even number (i.e., `2, 4, 6`).

Sorting Data with LINQ:

LINQ can also be used to sort collections. You can use the `Order By` clause to sort data in ascending or descending order.

Example: Sorting a List of integers

```
Dim numbers As New List(Of Integer)({5, 2, 9, 1, 4})
Dim sortedNumbers = From n In numbers Order By n Select n
For Each num In sortedNumbers
    Console.WriteLine(num)
Next
```

- **Explanation:** The LINQ query `From n In numbers Order By n Select n` sorts the numbers in ascending order. The `For Each` loop prints the sorted numbers: `1, 2, 4, 5, 9.`

Other Collection Operations with LINQ

LINQ can be used for various other operations on collections such as:

- **Aggregating Data**: You can sum, average, count, or perform other aggregate operations.
  - Example: `Dim sum = numbers.Sum()`
- **Grouping Data**: You can group data based on a key.
  - Example: `Dim groupedNumbers = From n In numbers Group By n Mod 2 Into Group`
- **Joining Data**: LINQ can join multiple collections based on a common key.
  - Example: `Join` keyword can be used to combine two collections based on a matching field.

Key Takeaways:

- **Arrays** are fixed-size collections, ideal when the number of elements is known in advance and does not change.
- **Lists** are dynamic collections, offering flexibility for adding and removing elements during runtime.
- **Dictionaries** store key-value pairs and are ideal for fast lookups by key.
- **LINQ** makes querying and manipulating collections easy, allowing you to filter, sort, and aggregate data in a readable and declarative way.
- Collections like **Arrays**, **Lists**, and **Dictionaries** can be manipulated with LINQ to perform complex operations such as filtering, sorting, and grouping.

8.4 Windows Services in VB.NET

A **Windows Service** is a type of application that is designed to run in the background on a Windows operating system. It operates independently of user interaction and does not have a graphical user interface (GUI). Windows Services are typically used for tasks that need to run continuously or on a schedule, such as system maintenance tasks, monitoring services, or background operations like handling updates, backups, or long-running processes.

What is a Windows Service?

Windows Services are primarily used for the following purposes:

- **Monitoring system resources**: Services can monitor system activity such as disk space, CPU usage, network traffic, etc.
- **Handling periodic tasks**: Services can perform routine tasks at specific intervals (e.g., backing up files, sending email alerts, performing maintenance tasks).
- **Interacting with other applications**: Services often communicate with other services or applications in a seamless, background manner.

Key Characteristics of Windows Services:

- **Runs in the Background**: A Windows Service runs as a background process, meaning it doesn't need a user interface and doesn't interact with users directly.
- **No User Interface**: Services do not have windows, buttons, or GUI elements. They are meant to be managed through the Services Management Console or command-line tools.
- **Automatic Start**: A Windows Service can be configured to start automatically when the system boots up or to start manually.
- **System-Level Permissions**: Services usually run with higher system privileges and can perform tasks that require administrative access.

Creating and Deploying a Windows Service in VB.NET

1. Create a New Windows Service Project

In Visual Studio, you can create a Windows Service project by selecting "Windows Service" as the project type. This will generate a template that includes a base service class and methods for handling the service's lifecycle events.

Steps to create a Windows Service:

1. Open Visual Studio.
2. Select **File** > **New** > **Project**.
3. Choose **Windows Service** from the list of project templates.
4. Name the project and click **Create**.

Visual Studio will create a basic `Service1` class with a template that includes the `OnStart` and `OnStop` methods, which are used to define the behavior of the service when it starts and stops.

2. Write Service Code

In a Windows Service, the logic for starting and stopping the service is written in the **`OnStart`** and **`OnStop`** methods, which are overridden from the base `ServiceBase` class.

Here's an example of a simple service:

```
Imports System.ServiceProcess
Imports System.Diagnostics

Public Class Service1
    Inherits ServiceBase

    ' Constructor to set the service name
    Public Sub New()
        Me.ServiceName = "MyBackgroundService"
    End Sub

    ' Code to execute when the service starts
    Protected Overrides Sub OnStart(ByVal args() As String)
        ' Write a log entry or initialize resources
        EventLog.WriteEntry("Service Started")
    End Sub

    ' Code to execute when the service stops
    Protected Overrides Sub OnStop()
        ' Clean up or release resources
        EventLog.WriteEntry("Service Stopped")
    End Sub

End Class
```

In this example:

- The **`OnStart`** method contains the logic that will be executed when the service is started (e.g., opening a file, initiating a process, logging an event).
- The **`OnStop`** method contains the logic to be executed when the service is stopped (e.g., closing files, stopping threads).

3. Install the Service

Once you have written your service code, you need to **install** it onto the system. This allows Windows to manage and control the service.

To install a Windows Service:

1. **Build the service project** in Visual Studio (make sure the service is compiled).
2. **Use InstallUtil** to install the service:

- Open the **Command Prompt** as Administrator.
- Navigate to the folder containing your compiled `.exe` file.
- Run the following command:

```
InstallUtil YourService.exe
```

- **InstallUtil** is a tool provided by the .NET Framework that installs the service and registers it with Windows. Once installed, the service will appear in the **Services Management Console**.

4. Start and Manage the Service

Once the service is installed, you can manage it through the **Services** management console in Windows. The console allows you to:

- **Start** the service
- **Stop** the service
- **Pause** or **Resume** the service
- **Restart** the service
- **Set service properties**, including startup type (automatic, manual, or disabled)

To access the Services console:

1. Press `Win + R`, type `services.msc`, and press **Enter**.
2. Find your service by its name and right-click to manage it.

5. Deploying the Service

To deploy a Windows Service to another machine:

1. Create a **deployment package** that includes the service executable, configuration files, and any dependencies.
2. Use **InstallUtil** to install the service on the target machine.
3. Alternatively, you can create an **Installer Project** in Visual Studio to automate the installation and setup process, which is useful for deployment across multiple systems.

Managing Windows Services

Windows Services can be managed and configured using several tools in addition to the Services Management Console:

- **Service Control Manager (SCM)**: A Windows component used to start, stop, and configure services from the command line. You can use the `sc` command to interact with services. For example:

```
sc start MyBackgroundService
sc stop MyBackgroundService
```

- **Task Scheduler**: Windows Services can be configured to run at specific times or after certain triggers using the **Task Scheduler**.
- **PowerShell**: You can manage services via PowerShell commands such as `Start-Service`, `Stop-Service`, and `Get-Service`.

Windows Service Lifecycle

A Windows Service has a well-defined lifecycle:

1. **Installation**: The service is installed and registered with the Windows operating system.
2. **Start**: The service is started either manually or automatically, and the `OnStart` method is invoked.
3. **Running**: The service performs its operations as designed (e.g., monitoring, processing tasks).
4. **Stop**: When the service is stopped, the `OnStop` method is invoked to clean up resources.
5. **Uninstallation**: The service is uninstalled, which removes it from the system.

Benefits of Using Windows Services

- **Background Operations**: Windows Services run independently of user sessions, making them ideal for long-running or periodic background tasks.
- **No User Interaction**: Services do not require user interaction, making them suitable for system-level tasks.
- **Automatic Start**: Windows Services can be configured to start automatically when the system boots, ensuring that critical background tasks are always running.
- **System Resources**: Services can be set to run with elevated privileges, allowing them to access system resources and perform operations that require admin rights.

30 multiple-choice questions (MCQs):

8.1 Working with Files and Streams

Reading and Writing Files in VB.NET / File Handling with StreamReader and StreamWriter

1. **Which class in VB.NET is used to read text from a file?**
   - A) FileStream
   - B) StreamReader
   - C) FileReader
   - D) FileReaderStream

- **Answer:** B) StreamReader

2. **Which method is used to write text to a file in VB.NET?**
   - A) WriteText
   - B) StreamWriter.Write
   - C) File.Write
   - D) StreamReader.Write
   - **Answer:** B) StreamWriter.Write
3. **How can you read the entire contents of a file as a string in VB.NET?**
   - A) File.ReadAllText
   - B) StreamReader.ReadToEnd
   - C) File.ReadLine
   - D) StreamReader.ReadLine
   - **Answer:** A) File.ReadAllText
4. **Which method reads a line from a file using the StreamReader class?**
   - A) ReadByte()
   - B) ReadLine()
   - C) ReadText()
   - D) ReadString()
   - **Answer:** B) ReadLine()
5. **What happens if you attempt to read past the end of a file using StreamReader?**
   - A) The program crashes.
   - B) An exception is thrown.
   - C) It returns `null` or an empty string.
   - D) It starts reading from the beginning.
   - **Answer:** C) It returns `null` or an empty string.
6. **Which method is used to append text to a file using StreamWriter?**
   - A) AppendText()
   - B) WriteLine()
   - C) Write()
   - D) Append()
   - **Answer:** A) AppendText()
7. **What should be done after using StreamReader or StreamWriter to ensure resources are freed?**
   - A) Close() method should be called.
   - B) Dispose() method should be called.
   - C) File should be closed manually.
   - D) Both A and B are correct.
   - **Answer:** D) Both A and B are correct.
8. **Which of the following is true when writing to a file using StreamWriter?**
   - A) It overwrites the existing file by default.
   - B) It appends to the existing file by default.
   - C) It throws an error if the file exists.
   - D) It creates a new file even if one exists.
   - **Answer:** A) It overwrites the existing file by default.
9. **Which class in VB.NET is used to handle binary file reading and writing?**
   - A) BinaryReader
   - B) FileReader
   - C) StreamWriter

- D) FileStream
- **Answer:** A) BinaryReader

8.2 Multithreading in VB.NET

Introduction to Threads / Creating and Managing Threads

10. **Which namespace is used for working with threads in VB.NET?**

- A) System.Threading
- B) System.Task
- C) System.Collections
- D) System.IO
- **Answer:** A) System.Threading

11. **Which method is used to start a new thread in VB.NET?**

- A) Start()
- B) Run()
- C) Execute()
- D) Begin()
- **Answer:** A) Start()

12. **What method is used to pause the execution of the current thread for a specified time in VB.NET?**

- A) Wait()
- B) Pause()
- C) Sleep()
- D) Halt()
- **Answer:** C) Sleep()

13. **Which property of a thread in VB.NET is used to check if the thread is still running?**

- A) IsAlive
- B) IsRunning
- C) Status
- D) IsActive
- **Answer:** A) IsAlive

14. **Which of the following is used to make the main thread wait for another thread to finish?**

- A) Join()
- B) Wait()
- C) Sleep()

- D) Await()
- **Answer:** A) Join()

15. **Which of the following statements is true about threads in VB.NET?**

- A) Each thread has its own memory space.
- B) Threads share the memory space of the process.
- C) Threads cannot share resources like variables.
- D) Threads cannot execute in parallel.
- **Answer:** B) Threads share the memory space of the process.

16. **What is the purpose of the `Thread.Abort()` method?**

- A) To forcibly stop a thread.
- B) To pause a thread.
- C) To restart a thread.
- D) To join a thread.
- **Answer:** A) To forcibly stop a thread.

8.3 Working with Collections

Lists, Arrays, and Dictionaries / Collection Manipulation and LINQ

17. **Which of the following is a fixed-size collection in VB.NET?**

- A) List(Of T)
- B) Dictionary(Of TKey, TValue)
- C) Array
- D) Queue
- **Answer:** C) Array

18. **Which collection type is ideal for dynamically adding and removing elements in VB.NET?**

- A) Array
- B) Dictionary
- C) List(Of T)
- D) Stack
- **Answer:** C) List(Of T)

19. **Which collection type stores key-value pairs in VB.NET?**

- A) List(Of T)
- B) Dictionary(Of TKey, TValue)
- C) Array
- D) Queue

- **Answer:** B) Dictionary(Of TKey, TValue)

20. **Which LINQ query operator can be used to filter elements based on a condition in VB.NET?**

- A) Select
- B) Where
- C) OrderBy
- D) GroupBy
- **Answer:** B) Where

21. **Which method is used to sort a collection in ascending order using LINQ?**

- A) SortBy()
- B) OrderBy()
- C) AscendingOrder()
- D) Sort()
- **Answer:** B) OrderBy()

22. **How do you access an element in a Dictionary by its key in VB.NET?**

- A) dictionary(key)
- B) dictionary.Item(key)
- C) dictionary.GetItem(key)
- D) Both A and B
- **Answer:** D) Both A and B

23. **What does the `FirstOrDefault()` method do in LINQ?**

- A) Returns the first element in a collection.
- B) Returns the first element or a default value if the collection is empty.
- C) Throws an exception if the collection is empty.
- D) Returns the last element in the collection.
- **Answer:** B) Returns the first element or a default value if the collection is empty.

24. **Which of the following methods can be used to add an element to a List in VB.NET?**

- A) Add()
- B) Insert()
- C) Append()
- D) Both A and B
- **Answer:** D) Both A and B

25. **Which LINQ method can be used to group elements based on a specified key in VB.NET?**

- A) GroupBy
- B) Aggregate
- C) Join

- D) SelectMany
- **Answer:** A) GroupBy

8.4 Windows Services in VB.NET

What is a Windows Service? / Creating and Deploying a Windows Service

26. **Which of the following is a primary characteristic of a Windows Service?**

- A) It has a graphical user interface.
- B) It runs in the background without user interaction.
- C) It can be run only from a web browser.
- D) It interacts with users through dialog boxes.
- **Answer:** B) It runs in the background without user interaction.

27. **In VB.NET, which method is overridden to define the behavior when a service starts?**

- A) OnStart()
- B) Start()
- C) Initialize()
- D) Begin()
- **Answer:** A) OnStart()

28. **Which method is used to stop a Windows Service in VB.NET?**

- A) OnEnd()
- B) OnStop()
- C) Stop()
- D) End()
- **Answer:** B) OnStop()

29. **What is required to install a Windows Service on a machine?**

- A) InstallUtil
- B) WebDeploy
- C) ClickOnce
- D) Windows Installer
- **Answer:** A) InstallUtil

30. **How do you create a new Windows Service project in Visual Studio?**

- A) Select "Windows Forms Application" project type.
- B) Select "Console Application" project type.
- C) Select "Windows Service" project type.
- D) Select "Web Application" project type.

- **Answer:** C) Select "Windows Service" project type.

8.1 Working with Files and Streams

Reading and Writing Files in VB.NET / File Handling with StreamReader and StreamWriter

1. Write a program that reads a text file line by line and prints its content to the console.

Answer:

```
Imports System.IO

Module Module1
    Sub Main()
        Dim reader As New StreamReader("C:\path\to\yourfile.txt")
        While Not reader.EndOfStream
            Console.WriteLine(reader.ReadLine())
        End While
        reader.Close()
    End Sub
End Module
```

---

2. Write a program that writes "Hello, World!" to a text file.

Answer:

```
Imports System.IO

Module Module1
    Sub Main()
        Dim writer As New StreamWriter("C:\path\to\yourfile.txt")
        writer.WriteLine("Hello, World!")
        writer.Close()
    End Sub
End Module
```

---

3. Write a program that appends a new line to an existing file.

Answer:

```
Imports System.IO

Module Module1
    Sub Main()
        Dim writer As New StreamWriter("C:\path\to\yourfile.txt", True) '
True to append
        writer.WriteLine("This is a new line.")
        writer.Close()
    End Sub
```

```
End Module
```

---

4. Write a program that reads a file and counts the number of lines in the file.

Answer:

```
Imports System.IO

Module Module1
    Sub Main()
        Dim reader As New StreamReader("C:\path\to\yourfile.txt")
        Dim lineCount As Integer = 0
        While Not reader.EndOfStream
            reader.ReadLine()
            lineCount += 1
        End While
        reader.Close()
        Console.WriteLine("Number of lines: " & lineCount)
    End Sub
End Module
```

---

5. Write a program that reads the entire contents of a file into a string and prints it.

Answer:

```
Imports System.IO

Module Module1
    Sub Main()
        Dim content As String = File.ReadAllText("C:\path\to\yourfile.txt")
        Console.WriteLine(content)
    End Sub
End Module
```

8.2 Multithreading in VB.NET

Introduction to Threads / Creating and Managing Threads

6. Write a program that creates a thread to print numbers from 1 to 10 with a delay of 1 second between each.

Answer:

```
Imports System.Threading

Module Module1
    Sub Main()
        Dim t As New Thread(AddressOf PrintNumbers)
```

```
        t.Start() ' Start the thread
    End Sub

    Sub PrintNumbers()
        For i As Integer = 1 To 10
            Console.WriteLine(i)
            Thread.Sleep(1000) ' Sleep for 1 second
        Next
    End Sub
End Module
```

---

7. Write a program that creates a thread to print "Hello, World!" five times and then waits for the thread to finish using `Join()`.

Answer:

```
Imports System.Threading

Module Module1
    Sub Main()
        Dim t As New Thread(AddressOf PrintHello)
        t.Start()
        t.Join() ' Wait for the thread to finish
        Console.WriteLine("Thread finished execution.")
    End Sub

    Sub PrintHello()
        For i As Integer = 1 To 5
            Console.WriteLine("Hello, World!")
            Thread.Sleep(500) ' Sleep for 500ms
        Next
    End Sub
End Module
```

---

8. Write a program that demonstrates the use of `IsAlive` property to check if a thread is running.

Answer:

```
Imports System.Threading

Module Module1
    Sub Main()
        Dim t As New Thread(AddressOf PrintNumbers)
        t.Start()

        While t.IsAlive
            Console.WriteLine("Thread is still running.")
            Thread.Sleep(500)
        End While
```

```
        Console.WriteLine("Thread has finished execution.")
    End Sub

    Sub PrintNumbers()
        For i As Integer = 1 To 5
            Console.WriteLine(i)
            Thread.Sleep(1000) ' Sleep for 1 second
        Next
    End Sub
End Module
```

---

9. Write a program that creates a thread and forcibly stops it using `Abort()`. (Note: Using `Abort()` is not recommended in production environments)

Answer:

```
Imports System.Threading

Module Module1
    Sub Main()
        Dim t As New Thread(AddressOf PrintNumbers)
        t.Start()
        Thread.Sleep(2000) ' Let the thread run for 2 seconds
        t.Abort() ' Forcefully stop the thread
        Console.WriteLine("Thread has been aborted.")
    End Sub

    Sub PrintNumbers()
        For i As Integer = 1 To 10
            Console.WriteLine(i)
            Thread.Sleep(500)
        Next
    End Sub
End Module
```

8.3 Working with Collections

Lists, Arrays, and Dictionaries / Collection Manipulation and LINQ

10. Write a program that creates an array of integers and prints the elements at index 2 and 4.

Answer:

```
Module Module1
    Sub Main()
        Dim numbers() As Integer = {10, 20, 30, 40, 50}
        Console.WriteLine("Element at index 2: " & numbers(2))
        Console.WriteLine("Element at index 4: " & numbers(4))
    End Sub
```

```
End Module
```

---

11. Write a program that adds 3 elements to a `List(Of Integer)` and prints them.

Answer:

```
Module Module1
    Sub Main()
        Dim numbers As New List(Of Integer)()
        numbers.Add(10)
        numbers.Add(20)
        numbers.Add(30)

        For Each num In numbers
            Console.WriteLine(num)
        Next
    End Sub
End Module
```

---

12. Write a program that uses a `Dictionary(Of String, String)` to store student names as keys and grades as values. Print all students and their grades.

Answer:

```
Module Module1
    Sub Main()
        Dim studentGrades As New Dictionary(Of String, String)()
        studentGrades.Add("Alice", "A")
        studentGrades.Add("Bob", "B")
        studentGrades.Add("Charlie", "C")

        For Each student In studentGrades
            Console.WriteLine(student.Key & ": " & student.Value)
        Next
    End Sub
End Module
```

---

13. Write a program that uses LINQ to filter even numbers from a list of integers and prints them.

Answer:

```
Module Module1
    Sub Main()
        Dim numbers As New List(Of Integer)({1, 2, 3, 4, 5, 6, 7, 8, 9})
        Dim evenNumbers = From n In numbers Where n Mod 2 = 0 Select n

        For Each num In evenNumbers
            Console.WriteLine(num)
```

```
        Next
    End Sub
End Module
```

---

14. Write a program that uses LINQ to sort a list of integers in descending order and prints the result.

Answer:

```
Module Module1
    Sub Main()
        Dim numbers As New List(Of Integer)({5, 2, 9, 1, 4})
        Dim sortedNumbers = From n In numbers Order By n Descending Select n

        For Each num In sortedNumbers
            Console.WriteLine(num)
        Next
    End Sub
End Module
```

---

15. Write a program that demonstrates the use of LINQ's `GroupBy` to group a list of integers by their remainder when divided by 2.

Answer:

```
Module Module1
    Sub Main()
        Dim numbers As New List(Of Integer)({1, 2, 3, 4, 5, 6})
        Dim grouped = From n In numbers Group n By n Mod 2 Into Group

        For Each grp In grouped
            Console.WriteLine("Remainder " & grp.Key & ": " & String.Join(",
", grp.Group))
        Next
    End Sub
End Module
```

CHAPTER 9: DESIGNING AND BUILDING A COMPLETE VB.NET APPLICATION

9.1 Project Planning and Design

Project planning and design are critical steps in ensuring the success of any software development effort. These steps help clarify the purpose, goals, and features of the application, as well as how it will function and meet user expectations. Effective planning and design also lay the groundwork for a more efficient development process, better quality assurance, and successful deployment.

Setting Objectives and Requirements

The first step in any project is understanding what needs to be achieved. This involves defining both **objectives** (what the application aims to do) and **requirements** (the necessary functionalities and conditions the application must meet).

Setting Objectives

- **Purpose of the Application**:
  - Before starting, it's crucial to understand the problem the application is solving or the need it is addressing. For example, if you're developing a **Customer Relationship Management (CRM)** system, the primary goal might be to help users manage customer data, interactions, and sales pipelines.
  - The application might aim to provide a tool for **improving workflow efficiency**, such as automating certain tasks or streamlining communication.
  - Or, the goal could be **providing real-time data** for business decision-making, making it accessible to multiple departments within an organization.
- **Main Goals of the Project**:
  - **Functionality Goals**: These could include facilitating certain workflows like easy **data entry**, generating **reports**, or ensuring that tasks are automated (such as **email notifications**).
  - **Business Goals**: Beyond technical features, it might be necessary to define business goals, such as **increasing sales**, **improving customer satisfaction**, or **reducing response times** to inquiries.

Defining Requirements

Once the objectives are established, you need to break down the requirements for the system. This can be split into two categories: **functional** and **non-functional** requirements.

- **Functional Requirements**:
  - These describe what the application should *do*—the features and actions the system must support. For example:
    - **User Management**: Allow users to create, update, and delete accounts.
    - **Reporting**: The system should generate weekly sales reports.

        - **Notification System**: The app should send email alerts when specific events occur (e.g., new lead, task deadline approaching).
        - **Search and Filtering**: Enable users to search for specific data like customers or transactions using filters such as date ranges, status, or location.
- **Non-functional Requirements**:
    - These describe how the system should *perform*—criteria that affect the user experience but are not directly related to specific features. For example:
        - **Performance**: The application should be able to handle **500 simultaneous users** without lagging.
        - **Scalability**: The system should be able to scale to accommodate additional users and data without major rewrites.
        - **Security**: Sensitive user data should be encrypted, and the system should comply with industry standards like **GDPR**.
        - **Usability**: The application should be easy to use, with minimal training required for new users.

Feasibility Study

Before diving into the development process, it's important to analyze whether the project objectives are achievable given the constraints:

- **Time**: Is there enough time to build the application within the project deadlines?
- **Budget**: Does the project have the resources it needs, both in terms of funding and human capital?
- **Technology**: Do you have access to the necessary tools, platforms, or frameworks? Do team members have the required expertise?

A feasibility study helps ensure the project's success by identifying potential risks early and adjusting timelines or resources accordingly.

User Stories or Use Cases

To better understand how end-users will interact with the system, **user stories** or **use cases** are created. These help identify features and functionality and ensure the application is user-centered.

- **User Stories**:
    - A **user story** typically follows this format:
        - *As a [type of user], I want to [perform an action] so that [I can achieve a goal].*
        - Example: "As a sales representative, I want to add new customer information so that I can track their purchases."
- **Use Cases**:
    - A **use case** describes how users will interact with a system to achieve a specific goal. It typically outlines a series of steps and the expected results.
        - Example: "Use case for generating a report: The user selects a date range, chooses report type, clicks 'Generate,' and the system produces a downloadable PDF report."

These help clarify the functionality from the user's perspective and ensure the development team understands the end goals.

Designing the User Interface (UI)

The user interface (UI) is the visual and interactive element of the application that users will interact with directly. Its design is critical because it influences both the usability and overall user experience of the application.

Wireframes and Prototypes

Wireframes are low-fidelity sketches that provide a basic layout of the user interface. They help visualize the app's structure and allow for early feedback before development begins.

- **Wireframes**:
  - Create rough sketches or digital wireframes to determine how different pages and elements (buttons, navigation menus, forms) will be structured.
  - Tools like **Sketch**, **Figma**, and **Adobe XD** are often used to create these designs.
- **Prototypes**:
  - Prototypes are more interactive than wireframes. They simulate the user interface and provide a better sense of how the application will work.

Usability and Accessibility

A well-designed UI should be intuitive and easy to navigate. This includes the following considerations:

- **Usability**:
  - Ensure the design is **intuitive** and **easy to use**. Users should be able to complete tasks with minimal training or guidance.
  - **Navigation** should be simple, with clear labels and actions that make it easy for users to move through the application.
- **Accessibility**:
  - Make sure the design accommodates users with different needs. This could include features like high-contrast modes, text resizing, or support for screen readers for users with visual impairments.

Consistency

Consistency in design ensures a **cohesive experience** across the application. This involves maintaining uniformity in elements like:

- **Color Scheme**: Use a consistent set of colors that align with the application's branding and ensure sufficient contrast for readability.

- **Fonts**: Choose readable fonts and maintain consistency in font sizes across headings, body text, and buttons.
- **Button Styles**: Ensure buttons look and behave similarly throughout the app.

Responsive Design

Since modern applications need to function across multiple devices (e.g., desktops, tablets, smartphones), a **responsive design** is crucial. This means the UI will adjust dynamically based on the device's screen size and orientation.

- **Mobile-first design**: Start by designing for the smallest screen sizes (mobile devices) and then scale up to tablets and desktops.
- **Media Queries**: Use media queries in CSS to change the layout based on the device's screen width.

By focusing on **responsive design**, you ensure the application works well on a variety of devices, providing a seamless experience for all users.

9.2 Application Architecture

Choosing an Architecture for Your Application

Choosing the right architecture for your application is essential for ensuring that it remains scalable, maintainable, and performant. A well-chosen architecture provides a structured approach for developers to follow, making it easier to manage, extend, and troubleshoot the system. Below are some common architectures:

1. Layered Architecture

Layered architecture is a classic and widely used approach for organizing an application into distinct layers, each with specific responsibilities. This separation of concerns makes the application easier to maintain, extend, and test.

- **Presentation Layer**:
  - This layer is responsible for the user interface (UI). It deals with how the application interacts with the user, taking user input, displaying results, and managing the interface logic.
- **Business Logic Layer (BLL)**:
  - This layer contains the core functionality of the application, such as rules, calculations, and operations. It works independently from the presentation layer and can be reused across different parts of the system.
- **Data Access Layer (DAL)**:
  - The DAL handles the interaction with data storage, typically a database. It encapsulates the logic for retrieving and persisting data to avoid direct database calls from the business layer, thereby promoting cleaner code and separation of concerns.
- **Benefits**:
  - **Modularity**: Each layer is independent, making it easier to modify or replace a specific layer without affecting the others.

- **Maintainability**: The separation allows for easier maintenance and scalability as the application grows.
- **Testability**: You can test each layer independently.

2. MVC (Model-View-Controller)

The **Model-View-Controller (MVC)** pattern is one of the most common architectural patterns, especially for web and desktop applications. It splits the application into three interconnected components, ensuring separation of concerns and better organization.

- **Model**:
  - This component handles the core data and logic of the application. It represents the state and business logic, including retrieving and storing data, as well as performing any required calculations or manipulations.
- **View**:
  - The View is the user interface of the application. It displays the data provided by the model in a format that is easy for the user to interact with. The View is usually decoupled from the business logic.
- **Controller**:
  - The Controller acts as a mediator between the Model and the View. It processes user inputs, communicates with the Model, and updates the View. When the user interacts with the View (such as clicking a button), the Controller decides how to respond.
- **Benefits**:
  - **Separation of concerns**: This makes the application easier to maintain and extend.
  - **Testability**: Individual components (Model, View, Controller) can be unit-tested.
  - **Flexibility**: Changes to the UI or business logic can be made independently of each other.

3. MVVM (Model-View-ViewModel)

The **Model-View-ViewModel (MVVM)** pattern is specifically designed for applications that use data binding, such as Windows Presentation Foundation (WPF) applications or applications built with Xamarin.Forms. MVVM is similar to MVC but provides a better way to manage the UI state and interaction.

- **Model**:
  - Like MVC, the Model in MVVM handles the data and business logic. It provides the core functionality of the application.
- **View**:
  - The View is still the UI, but in MVVM, it is closely tied to the **ViewModel** through data-binding.
- **ViewModel**:
  - The ViewModel serves as an intermediary between the View and the Model. It holds the state of the View and provides data to be displayed by the View. The ViewModel can transform the data from the Model into a format that can be easily consumed by the View.
- **Benefits**:

- **Two-way data binding**: Changes in the UI automatically update the underlying data and vice versa, reducing boilerplate code.
- **Separation of concerns**: The View is decoupled from both the business logic and the data, making the application easier to maintain and test.
- **Testability**: The ViewModel is designed to be testable without involving the UI.

4. Microservices Architecture

Microservices architecture is ideal for larger applications where the system is divided into independent, self-contained services. Each microservice performs a specific function (e.g., user management, order processing) and communicates with others via APIs.

- **Microservices**:
  - Each microservice is responsible for a distinct feature or function and can be developed, deployed, and maintained independently of the others.
- **Benefits**:
  - **Scalability**: Services can be scaled independently based on demand, allowing for more efficient use of resources.
  - **Flexibility**: Developers can use different technologies for different services (e.g., one service could use a NoSQL database while another uses a relational database).
  - **Resilience**: If one microservice fails, it does not bring down the entire application.
- **Challenges**:
  - Microservices require careful orchestration and management, and the complexity of deployment increases as the number of services grows.

5. Event-Driven Architecture

Event-driven architecture is particularly useful for real-time systems where actions in the system are triggered by events. This pattern is based on the idea that components respond to specific events and change the system's state accordingly.

- **Components**:
  - **Event Producers**: These generate events based on user actions or system changes.
  - **Event Consumers**: These listen for events and take action when the event is received (e.g., updating the UI, processing data).
  - **Event Bus**: The communication medium where events are sent and received.
- **Benefits**:
  - **Reactivity**: Suitable for systems that need to respond quickly to user inputs or external changes (e.g., stock market applications, real-time chat apps).
  - **Decoupling**: Producers and consumers are decoupled, meaning changes to one component don't directly affect others.
- **Challenges**:
  - Event-driven systems can become difficult to manage as the number of events and listeners increases. It requires robust handling to avoid race conditions, message loss, or failure in communication.

Best Practices for Design Patterns

Design patterns provide reusable solutions to common design problems. These patterns are widely accepted best practices that have been proven effective over time.

1. Singleton Pattern

The Singleton pattern ensures that a class has only one instance, providing a global point of access to that instance. This is particularly useful for managing shared resources, such as database connections or configuration settings.

- **Example**: A database connection pool manager may use the Singleton pattern to ensure there is only one instance managing all connections.

2. Factory Pattern

The Factory pattern abstracts the creation of objects. It is used when the object creation process is complex or involves many variations. Instead of directly creating objects, the factory provides a method for creating them, which helps decouple the client code from the instantiation logic.

- **Example**: A **LoggerFactory** can decide which type of logging mechanism (e.g., file logger, console logger) should be used based on configuration.

3. Repository Pattern

The Repository pattern is used to manage data access. It provides an abstraction layer between the business logic and the data access layer, offering a collection-like interface for interacting with data. This allows the underlying data storage implementation to change without affecting the business logic.

- **Example**: A **CustomerRepository** might provide methods to add, remove, or find customers in the database without exposing the details of the database queries.

4. Observer Pattern

The Observer pattern is used to notify multiple objects of a change in state. It's particularly useful in applications that need to reflect real-time changes in a large number of components, such as **UI updates** or **event notifications**.

- **Example**: In a **real-time chat application**, every time a new message is sent, the observers (chat windows) need to update to display the message.

5. Strategy Pattern

The Strategy pattern allows you to select an algorithm or behavior at runtime. This is useful when an application needs to switch between different strategies or operations, such as various payment processing methods.

- **Example**: A **PaymentService** might use the Strategy pattern to switch between different payment gateways, like PayPal, Stripe, or credit card processing, based on user preferences.

9.3 Implementing Core Functionality

1. Connecting to Databases

When implementing core functionality in your application, connecting to and interacting with databases is often central to storing and retrieving data. The two most common approaches in VB.NET for connecting to relational databases are ADO.NET and Entity Framework (EF).

Database Connections:

- **ADO.NET**:
  - ADO.NET is a low-level data access framework provided by the .NET framework. It allows you to connect to relational databases like SQL Server using a set of objects such as `SqlConnection`, `SqlCommand`, and `SqlDataReader`. You can perform operations such as querying, inserting, updating, and deleting data.

  Example using ADO.NET:

```
Dim connectionString As String = "Your_Connection_String"
Using connection As New SqlConnection(connectionString)
    connection.Open()

    Dim query As String = "SELECT * FROM Customers"
    Using command As New SqlCommand(query, connection)
        Using reader As SqlDataReader = command.ExecuteReader()
            While reader.Read()
                Console.WriteLine(reader("CustomerName").ToString())
            End While
        End Using
    End Using
End Using
```

  - In this example, a connection is established to the SQL Server, and a query is executed to retrieve data from the `Customers` table.
- **Entity Framework (EF):**
  - Entity Framework is an Object-Relational Mapping (ORM) framework that simplifies database interactions by allowing you to work with data as objects (entities) rather than writing raw SQL. It abstracts away the complexity of direct database operations and is useful for applications that require a high-level interaction with the database.

Example using Entity Framework:

```
Dim dbContext As New YourDbContext()
Dim customers = dbContext.Customers.ToList()
For Each customer In customers
    Console.WriteLine(customer.Name)
Next
```

- Here, `YourDbContext` represents your EF data context, and `Customers` is a DbSet that maps to a `Customers` table in the database. The data is retrieved as a collection of `Customer` objects, and you don't need to write raw SQL.

Handling SQL Queries:

- **Parameterized Queries:**
  - To prevent SQL injection attacks, always use parameterized queries instead of concatenating strings to create SQL statements. A parameterized query uses placeholders for user inputs, and the database engine ensures proper sanitization of the input values.

Example using ADO.NET with Parameterized Queries:

```
Dim query As String = "SELECT * FROM Customers WHERE City = @City"
Using command As New SqlCommand(query, connection)
    command.Parameters.AddWithValue("@City", cityName)
    Using reader As SqlDataReader = command.ExecuteReader()
        While reader.Read()
            Console.WriteLine(reader("CustomerName"))
        End While
    End Using
End Using
```

- Here, `@City` is a parameterized placeholder, and `command.Parameters.AddWithValue` ensures the parameter is safely added to the query.

Database Design:

- **Schema Design:**
  - Designing a well-structured database schema is fundamental to the core functionality of the application. This includes determining tables, relationships (one-to-many, many-to-many), primary keys, and foreign keys.
  - **Normalization**:
    - Normalization is the process of organizing data to minimize redundancy and ensure data integrity. The database should be normalized (usually up to 3NF – Third Normal Form) to avoid data anomalies like update, insert, or delete anomalies.
  - **Foreign Keys**:

- Foreign keys are used to establish relationships between tables. For example, a `Customer` table might have a `CustomerID` as the primary key, and an `Orders` table might include a `CustomerID` as a foreign key to indicate which customer placed the order.

2. Business Logic and Validation

Once data is successfully retrieved or input, the next step is to implement the core functionality of your application. Business logic governs the rules and decisions that drive the behavior of your application.

Business Logic:

- The business logic layer is responsible for carrying out the core operations of the application, such as:
    - **Processing Data**: For example, calculating discounts, taxes, or shipping costs based on user input.
    - **Decision Making**: Making decisions based on specific conditions like whether a user is eligible for a certain service or whether a product is in stock.
    - **Application Flow**: Managing the flow of information and processes within the application (e.g., navigating between forms or windows, sending data to the database).

Example of business logic (calculating a discount):

```
Function CalculateDiscount(price As Decimal, discountPercentage As
Decimal) As Decimal
    Return price - (price * (discountPercentage / 100))
End Function
```

- This function calculates the discount based on a price and discount percentage.

Data Validation:

- **Input Validation**:
    - Before processing or saving data, it is important to validate user input. This ensures that the data adheres to the expected format and prevents incorrect or malicious data from entering the system.
    - For example, validating an email address, checking that a phone number matches a valid format, or verifying that a user's age falls within an acceptable range.

Example of validating an email address:

```
Function IsValidEmail(email As String) As Boolean
    Dim regex As New Regex("^[^@]+@[^@]+\.[^@]+$")
    Return regex.IsMatch(email)
End Function
```

- This function checks if the email matches a simple regular expression pattern for valid email addresses.

- **Validation Before Database Operations:**
  - Always validate data before sending it to the database to avoid errors and inconsistencies. For example, if inserting a user record, you may want to check if a username already exists in the system.

  Example of checking if a username already exists:

```
Function UsernameExists(username As String) As Boolean
    Dim query As String = "SELECT COUNT(*) FROM Users WHERE Username =
@Username"
    Using command As New SqlCommand(query, connection)
        command.Parameters.AddWithValue("@Username", username)
        Dim count As Integer = Convert.ToInt32(command.ExecuteScalar())
        Return count > 0
    End Using
End Function
```

  - This function checks if a given username already exists in the database.

Error Handling:

- Proper error handling ensures that your application can gracefully handle unexpected conditions and provide helpful feedback to the user.
- **Try...Catch Blocks**:
  - In VB.NET, you can use the `Try...Catch` block to handle exceptions. This is useful for catching runtime errors (e.g., database connection failures, invalid inputs) and providing meaningful error messages.

  Example of handling a database connection error:

```
Try
    connection.Open()
Catch ex As SqlException
    MessageBox.Show("Error: Unable to connect to the database. Please
try again later.")
Finally
    connection.Close()
End Try
```

  - This code ensures that if a database connection fails, the user sees a clear message and the connection is closed properly.
- **Logging Errors**:
  - In addition to displaying error messages to users, it is important to log errors to help developers debug the application. You can use logging frameworks such as **NLog** or **Log4Net** to log exceptions to files, databases, or external systems.

  Example of logging an error using NLog:

```
Dim logger As Logger = LogManager.GetCurrentClassLogger()
Try
    ' Some code that may throw an exception
Catch ex As Exception
    logger.Error(ex, "An error occurred while processing the request.")
End Try
```

- This code logs an exception message with details, which can later be reviewed for debugging.

9.4 Testing and Debugging the Application

Testing and debugging are critical phases in the software development lifecycle, ensuring that your application behaves as expected, and that issues are quickly identified and resolved. Let's break down both testing and debugging processes in detail, focusing on the core practices for ensuring that your VB.NET applications are robust, reliable, and error-free.

Unit Testing in VB.NET

Unit testing involves validating that individual components or functions of your application behave as expected. These tests focus on small units of functionality, ensuring that each one works independently.

Writing Unit Tests:

Unit testing in VB.NET can be done using testing frameworks such as **MSTest**, **NUnit**, or **xUnit**. These frameworks provide tools to write, run, and manage unit tests.

- **MSTest**: MSTest is a testing framework that's integrated with Visual Studio. To write unit tests using MSTest, you need to create a test project, which contains test methods marked with `[TestMethod]`.

  Example:

```
Imports Microsoft.VisualStudio.TestTools.UnitTesting

<TestClass>
Public Class MathTests
    <TestMethod>
    Public Sub TestAddNumbers()
        Dim result As Integer = AddNumbers(2, 3)
        Assert.AreEqual(5, result)
    End Sub

    Public Function AddNumbers(a As Integer, b As Integer) As Integer
        Return a + b
    End Function
End Class
```

    - The `TestAddNumbers` method tests the `AddNumbers` function to ensure it returns the correct result.
- **NUnit:** NUnit is another popular testing framework that is often used for unit testing in .NET applications. It works similarly to MSTest, but you can add `NUnit` attributes such as `[Test]`.

  Example using NUnit:

```
Imports NUnit.Framework

<TestFixture>
Public Class CalculatorTests
    <Test>
    Public Sub TestMultiplyNumbers()
        Dim result As Integer = MultiplyNumbers(4, 5)
        Assert.AreEqual(20, result)
    End Sub

    Public Function MultiplyNumbers(a As Integer, b As Integer) As
Integer
        Return a * b
    End Function
End Class
```

- **Running Tests:** Once you've written the tests, you can run them using Visual Studio's Test Explorer or through the **dotnet test** command in the command line.

Mocking Dependencies:

In unit testing, you often need to test a unit of code in isolation, which means mocking external dependencies like databases, web services, or external APIs.

- **Mocking** helps simulate these dependencies so that your tests focus on the unit being tested rather than the external systems it interacts with.
- **Moq** is a popular library used for mocking in .NET. It allows you to create mock objects for interfaces or classes that your code depends on.

Example using Moq:

```
Imports Moq

Public Class DataServiceTests
    <TestMethod>
    Public Sub TestGetCustomerData()
        Dim mockRepo As New Mock(Of ICustomerRepository)()
        mockRepo.Setup(Function(repo) repo.GetCustomerData(It.IsAny(Of
Integer))) _
                .Returns(New Customer With {.Name = "John Doe", .Id = 1})

        Dim service As New CustomerService(mockRepo.Object)
        Dim customer As Customer = service.GetCustomer(1)
```

```
        Assert.AreEqual("John Doe", customer.Name)
    End Sub
End Class
```

- In this example, `ICustomerRepository` is mocked so that the test focuses on the logic in `CustomerService` without needing a real database connection.

Test Coverage:

To ensure your application behaves correctly, you need to cover various scenarios in your tests:

- **Edge cases**: Consider boundary conditions, such as an empty list, maximum values, or invalid inputs.
- **Error scenarios**: Test for cases where errors could occur, such as invalid data or database connection failures.
- **Typical usage scenarios**: Ensure that your tests cover the most common use cases in your application.

Example edge case test:

```
<TestMethod>
Public Sub TestDivideByZero()
    Try
        Dim result As Integer = DivideNumbers(10, 0)
    Catch ex As DivideByZeroException
        Assert.AreEqual("Cannot divide by zero", ex.Message)
    End Try
End Sub
```

Automated Testing:

Automated testing can be integrated into a **Continuous Integration (CI)** pipeline. This helps run your unit tests automatically every time you make changes to the codebase. This ensures that new changes do not break existing functionality and provides early detection of issues.

- **CI tools** like **Jenkins**, **Azure DevOps**, and **GitHub Actions** can be configured to automatically run unit tests whenever code is pushed to the repository.

Debugging Techniques and Tools

Debugging is the process of identifying and fixing issues in your code, and **Visual Studio** provides powerful debugging tools for VB.NET developers.

Debugging with Visual Studio:

Visual Studio provides several tools to help you debug your application:

- **Breakpoints**: Breakpoints are markers that pause the execution of your application at specific lines of code, allowing you to inspect the current state of variables, the flow of execution, and the call stack.

  Setting a Breakpoint:

  - Click on the left margin next to a line of code in the editor to set a breakpoint. When the breakpoint is hit during execution, Visual Studio will pause and allow you to inspect values.
  - You can use the **Immediate Window** to execute expressions, view variable values, or call functions while debugging.
- **Stepping Through Code**: You can use the **Step Over**, **Step Into**, and **Step Out** options to control how the debugger moves through your code.
  - **Step Over**: Runs the current line and moves to the next one (skipping over function calls).
  - **Step Into**: Moves into the function or method on the current line.
  - **Step Out**: Steps out of the current function and continues execution from the calling method.
- **Watch and Locals Windows**: You can use these windows to monitor variable values while debugging. This helps identify where the values deviate from what you expect, which is useful for diagnosing issues.

Exception Handling:

- **Try...Catch Blocks**:
  - Exception handling allows your application to handle unexpected errors in a controlled way, preventing crashes and providing meaningful feedback to users.

  Example of exception handling:

```
Try
    ' Code that may throw an exception
    Dim result As Integer = DivideNumbers(10, 0)
Catch ex As DivideByZeroException
    MessageBox.Show("Cannot divide by zero")
Catch ex As Exception
    MessageBox.Show("An unexpected error occurred: " & ex.Message)
End Try
```

- **Logging**:
  - You can use **logging frameworks** like **NLog** or **Log4Net** to capture and log exceptions for debugging purposes. This allows you to store error information in log files, which can be analyzed later.

  Example using NLog:

```
Dim logger As Logger = LogManager.GetCurrentClassLogger()
Try
    ' Code that may throw an exception
```

```
Catch ex As Exception
    logger.Error(ex, "An error occurred")
End Try
```

- **Event Logs**:
  - Writing logs to the Windows Event Log or using external log servers (e.g., Elasticsearch or Splunk) can help in diagnosing and monitoring application behavior in production environments.

Unit Test Debugging:

- When running unit tests, **Visual Studio** allows you to debug failing tests. You can set breakpoints in your unit test code or in the code being tested, and Visual Studio will stop at the breakpoints when running the test.
- **Debugging Failing Tests**:
  - When a unit test fails, you can right-click the failed test in the **Test Explorer** and choose **Debug** to step through the test and examine why it failed.

9.5 Deploying the Application

Deploying an application involves packaging and distributing it in such a way that users can install and run it on their systems. A successful deployment process ensures that the application reaches the users, works correctly in various environments, and allows for easy updates. There are various methods for packaging, distributing, and installing applications depending on their type and target platforms.

Packaging and Distribution Options

Packaging refers to the process of preparing the application for distribution. The goal is to make it easy for users to install the application, whether they are using local machines, a network share, or cloud environments.

Creating a Deployable Package:

A deployable package is a file or set of files that contain all the necessary components for the application to run on the target system. Here are some of the common types of deployable packages:

- **EXE Files**: An executable (EXE) file is a standalone file that can be launched directly by double-clicking it. This is common for desktop applications but often requires that the system has the appropriate runtime environment (e.g., .NET Framework, .NET Core) installed.

- **Windows Installer (MSI) Files**: MSI files are used for installing applications on Windows. They include not only the application's executable but also configuration files, registry entries, shortcuts, and other required resources. MSI files are often used for more robust, system-level installations where you need to configure the system environment (like setting registry keys, adding environment variables, etc.).
- **Docker Images**: If you're deploying an application in a containerized environment, you can package the application as a Docker image. Docker images contain everything needed to run the application, including the operating system, runtime, libraries, and the application itself. These images can be deployed to container orchestration platforms like Kubernetes or cloud services like AWS ECS or Azure Kubernetes Service.

ClickOnce Deployment:

ClickOnce is a deployment technology that enables developers to easily deploy Windows-based applications. With ClickOnce, users can install and run the application directly from a web browser, network share, or even a CD/DVD. It also provides automatic updates whenever a new version is available.

- **How ClickOnce Works:**
  - When an application is deployed using ClickOnce, the application is first published to a server or website. The users can access the installation via a link.
  - Once the user clicks the link, ClickOnce installs the application automatically, and users can start using it right away.
  - **Automatic Updates**: ClickOnce supports automatic updates by checking for new versions each time the application starts. If a new version is available, it is downloaded and installed automatically.
  - **Deployment from Various Sources**: You can deploy via HTTP, file shares, or even from a CD/DVD.

Example of ClickOnce Deployment:

- Publish the project in Visual Studio:
  - Go to the **Project** menu, select **Publish**.
  - Specify the publish location (e.g., a web server, file share).
  - Configure update settings (e.g., check for updates on launch).
  - After publishing, users can click the provided URL or setup link to install the application.

Web Deployment:

For **web applications**, deployment typically involves uploading the application to a web server. The two most common ways to deploy a web application are:

- **IIS (Internet Information Services)**: IIS is the web server for Windows, and it's commonly used to deploy web applications written in ASP.NET, ASP.NET Core, and other web technologies.

    - You'll need to deploy the application files (e.g., HTML, CSS, JavaScript, DLLs) to the IIS server.
    - Configuration, such as database connections and application settings, will often be stored in web.config or appsettings.json files.
- **Cloud Deployment**: Modern web applications are often deployed to cloud platforms like **Azure** or **AWS** for scalability and ease of management.
    - **Azure**: Azure App Service is commonly used to deploy .NET applications. It supports automatic scaling, continuous integration (CI), and various configurations (e.g., deployment slots).
    - **AWS**: AWS provides services like Elastic Beanstalk or EC2 instances to host web applications. These allow easy scaling and deployment using continuous deployment tools like AWS CodeDeploy.

Creating Installers

After you have packaged your application, creating an installer is the next step. Installers help automate the process of copying files, setting up the environment, and ensuring the application is correctly configured.

Windows Installer (MSI):

MSI installers are a popular choice for Windows applications. They allow the user to install the application with a standard installation process. You can create MSI installers using various tools, including:

- **WiX (Windows Installer XML)**: WiX is an open-source toolset that lets you create MSI-based installers. WiX allows you to define the entire setup process in an XML file, including installing files, creating registry entries, and setting up shortcuts.

  WiX Example:

    - Define an installer in an XML format, specifying which files to install and where.
    - Use WiX Toolset to compile the XML into an MSI installer.
- **InstallShield**: InstallShield is a commercial tool that provides a visual interface to create MSI-based installers. It is more feature-rich than WiX, offering advanced configuration options for enterprise-level applications.

Custom Installers:

Custom installers are useful when you need more control over the installation process, such as displaying a custom user interface, adding additional steps, or configuring specific system settings.

- **Features of Custom Installers**:

- **Custom UI**: You can create custom forms to prompt the user for information during the installation process (e.g., ask for database connection strings or license keys).
- **Conditional Installation**: Custom installers can provide conditions for installing certain components based on the user's selection.
- **Third-party Integrations**: You can integrate the installer with other tools or scripts (e.g., running database migration scripts before installing the application).

Example: Use **Inno Setup** or **NSIS (Nullsoft Scriptable Install System)** to create an installer that displays custom messages, asks for user input, and installs the application in a user-specified directory.

Installer Deployment:

Once the installer is created, the next step is distributing it to your users. There are several methods to distribute an installer:

- **Software Distribution Tools**: If your company uses software distribution platforms (e.g., **SCCM** or **Intune**), the installer can be pushed to users' machines automatically.
- **Shared Network Locations**: You can place the installer on a shared network drive, allowing users to download and install the application.
- **Web Downloads**: You can host the installer on a website for users to download. This is often done for commercial or public-facing applications.

---

30 multiple-choice questions (MCQs):

9.1 Project Planning and Design

Setting Objectives and Requirements

1. **What is the primary purpose of defining project objectives in the planning phase?**
   - a) To describe how the application will be implemented
   - b) To determine the tools and technologies used
   - c) To ensure the project meets the intended goals and addresses the problem
   - d) To select team members
   - **Answer**: c) To ensure the project meets the intended goals and addresses the problem
2. **Which of the following is an example of a functional requirement?**
   - a) The application should be able to handle 500 simultaneous users
   - b) The application should run on Windows 10 or higher
   - c) The application should allow users to log in and view their profile
   - d) The application should have a response time of less than 2 seconds
   - **Answer**: c) The application should allow users to log in and view their profile
3. **What is the main goal of a feasibility study during project planning?**
   - a) To evaluate if the project is achievable within constraints such as time and resources
   - b) To design the user interface
   - c) To assign roles to the development team

- d) To write the initial codebase
- **Answer**: a) To evaluate if the project is achievable within constraints such as time and resources

Designing the User Interface

4. **Which of the following is the purpose of creating wireframes during UI design?**
   - a) To define the functionality of the application
   - b) To visualize and plan the layout and user interaction elements
   - c) To create the final production code for the application
   - d) To select the programming language
   - **Answer**: b) To visualize and plan the layout and user interaction elements
5. **What is an important factor to consider in designing a responsive UI?**
   - a) Using a large font size for all text
   - b) Ensuring the application adapts to different screen sizes and devices
   - c) Having a fixed layout for all users
   - d) Ignoring accessibility features to improve speed
   - **Answer**: b) Ensuring the application adapts to different screen sizes and devices

---

9.2 Application Architecture

Choosing an Architecture for Your Application

6. **Which of the following is a characteristic of the MVC (Model-View-Controller) architecture?**
   - a) It separates data access and business logic from user interface design
   - b) It is mainly used in monolithic applications
   - c) The view handles both the logic and the data
   - d) It uses a single class for handling business logic and user interface
   - **Answer**: a) It separates data access and business logic from user interface design
7. **Which application architecture is best suited for applications that require independent, loosely coupled services?**
   - a) Layered Architecture
   - b) Microservices Architecture
   - c) MVC Architecture
   - d) Event-Driven Architecture
   - **Answer**: b) Microservices Architecture
8. **What is the primary benefit of using the MVVM (Model-View-ViewModel) architecture in WPF applications?**
   - a) It simplifies communication between the model and view by binding data
   - b) It minimizes the use of database interactions
   - c) It allows models to perform complex computations directly
   - d) It uses a single controller to manage business logic
   - **Answer**: a) It simplifies communication between the model and view by binding data

9. **Which design pattern ensures a class has only one instance, often used for database connection pooling?**
   - a) Factory Pattern
   - b) Singleton Pattern
   - c) Observer Pattern
   - d) Strategy Pattern
   - **Answer**: b) Singleton Pattern
10. **What does the Factory Pattern help achieve in object creation?**
    - a) It allows for direct instantiation of objects without any intermediate logic
    - b) It creates objects with complex initialization logic while hiding the instantiation process
    - c) It manages database connections
    - d) It ensures that an object is only created once
    - **Answer**: b) It creates objects with complex initialization logic while hiding the instantiation process
11. **Which pattern is used to manage data access in an application by providing a collection-like interface for interacting with domain objects?**
    - a) Repository Pattern
    - b) Strategy Pattern
    - c) Singleton Pattern
    - d) Adapter Pattern
    - **Answer**: a) Repository Pattern

9.3 Implementing Core Functionality

Connecting to Databases

12. **Which ADO.NET class is used to execute SQL queries and retrieve data from a database?**
    - a) SqlConnection
    - b) SqlCommand
    - c) SqlDataReader
    - d) SqlTransaction
    - **Answer**: b) SqlCommand
13. **When using parameterized queries in ADO.NET, what is the main advantage?**
    - a) It helps execute SQL queries faster
    - b) It prevents SQL injection attacks
    - c) It automatically formats the query string
    - d) It generates SQL commands dynamically
    - **Answer**: b) It prevents SQL injection attacks
14. **Which ORM (Object-Relational Mapping) framework is commonly used in VB.NET for easier database interaction?**
    - a) ADO.NET

- b) Entity Framework
- c) LINQ to SQL
- d) Dapper
- **Answer**: b) Entity Framework

Business Logic and Validation

15. **What is the primary purpose of business logic in an application?**
    - a) To format user input
    - b) To handle core operations such as calculations or decision-making rules
    - c) To manage user authentication
    - d) To display the user interface
    - **Answer**: b) To handle core operations such as calculations or decision-making rules
16. **Why is data validation important before processing or storing data?**
    - a) To ensure data is correctly formatted and meets required conditions
    - b) To improve the appearance of the data
    - c) To save processing time
    - d) To allow users to enter incorrect data
    - **Answer**: a) To ensure data is correctly formatted and meets required conditions
17. **Which technique is commonly used in VB.NET to handle exceptions during application execution?**
    - a) If...Else Statements
    - b) Try...Catch Blocks
    - c) Switch...Case Statements
    - d) For...Next Loops
    - **Answer**: b) Try...Catch Blocks

9.4 Testing and Debugging the Application

Unit Testing in VB.NET

18. **What is the purpose of unit testing in VB.NET?**
    - a) To ensure that individual components or functions of the application work as expected
    - b) To ensure the application works across all devices
    - c) To test the application's integration with external services
    - d) To test the entire system's user interface
    - **Answer**: a) To ensure that individual components or functions of the application work as expected
19. **Which testing framework is commonly used for unit testing in VB.NET?**
    - a) JUnit
    - b) MSTest
    - c) PHPUnit
    - d) PyTest
    - **Answer**: b) MSTest

20. **Which tool can be used to mock dependencies when writing unit tests in VB.NET?**
    - a) Moq
    - b) NUnit
    - c) TestComplete
    - d) SoapUI
    - **Answer**: a) Moq

Debugging Techniques and Tools

21. **Which feature of Visual Studio allows you to pause the program execution and inspect variable values during debugging?**
    - a) Breakpoints
    - b) Code Completion
    - c) Live Reload
    - d) Profiling
    - **Answer**: a) Breakpoints
22. **Which of the following is useful for logging detailed information about application errors and exceptions?**
    - a) Breakpoints
    - b) Exception Handling and Logging
    - c) Unit Tests
    - d) Code Reviews
    - **Answer**: b) Exception Handling and Logging
23. **When debugging a unit test, which Visual Studio feature allows you to step through the code of a failing test to identify the issue?**
    - a) Performance Profiler
    - b) Test Explorer
    - c) Debugger
    - d) Code Lens
    - **Answer**: c) Debugger

9.5 Deploying the Application

Packaging and Distribution Options

24. **Which deployment method is used to allow users to install applications directly from a web browser or network share?**
    - a) Docker Containers
    - b) ClickOnce Deployment
    - c) Manual Installation
    - d) Microsoft Store
    - **Answer**: b) ClickOnce Deployment
25. **For web applications, which hosting service can be used to deploy applications on the cloud?**
    - a) Internet Information Services (IIS)

- b) Docker Swarm
- c) Azure or AWS
- d) Web API Hosting
- **Answer**: c) Azure or AWS

26. **Which tool is commonly used to create MSI-based installers for Windows applications?**
    - a) InstallShield
    - b) Visual Studio Code
    - c) Eclipse
    - d) IntelliJ IDEA
    - **Answer**: a) InstallShield

Creating Installers

27. **Which of the following is a feature of a custom installer?**
    - a) It performs automatic testing of the application
    - b) It allows users to configure options during the installation process
    - c) It ensures the application has no bugs
    - d) It creates a backup of all installed files
    - **Answer**: b) It allows users to configure options during the installation process
28. **What is the advantage of using an MSI installer?**
    - a) It is easy to create and does not require configuration
    - b) It provides an automated way to configure registry keys, file copies, and other installation tasks
    - c) It requires manual installation steps
    - d) It cannot be used on Windows systems
    - **Answer**: b) It provides an automated way to configure registry keys, file copies, and other installation tasks
29. **Which method can be used to distribute application installers to users?**
    - a) Push notifications
    - b) Software Distribution Tools
    - c) Direct mail
    - d) Chatbots
    - **Answer**: b) Software Distribution Tools
30. **What is the key benefit of using a Windows Installer (MSI)?**
    - a) Simplifies the application's source code
    - b) Automates the installation process with built-in support for system configuration
    - c) Allows for real-time updates
    - d) Increases the speed of the application
    - **Answer**: b) Automates the installation process with built-in support for system configuration

CHAPTER 10: BEST PRACTICES AND CODE OPTIMIZATION

10.1 Writing Clean and Maintainable Code

Writing clean and maintainable code is a critical practice for any developer. It ensures that code can be easily understood, modified, and extended in the future. Clean code is not just about solving problems; it's also about making the solution readable and easy to follow.

Commenting and Documenting Code

Effective commenting and documentation help both the developer and other collaborators understand the code's intent and functionality, and maintain it in the future.

1. Commenting

Purpose: Comments explain what the code does, why specific decisions were made, and provide additional context that is not immediately obvious from the code itself. This is important when working in teams or when revisiting the code after a period of time.

Types of Comments:

- **Inline Comments**: These comments are placed on the same line or just next to a line of code. They provide an explanation for that specific line or statement.
  - **Example**:

    ```
    Dim totalPrice As Double = price * 1.2 ' Multiply price by tax rate (20%)
    ```

    Here, the inline comment explains why the price is multiplied by 1.2 (to account for a 20% tax rate).

- **Block Comments**: These comments are used to explain larger sections of code or more complex logic. A block comment usually spans multiple lines and gives a deeper explanation of what the code is doing.
  - **Example**:

    ```
    ' This block of code calculates the total amount after applying various discounts.
    ' We first apply a standard 10% discount for all items, then an additional 5% discount for items over $100.
    Dim discountAmount As Double = totalAmount * 0.10
    If totalAmount > 100 Then
        discountAmount += totalAmount * 0.05
    End If
    ```

Best Practices:

- Avoid redundant comments that simply restate what the code is doing (e.g., `i = i + 1` is clear enough without the comment `'increment i by 1`).
- Comments should **not** be used to explain poorly written code; instead, the code should be refactored to make it more understandable.
- Comments should be **up-to-date** with code changes. Outdated comments can confuse developers more than no comments at all.

2. Documenting Code

While comments provide inline explanations, **documentation** offers a more structured, high-level overview of your codebase. It gives context and purpose for methods, classes, and modules.

Tools for Documentation in VB.NET: In VB.NET, you can use **XML Documentation Comments**, which are specialized comments that provide structured metadata about methods, parameters, and classes. These comments can be processed by tools like **Visual Studio** to generate API documentation, making it easier to maintain and use the codebase.

Method-level Documentation: Every method should have clear documentation that describes:

- What the method does.
- The parameters it accepts.
- The value it returns.

Example:

```
''' <summary>
''' This function calculates the discount price based on the original price
and discount percentage.
''' </summary>
''' <param name="originalPrice">The original price of the product</param>
''' <param name="discountPercentage">The discount percentage to apply</param>
''' <returns>The price after the discount is applied</returns>
Public Function CalculateDiscountPrice(ByVal originalPrice As Double, ByVal
discountPercentage As Double) As Double
    Return originalPrice * (1 - discountPercentage / 100)
End Function
```

This example explains the purpose of the method, what parameters it expects, and what it returns. Tools like Visual Studio can extract these comments to provide hover-over tooltips or generate external documentation files.

Class-level Documentation: Just as methods need documentation, classes should be documented to explain their purpose and behavior. This helps new developers quickly understand the role of a class within the application.

Example:

```
''' <summary>
''' The Customer class represents a customer in the system.
```

```
''' It stores basic customer information and allows updates to their details.
''' </summary>
Public Class Customer
    ' Class properties and methods go here
End Class
```

Naming Conventions and Formatting

1. Naming Conventions

Following consistent naming conventions across your code makes it more readable and maintainable. It ensures that developers can quickly recognize the purpose and type of variables, methods, and classes.

Common Naming Guidelines in VB.NET:

- **Classes/Modules/Interfaces**: Use **PascalCase** (first letter capitalized for each word) for classes, modules, and interfaces.
  - **Example:** `CustomerOrder`, `InvoiceManager`, `IOrderProcessor`
- **Methods/Properties**: Use **PascalCase** for methods and properties. The name should represent an action or the purpose of the property.
  - **Example:** `CalculateTotalAmount`, `GetCustomerDetails`
- **Variables/Parameters**: Use **camelCase** (first letter lowercase, with subsequent words capitalized) for variables and parameters.
  - **Example:** `totalAmount`, `customerList`, `orderNumber`
- **Constants**: Constants are typically written in **uppercase** with underscores separating words.
  - **Example:** `MAX_SIZE`, `PI`, `DATABASE_URL`
- **Enumerations**: Use **PascalCase** for enums.
  - **Example:** `OrderStatus`, `PaymentType`
- **Private Fields**: Prefix private fields with an underscore (_) to distinguish them from public properties or methods.
  - **Example:** `_customerName`, `_orderTotal`

Best Practices:

- Choose meaningful names that clearly describe the purpose of the variable, method, or class.
- Avoid single-letter variables except for loop counters (e.g., `i`, `j`).
- Avoid using abbreviations unless they are well-known and unambiguous.

---

2. Formatting

Proper formatting enhances the readability of the code and ensures that it follows a consistent structure. Formatting should be consistent throughout the entire codebase to avoid confusion.

Best Practices:

- **Indentation**: Use consistent indentation, typically 4 spaces per indentation level. Indentation helps to distinguish blocks of code (e.g., inside loops, conditionals, or functions).
- **Brackets**: Always use curly braces ({ }) for loops, conditionals, and method definitions, even if the block contains only one line of code. This reduces the risk of errors when modifying code.
  - **Example**:

```
If radius <= 0 Then
    Throw New ArgumentException("Radius must be greater than
zero.")
End If
```

- **Line Length**: Keep lines of code to a maximum of 80-100 characters. This ensures that code is readable on most screens and avoids horizontal scrolling.
  - If a line is too long, split it logically across multiple lines.
  - **Example**:

```
Dim totalAmount As Double = (price + tax) * quantity +
shippingCost
```

- **Spacing**: Ensure that there is adequate space around operators to make expressions easier to read.
  - **Example**:

```
Dim totalAmount As Double = price + tax ' Correct formatting
```

  - Incorrect formatting would look like this:

```
Dim totalAmount As Double = price+tax ' Harder to read and
understand
```

Example of Well-Formatted and Documented Code:

```
''' <summary>
''' This function calculates the area of a circle given its radius.
''' It throws an exception if the radius is non-positive.
''' </summary>
''' <param name="radius">The radius of the circle</param>
''' <returns>The area of the circle</returns>
Public Function CalculateArea(ByVal radius As Double) As Double
    ' Validate the radius value
    If radius <= 0 Then
        Throw New ArgumentException("Radius must be greater than zero.")
    End If

    ' Calculate and return the area
```

```
    Return Math.PI * radius * radius
End Function
```

In this example:

- **Documenting**: The method is thoroughly documented, describing its purpose, parameters, and return values.
- **Commenting**: Inline comments explain specific logic (e.g., validation of the radius).
- **Naming**: Proper naming conventions are used (`CalculateArea`, `radius`), making it clear what the method does and what data it processes.
- **Formatting**: The code is indented correctly, with space around operators and consistent use of curly braces.

10.2 Performance Tuning and Optimization

Performance tuning and optimization are crucial in developing high-performing applications. Slow-performing applications not only lead to a poor user experience but can also incur higher resource costs (e.g., CPU, memory, and network resources). By identifying performance bottlenecks and optimizing specific areas, you can significantly improve your application's speed and scalability.

Identifying Bottlenecks in Code

A bottleneck refers to a part of the system where the performance is hindered due to inefficient processes or resource limitations. Identifying bottlenecks is the first step in optimizing performance.

1. Performance Bottlenecks

Definition: A performance bottleneck occurs when a particular component or operation in your application takes longer to execute than expected or required, thereby slowing down the entire system. This can lead to delays, timeouts, and poor user experience.

Common Causes:

- **I/O operations**: Reading and writing data to files or databases can be slow, especially if the data is large or if the system's disk I/O speed is slow.
- **Database queries**: Inefficient or unoptimized queries (e.g., complex joins, large data sets, lack of indexing) can slow down application performance.
- **Nested loops**: Using nested loops without proper optimization can result in excessive time complexity, making the application slower as the dataset grows.
- **Large memory allocations**: Handling large amounts of data or creating large objects can consume a lot of memory and take time.
- **Network latency**: Calls to external APIs or services over the network can introduce delays due to slow or unreliable network connections.

2. Techniques for Identifying Bottlenecks

- **Profiling Tools**: Profiling tools are essential for identifying performance bottlenecks. These tools analyze the application's execution and provide insights into where the application spends the most time. For example:
    - **Visual Studio Profiler**: It offers a detailed view of CPU usage, memory consumption, and time spent in different parts of your application.
    - **Third-party tools**: Tools like **dotTrace**, **Ants Profiler**, or **Redgate's ANTS Performance Profiler** can provide in-depth insights into performance issues.
- **Code Review**: Code reviews help in identifying inefficient or suboptimal coding practices. Look for code with:
    - Nested loops with high time complexity (e.g., $O(n^2)$ or higher).
    - Inefficient algorithms that can be optimized (e.g., sorting, searching).
    - Operations that access external resources (e.g., file I/O, database queries) repeatedly in a loop.
- **Benchmarking**: By testing specific parts of your code and measuring execution time, you can pinpoint slow segments. This can be done using **Stopwatch** in .NET or other timing tools. You might also use custom test cases or performance metrics.
    - **Example**:

```
Dim stopwatch As New Stopwatch()
stopwatch.Start()

' Code to measure performance
SomeMethod()

stopwatch.Stop()
Console.WriteLine("Execution time: " &
stopwatch.ElapsedMilliseconds & " ms")
```

- **Common Bottlenecks**:
    - **I/O Operations**: Writing and reading data to/from disk, file systems, or databases can be slow.
    - **Database Queries**: Poorly written or unoptimized queries that don't use indexes or retrieve unnecessary data.
    - **Nested Loops**: Repeated processing of large datasets in nested loops (e.g., $O(n^2)$) can be very slow as data size grows.
    - **Large Memory Allocations**: Allocating and releasing large chunks of memory frequently can cause performance degradation.

3. Reducing Bottlenecks

Once you identify the bottleneck, you can apply various techniques to reduce it:

- **Refactor Code**: Refactor inefficient code to use better algorithms and more efficient data structures. For instance:
    - Use **hash tables** instead of nested loops for lookup operations.

    - Replace **recursion** with **iteration** if recursion depth is large and could cause stack overflows.
    - Use **caching** or **memoization** techniques to avoid repeated expensive calculations.
- **Parallel Processing / Multi-threading**: Use **multithreading** or **parallel processing** to distribute computational tasks across multiple threads or processors. This approach allows for better utilization of CPU resources and can significantly speed up computations in CPU-bound applications.
    - **Example** (Using `Task` for parallelism):

```
Dim tasks As New List(Of Task)()
For i As Integer = 1 To 10
    tasks.Add(Task.Run(Sub() ProcessData(i)))
Next
Task.WhenAll(tasks).Wait()
```

- **Caching Results**: Cache the results of expensive operations (e.g., calculations or database queries) if the data is reused multiple times. This avoids the need for repeated calculations or queries, saving both time and resources. You can use simple in-memory caching mechanisms or more sophisticated tools like **MemoryCache** in .NET.
    - **Example** (Simple caching using `Dictionary`):

```
Dim cache As New Dictionary(Of String, Object)()

If Not cache.ContainsKey("expensiveData") Then
    cache("expensiveData") = GetExpensiveData()
End If
Dim result = cache("expensiveData")
```

Optimizing Database Queries

Database performance is critical in many applications, and inefficient queries can lead to significant slowdowns, especially when dealing with large datasets.

1. Database Query Optimization

Here are several strategies for improving database query performance:

- **Indexes**: Indexing frequently queried columns improves the speed of data retrieval. Indexes speed up search operations by allowing the database engine to quickly locate the required rows instead of scanning the entire table.
    - **Example**:
        - **Without Index:** `SELECT * FROM Customers WHERE LastName = 'Smith'`
        - **With Index:** `CREATE INDEX idx_lastname ON Customers(LastName);`
        - Query: `SELECT * FROM Customers WHERE LastName = 'Smith'`
- **Optimize Joins**: Joins are powerful but can be slow if not used carefully. Make sure to use the appropriate join type (`INNER JOIN`, `LEFT JOIN`, etc.) and avoid unnecessary joins, especially when dealing with large datasets.

- **Example**: If you're joining two large tables but only need some specific columns, avoid unnecessary joins.

```
-- Bad: JOINing unnecessarily
SELECT *
FROM Orders O
JOIN Customers C ON O.CustomerID = C.CustomerID

-- Good: Only select necessary fields and avoid unnecessary joins
SELECT O.OrderID, O.OrderDate
FROM Orders O
WHERE O.CustomerID = @CustomerID
```

- **Limit Data Retrieved**: Instead of using `SELECT *`, always select only the columns you need. This reduces the amount of data transferred and improves query execution time.
  - **Example**:
    - **Bad**: `SELECT * FROM Orders`
    - **Good**: `SELECT OrderID, CustomerName FROM Orders WHERE OrderDate > @startDate`
- **Parameterized Queries**: Always use parameterized queries instead of concatenating strings. This improves performance, reduces the risk of SQL injection, and allows the query plan to be reused.
  - **Example** (Using Parameterized Query in VB.NET):

```
Dim cmd As New SqlCommand("SELECT OrderID, CustomerName FROM
Orders WHERE OrderDate > @startDate", connection)
cmd.Parameters.AddWithValue("@startDate", startDate)
```

2. Database Connection Management

Efficient connection management is key to avoiding resource exhaustion and improving database query performance.

- **Open Connections Late and Close Early**: Always open database connections as late as possible and close them as soon as you are done using them. Keeping connections open for longer than necessary can result in resource wastage.
  - **Example**:

```
Using connection As New SqlConnection(connectionString)
    connection.Open()
    ' Perform database operations
End Using
```

- **Connection Pooling**: Connection pooling allows the reuse of existing connections rather than opening a new one every time. This can drastically reduce connection overhead and improve application performance.
  - In .NET, **ADO.NET** handles connection pooling by default, so you don't need to manually manage connections unless you're working in a non-standard environment.

10.3 Code Refactoring Techniques

Code refactoring is the process of improving the structure, readability, and maintainability of your code without changing its external behavior. Refactoring helps reduce complexity, improves performance, and makes the code more reusable and easier to understand. Below are some of the key techniques for refactoring code effectively.

1. Making Code More Modular and Reusable

The goal of modularity and reusability is to break down complex code into smaller, self-contained components that can be reused throughout the application. This not only simplifies maintenance but also ensures that changes made to one part of the system do not affect other parts.

Modularity:

Modularity refers to breaking down large and complex functions or classes into smaller, more manageable pieces. Each function or class should have a single responsibility and should operate independently, making it easier to modify and test.

- **Single Responsibility Principle**: Each function should do one thing, and do it well. By adhering to this principle, you ensure that functions are small, focused, and easier to understand.
- **Example**: Let's say you have a function that performs multiple tasks such as fetching data from the database, processing it, and displaying it. You should refactor it into smaller, focused functions.

  Before Refactoring:

  ```
  Public Sub ProcessAndDisplayData()
      Dim data As DataTable = GetDataFromDatabase()
      ' Perform processing
      ' Display data
  End Sub
  ```

  After Refactoring:

  ```
  Public Function GetDataFromDatabase() As DataTable
      ' Fetch data from database
      Return New DataTable()
  End Function

  Public Sub ProcessData(ByVal data As DataTable)
      ' Process the data
  End Sub

  Public Sub DisplayData(ByVal data As DataTable)
      ' Display the data
  End Sub
  ```

Now, each function has a clear responsibility, and they can be reused elsewhere in the application.

Reusable Components:

Identifying repetitive code and creating reusable methods, classes, or libraries to handle common functionality is a powerful refactoring strategy. By creating utility classes or services, you avoid duplicating logic across multiple places in your code.

- **Example**: You might have multiple places in your code where you are logging messages. Instead of repeating the same logging logic everywhere, you can create a utility class for logging.

  Reusable Component Example:

  ```
  Public Class Logger
      Public Sub LogMessage(ByVal message As String)
          ' Write message to log file
          ' Code to log message to a file or external system
      End Sub
  End Class
  ```

  Now, instead of having repetitive logging logic scattered across different classes or methods, you can simply call `Logger.LogMessage` whenever needed.

  Usage Example:

  ```
  Dim logger As New Logger()
  logger.LogMessage("User logged in")
  ```

This creates a more organized and manageable codebase, making the system easier to maintain and extend.

---

2. Removing Redundancy and Improving Readability

Eliminating Redundant Code:

Redundant code is code that appears multiple times throughout the system. It often indicates a lack of modularity or a need for abstraction. Refactoring this redundant code into a reusable method or function makes your code cleaner and easier to manage.

- **Example**: You may have similar conditions or logic appearing in multiple places. Instead of repeating the same code, extract that logic into a separate method.

  Before Refactoring (Redundant Code):

  ```
  If (userAge >= 18) Then
  ```

```
    ' Show voting rights
End If

If (userAge >= 18) Then
    ' Show driving rights
End If
```

In the above code, the `userAge >= 18` condition is repeated twice, which is redundant.

After Refactoring:

```
Public Sub CheckRights(ByVal userAge As Integer)
    If (userAge >= 18) Then
        ' Show voting and driving rights
    End If
End Sub
```

Now, by refactoring the redundant logic into the `CheckRights` method, you avoid duplication, and any changes to the logic will be centralized in one place.

Improving Readability:

Readability is one of the most important aspects of maintainable code. Code should be easy to follow and understand, not just for you but for anyone else who may work on the code in the future.

- **Refactor Complex Logic**: If you have complex expressions or logic in a single line, break them down into smaller, more readable components. This also makes debugging easier.

  Before Refactoring (Complex Logic):

  ```
  Dim finalPrice As Double = price * (1 - discount / 100) + tax
  ```

  After Refactoring:

  ```
  Dim discountAmount As Double = price * (discount / 100)
  Dim finalPrice As Double = price - discountAmount + tax
  ```

  Breaking down the logic into smaller, meaningful variables improves readability.

- **Meaningful Variable and Method Names**: The names of variables and methods should be descriptive and convey the purpose of the item. Avoid using abbreviations or vague names like `x`, `temp`, or `foo`.

  Before Refactoring (Bad Naming):

  ```
  Dim x As Integer
  Dim foo As String
  ```

After Refactoring (Better Naming):

```
Dim itemCount As Integer
Dim errorMessage As String
```

Use names that convey the purpose of the variable or method, making it easier for someone reading the code to understand its purpose without needing excessive comments.

- **Use Comments Where Necessary**: While code should be self-explanatory through good naming and clear structure, there will be times when you need to explain why certain decisions were made. Use comments to clarify complex or non-obvious logic, but avoid redundant comments.

  Example:

```
' Calculate the discount price
Public Function CalculateDiscountPrice(ByVal originalPrice As Double,
ByVal discountPercentage As Double) As Double
    ' Discount is calculated as the original price minus the discount
percentage
    Return originalPrice * (1 - discountPercentage / 100)
End Function
```

  A comment should explain **why** a particular approach is used or describe its logic if it is not immediately clear from the code itself.

10.4 Security Best Practices in VB.NET

Security is a critical aspect of software development, especially when dealing with sensitive user information such as passwords, personal details, and financial data. Ensuring your application is secure helps protect users and the application from malicious attacks. Below are the key security practices to follow when developing in VB.NET.

---

1. Protecting Sensitive Data

1.1 Encryption

Encryption is essential for protecting sensitive data, both at rest (in storage) and in transit (during transmission). When sensitive data, such as passwords, credit card numbers, or personal information, is stored or transmitted, it should be encrypted to prevent unauthorized access.

- **AES Encryption (Advanced Encryption Standard)**: AES is widely regarded as one of the most secure encryption algorithms for encrypting sensitive data. It is a symmetric key encryption standard, meaning the same key is used for both encryption and decryption.
- **Example**: Using AES for encryption in VB.NET

```
Dim aes As New AesManaged()
aes.Key = key  ' Key must be securely generated and stored
aes.IV = iv    ' Initialization vector, typically random for added security
Dim encryptor As ICryptoTransform = aes.CreateEncryptor(aes.Key, aes.IV)
Dim encryptedData As Byte() = encryptor.TransformFinalBlock(dataToEncrypt, 0,
dataToEncrypt.Length)
```

In this example:

- `aes.Key`: The encryption key used to encrypt and decrypt the data.
- `aes.IV`: The initialization vector (IV) is used to further secure the encryption.
- The encrypted data is generated using the `CreateEncryptor()` method, which returns an `ICryptoTransform` object used to encrypt the data.

1.2 Hashing

For data that does not need to be recovered (such as passwords), **hashing** is a better option than encryption. Hashing is a one-way function that converts data (e.g., a password) into a fixed-length value, making it difficult (if not impossible) to recover the original data.

- **Hashing for Passwords**: Always use a strong hash function like SHA-256 to hash passwords, and include a **salt** (a random value added to the password before hashing) to protect against rainbow table attacks.
- **Example**: Hashing a password using SHA-256 in VB.NET

```
Dim password As String = "user_password"
Dim salt As String = "random_salt_value"  ' Salt must be securely generated
and stored
Dim passwordWithSalt As String = password & salt
Dim hash As String =
Convert.ToBase64String(SHA256.Create().ComputeHash(Encoding.UTF8.GetBytes(pas
swordWithSalt)))
```

In this example:

- The password is concatenated with a salt value to create a unique input for the hash function.
- The result of the `SHA256.Create().ComputeHash()` function is a fixed-length hash value that is stored securely in the database. This hash is not reversible, making it impossible for attackers to retrieve the original password.

1.3 Secure Data Transmission

When transmitting sensitive data over the network, it is crucial to ensure that the data is encrypted during transmission. **HTTPS** (HyperText Transfer Protocol Secure) is the secure version of HTTP, which uses SSL/TLS protocols to encrypt the data sent between the client and server.

- **Always use HTTPS**: Ensure that all sensitive data, including login credentials and financial information, is transmitted over HTTPS to prevent man-in-the-middle attacks.
- **Example**: Enforcing HTTPS on a web application

```
' In the Web.config file, you can enforce the use of HTTPS for your web
application
<configuration>
  <system.webServer>
    <rewrite>
      <rules>
        <rule name="HTTPS Redirect" enabled="true" stopProcessing="true">
          <match url="(.*)" />
          <conditions>
            <add input="{HTTPS}" pattern="off" />
          </conditions>
          <action type="Redirect" url="https://{HTTP_HOST}/{R:1}" />
        </rule>
      </rules>
    </rewrite>
  </system.webServer>
</configuration>
```

In this example, any HTTP requests to the server are automatically redirected to HTTPS, ensuring that the data is always transmitted securely.

---

2. Preventing SQL Injection and Cross-Site Scripting (XSS)

2.1 SQL Injection Prevention

SQL injection occurs when an attacker manipulates a SQL query by injecting malicious SQL code into an input field. This can allow attackers to bypass authentication, steal data, or perform other harmful actions on the database.

- **Parameterized Queries**: To prevent SQL injection, always use **parameterized queries** or prepared statements, which separate SQL code from user input. This ensures that user input is treated as data, not executable SQL code.
- **Example**: Using parameterized queries in VB.NET

```
Dim cmd As New SqlCommand("SELECT * FROM Users WHERE Username = @username",
connection)
cmd.Parameters.AddWithValue("@username", userInput)  ' userInput is provided
by the user
Dim reader As SqlDataReader = cmd.ExecuteReader()
```

In this example:

- The query uses @username as a placeholder for the user input, which is then safely added to the query using cmd.Parameters.AddWithValue(). This prevents the user input from being directly concatenated into the SQL statement, thus eliminating the risk of SQL injection.

2.2 Cross-Site Scripting (XSS) Prevention

Cross-Site Scripting (XSS) occurs when an attacker injects malicious scripts (JavaScript, etc.) into a web page, which can then be executed in a user's browser. To prevent XSS, always sanitize user input and use encoding to ensure that input is treated as data, not executable code.

- **Sanitizing Input**: Always validate and sanitize user input to prevent malicious content from being injected into your web pages.
- **HTML Encoding**: Use HTML encoding to ensure that any special characters in the user input (like <, >, or &) are displayed as data, not interpreted as HTML tags.
- **Example**: Sanitizing and encoding user input to prevent XSS

```
Dim sanitizedInput As String = HttpUtility.HtmlEncode(userInput)
```

In this example:

- The HttpUtility.HtmlEncode() function converts special HTML characters into their corresponding HTML entities (e.g., < becomes <, > becomes >), ensuring that any HTML or script tags in the user input are rendered as plain text.

10.5 Future Trends in VB.NET Development

As software development trends continue to evolve, VB.NET (Visual Basic .NET) remains a key player in the .NET ecosystem. Over the years, VB.NET has adapted to new technology paradigms and continues to offer robust solutions for developers. Below, we explore the emerging trends that shape VB.NET's role in the industry, highlighting how it is adapting to meet modern development needs.

---

1. Cross-Platform Development

1.1 .NET Core and VB.NET's Cross-Platform Capabilities

One of the most significant changes in the .NET ecosystem is the evolution of .NET Core (now part of .NET 5/6 and beyond), which is a cross-platform, open-source framework. With the transition to .NET 5/6, VB.NET has become a first-class citizen in the cross-platform world, allowing developers to create applications that run on **Windows, Linux, and macOS**.

This shift allows VB.NET developers to:

- **Build applications for multiple platforms**: Developers can now target not only Windows but also other operating systems, which was previously challenging for VB.NET developers who were primarily focused on Windows-based development.
- **Transition legacy systems**: Many legacy applications written in VB.NET that were previously limited to Windows environments can now be migrated to a more modern, cross-platform architecture, making it easier for businesses to embrace newer technologies and platforms.

1.2 Increased Industry Relevance

- The **cross-platform capabilities** of VB.NET open up more opportunities for developers who need to maintain and modernize legacy systems. This is particularly useful for businesses that have existing VB.NET applications but want to move to a more flexible infrastructure.
- VB.NET is positioned to play a key role in enterprise environments, where cross-platform development is becoming increasingly important as companies embrace cloud services and containerized applications.

---

2. Integration with Modern Technologies

2.1 Cloud Computing with Azure

- **Azure** is Microsoft's cloud platform, and as cloud adoption grows, VB.NET is being integrated with Azure's vast array of services. Developers can use VB.NET to create cloud-native applications, including **web apps, serverless functions, and containerized services**, all of which can be deployed to Azure.
- VB.NET works seamlessly with **Azure SDKs**, allowing developers to interact with cloud services such as **Azure Storage**, **Azure Functions**, and **Azure Cosmos DB**, making it a compelling option for businesses moving their workloads to the cloud.

2.2 Artificial Intelligence and Machine Learning

- **Machine Learning (ML.NET)** is a machine learning framework developed by Microsoft that integrates with .NET languages, including VB.NET. ML.NET allows VB.NET developers to build custom machine learning models directly within their applications without needing to learn new languages or frameworks.
- **AI Integration**: With the rise of AI, VB.NET is becoming more integrated with modern AI and deep learning technologies. VB.NET developers can use libraries and APIs to incorporate AI functionalities into applications, such as **natural language processing (NLP)**, **image recognition**, and **predictive analytics**.

2.3 The Impact of AI and Cloud Computing on VB.NET

- The future of VB.NET will see more tools and frameworks developed to support **AI-powered solutions**. This will further integrate VB.NET into industries like healthcare, finance, and e-commerce, where data analytics and intelligent automation are becoming essential.
- As cloud services and AI models evolve, VB.NET will continue to receive updates to work seamlessly with these technologies, ensuring that it remains relevant in the rapidly changing tech landscape.

---

3. Focus on Web and Mobile Development

3.1 ASP.NET and Web Development

- **ASP.NET**, a powerful web development framework within the .NET ecosystem, has always supported VB.NET, enabling developers to build dynamic, data-driven web applications. VB.NET can be used for both **Web Forms** and **MVC (Model-View-Controller)** applications, and with the rise of **Blazor** (a framework for building interactive web applications using C# and .NET), VB.NET developers can also build modern, client-side web applications.
- **Blazor** enables developers to build **interactive web applications** with C# or VB.NET, running directly in the browser via WebAssembly (WASM). This makes VB.NET a viable language for building rich web applications that run efficiently in modern browsers.

3.2 Xamarin for Mobile Applications

- **Xamarin** is a framework that allows developers to build cross-platform mobile applications for **iOS** and **Android** using a single codebase. While Xamarin originally supported C#, it also supports VB.NET, allowing developers to write mobile apps for both platforms with the same codebase.
- As mobile development continues to grow, VB.NET developers have the opportunity to leverage Xamarin to expand their reach beyond traditional desktop or web apps to mobile platforms.

---

4. Community and Ecosystem

4.1 Open-Source and the .NET Ecosystem

- Microsoft has increasingly embraced open-source development, and **.NET** has followed this trend. **.NET Core**, which was the foundation for VB.NET's cross-platform capabilities, is open-source and freely available. This has made VB.NET more approachable for developers and has helped ensure its continued development and support.

- The **.NET Foundation**, which promotes the development and adoption of open-source .NET projects, is growing, and VB.NET developers are benefiting from a rich ecosystem of libraries, tools, and frameworks that are constantly evolving to meet modern development needs.

4.2 Cloud-First Solutions

- The emphasis on **cloud-first solutions** by Microsoft ensures that VB.NET remains relevant in cloud-based enterprise applications. As more businesses migrate to the cloud, VB.NET will continue to be supported in these cloud ecosystems, ensuring its place as a reliable technology for enterprise solutions.

4.3 Vibrant Developer Community

- Microsoft has a strong commitment to VB.NET's future, ensuring that developers have the tools, support, and documentation they need to succeed.
- The **VB.NET community** is active, with many developers contributing to forums, open-source projects, and user groups. This strong community support is essential for keeping VB.NET evolving and adapting to new industry trends.

APPENDICES

A: Common Error Codes and Solutions

Understanding common error codes and how to address them is essential for troubleshooting and resolving issues efficiently in VB.NET development. Here's a look at some typical VB.NET error codes and their possible solutions:

---

1. NullReferenceException

- **Cause**: This occurs when you try to access a member (method, property, or field) on an object that is `null`. It often happens when an object is not instantiated but is being referenced.
- **Solution**:
    - Always check if the object is `null` before trying to use it.
    - Example:

```
If myObject IsNot Nothing Then
    ' Safe to access properties and methods
End If
```

2. ArgumentNullException

- **Cause**: This error is thrown when a method receives a `null` argument that it doesn't allow.
- **Solution**: Ensure that method arguments are properly validated and not `null` before calling the method.
    - Example:

```
If myString Is Nothing Then
    Throw New ArgumentNullException("myString cannot be null")
End If
```

3. IndexOutOfRangeException

- **Cause**: This occurs when trying to access an index in an array or collection that is out of bounds.
- **Solution**: Check if the index is within valid bounds before attempting to access an element.
    - Example:

```
If index >= 0 AndAlso index < myArray.Length Then
    ' Safe to access myArray(index)
End If
```

4. InvalidCastException

- **Cause**: Happens when there is an invalid type casting, such as trying to cast an object to a type that it cannot be converted to.
- **Solution**: Ensure that the cast is valid by using `TryCast` or checking the type beforehand.
    - Example:

```
Dim myObject As Object = "Hello"
```

```
Dim myString As String = TryCast(myObject, String)
If myString IsNot Nothing Then
    ' Use myString safely
End If
```

5. FileNotFoundException

- **Cause**: This error occurs when an application tries to access a file that does not exist at the specified path.
- **Solution**: Check the file path for typos, or ensure the file is in the correct location.
    - Example:

```
If File.Exists(filePath) Then
    ' Proceed to open the file
Else
    ' Handle file not found
End If
```

6. TimeoutException

- **Cause**: This exception is raised when an operation exceeds the specified time limit or timeout.
- **Solution**: Increase the timeout duration or optimize the operation to complete faster.
    - Example:

```
' Increase timeout period if necessary
command.CommandTimeout = 60 ' Timeout after 60 seconds
```

7. UnauthorizedAccessException

- **Cause**: This exception occurs when the application attempts to access a resource (e.g., a file, directory, or network) for which it does not have permission.
- **Solution**: Ensure the application has the necessary permissions, or handle the exception with proper error messaging.
    - Example:

```
Try
    ' Attempt file access
Catch ex As UnauthorizedAccessException
    ' Handle the exception, maybe notify the user
End Try
```

B: VB.NET Shortcuts and Tips

Knowing useful keyboard shortcuts and tips can significantly improve your efficiency while developing in VB.NET.

1. Common Keyboard Shortcuts in Visual Studio

- **Ctrl + Shift + B**: Build the entire solution.
- **F5**: Start debugging the application.
- **Ctrl + F5**: Start the application without debugging.

- **F9**: Toggle breakpoints.
- **Ctrl + . (dot)**: Quick actions and refactorings (e.g., auto-generate code, rename variables).
- **Ctrl + K + D**: Format the entire document.
- **Ctrl + M + M**: Collapse or expand the current code block.
- **Ctrl + F**: Open the find dialog for searching code.
- **Ctrl + H**: Open the find-and-replace dialog.
- **Ctrl + Shift + F**: Find across all files.
- **Ctrl + Shift + N**: Create a new project.

2. Tips for Efficient Coding

- **Use IntelliSense**: Visual Studio provides IntelliSense to help you with autocompletion of code. Make sure to use it to speed up coding.
- **Use Snippets**: Visual Studio comes with predefined code snippets that you can quickly insert by typing a shortcut (e.g., `for` for a `For` loop, `prop` for a property, etc.).
- **Refactoring**: Use Visual Studio's refactoring tools (Ctrl + .) to easily rename variables, methods, or classes and perform other common refactoring tasks.
- **Navigation**: Press **Ctrl + T** to navigate to any file or symbol within the solution. You can also use **Ctrl + -** to go back to the previous location.
- **Commenting**: Use **Ctrl + K + C** to comment selected code and **Ctrl + K + U** to uncomment it.

www.ingramcontent.com/pod-product-compliance
Lightning Source LLC
LaVergne TN
LVHW060120070326
832902LV00019B/3060
* 9 7 9 8 3 0 8 7 7 7 1 9 9 *